Traces of Guilt

Traces of Guilt

Hunting our most dangerous computer criminals

NEIL BARRETT

BANTAM PRESS

LONDON · NEW YORK · TORONTO · SYDNEY · AUCKLAND

TRANSWORLD PUBLISHERS
61–63 Uxbridge Road, London W5 5SA
a division of The Random House Group Ltd

RANDOM HOUSE AUSTRALIA (PTY) LTD
20 Alfred Street, Milsons Point, Sydney,
New South Wales 2061, Australia

RANDOM HOUSE NEW ZEALAND LTD
18 Poland Road, Glenfield, Auckland 10, New Zealand

RANDOM HOUSE SOUTH AFRICA (PTY) LTD
Endulini, 5a Jubilee Road, Parktown 2193, South Africa

Published 2004 by Bantam Press
a division of Transworld Publishers

A catalogue record for this book is available from the British Library.
ISBN 0593 051866

Typeset in 12/14pt Times by
Falcon Oast Graphic Art Ltd.

Printed in Great Britain by
Clays Ltd, St Ives plc

1 3 5 7 9 10 8 6 4 2

Papers used by Transworld Publishers are natural, recyclable products made from
wood grown in sustainable forests. The manufacturing processes conform to the
environmental regulations of the country of origin.

As always, for my family

Contents

Acknowledgements

So many people helped in the creation of this book, most obviously by working alongside me as I carried out the activities described. My colleagues at the company Information Risk Management Plc; the police officers, academics and lawyers with whom I came into contact; and those who read and helped with the work in progress. In particular, I'd like to thank Patrick Walsh and his team of readers and reviewers; and my wife Diana for reading and commenting on the book, and for her patience as I hid myself away to write it.

Thank you.

Introduction

Imagine an all too plausible nightmare . . .

Returning home in the dark, you find your front door swinging open, a window smashed. The house has been ransacked, books and ornaments scattered across the floor. Spray paint and excrement have been daubed across your carefully decorated walls; the television has been kicked over, photograph frames smashed and trampled underfoot.

You make your way through the house, the scenes of devastation repeated in every room, until you reach the bedroom. Cheap jewellery from the dressing-table boxes has been scattered across the floor, trampled with shards of broken perfume bottles and ripped clothing. But the truly expensive jewellery – the heirlooms and special pieces – had been hidden at the back of an unobtrusive drawer. This, you quickly realize, has also been taken.

Obviously you have been robbed. But what exactly has happened?

Did someone find the door unlocked, following an opportunistic rattle at the handle? Did they go on a wild wrecking spree, breaking the window in the process? Were they not intending to steal anything, and so ignored the cheaper jewellery, but stumbled over the more expensive pieces and decided to take them anyway? That's almost a comfortable version of the crime; you were not a deliberate target of the events, there was no malice intended. It was a simple opportunistic incident and the fates decreed that this time it was your turn.

Alternatively, did someone watch and wait until you had left the house; and did they then walk up to the door and use the correct key, without fumbling or hesitation? Did they go directly to the bedside drawer and pocket the most expensive pieces, before methodically and calmly wrecking the house so as to cover their tracks? Were you the victim, in other words, of someone who knew you and your life intimately enough to know precisely what to do and how to cover their tracks?

For the police, the distinction between the two is vitally important. Are they looking for an opportunistic housebreaker or a former partner? Was the heirloom jewellery taken so as to be sold or as some form of revenge? And if there was a revenge motive, are you still at personal risk from the individual; if you had been at home, would you have been attacked?

Now, imagine that house had been fitted with a CCTV system in every room, the cameras carefully hidden away. The tapes will answer the questions: we will be able to see how many people entered the house and in what fashion; we will be able to see what they do and where they go. Of course, we will still have to catch them and we will still have to make sure that the tapes can be used as evidence; but our basic questions will have been answered.

Few houses are fitted with cameras, but all computers have equivalent mechanisms for tracking and recording activity – criminal or legitimate – that is carried out on them. Information is stored on computers in files, arranged in a hierarchical structure of directories or folders. Each file and each directory has a 'time stamp' associated with it, which records when the contents were last accessed or last altered. A computer engineer can follow these time stamps to see just what was done on the computer. In effect, it is as though a forensics expert could give a definite time for each of the fingerprints at a normal crime scene, allowing investigators to follow precisely the progress of an intruder through a house.

In the case of computer records, provided that the time stamps aren't altered by subsequent users of the computer – or by police investigators – they give a complete history of what was done and even an insight into the user's motives. Unfortunately, computer data is highly volatile: the data can be changed by the very act of examining it on a computer. Clumsy investigators, 'helpful' system administrators, curious colleagues: all can unwittingly overwrite the valuable time stamps that show when a file was last accessed, in effect smudging the traces of guilt beyond recovery.

Even where those traces are not inadvertently altered, there are still problems for the investigator to face. Most obviously, a computer can contain an unimaginably large amount of data. Even an average home computer can hold so much data that an investigator could spend their entire police career just reading through it. Hunting for a needle in a haystack would be easy in comparison to the task of picking through billions of items of data on a computer, looking for the handful of clues that might indicate guilt.

And naturally, those clues that *are* eventually uncovered need then to be explained and presented to courts, where very few jury members and judges – let alone counsel and lawyers – have sufficient experience with computers to understand their operation well enough to form an opinion, to challenge an assertion, or to phrase an argument involving them.

But the effort is well worth the toil. Just as computers are used now by us all in our day-to-day activities, they are also used by criminals: to communicate with one another, to plan, to exchange information – or simply to swap gossip. Amongst those impossibly complex, impossibly large, impossibly volatile collections of data are the handful that establish a criminal's identity, psychology, objectives and activities.

If the corpse is pathology's 'silent witness', the computer is a determinedly garrulous and articulate one, but one that requires careful handling if the story it tells is to be admissible and understandable in court. That, for me, is the interest and the challenge of 'computer forensics', a discipline that I have worked in for many years: as a practitioner, a teacher, and ultimately an expert witness in court.

I came into this world many years before I was first asked to appear in court, through working in a university, through specializing in information security, through being a computer hacker and then more recently through volunteering to teach police officers about the intricacies of computer-hacking. Since then, I have helped to establish the standards and practical approaches to investigating and prosecuting computer crime, not just in the UK but throughout the world. I have worked with prosecutors to train them in the nature of computer offences, and have worked on some of the more interesting and exciting parts of the British and other governments' response to high-tech crime. And, of course, I have appeared now in courtrooms throughout the UK.

Some of the cases that I have worked on have been deeply disturbing and have affected the way that I relate to my colleagues and my family; some have been of vital importance to the legal landscape, or even to national security. Some cases have been simply won; and some have been lost after bitter fighting over arcane points of technical detail.

But all of the cases have been entertaining and intellectually challenging. This is the story of a small number of them, written to show the way in which computer crimes have moved from the specialist to the mainstream, and the way in which law enforcement has been forced to respond. That response has sometimes been ineffective, sometimes too late, and sometimes uninformed; but the response has continued to improve and has given rise to a requirement for training, for specialists and for international co-operation between law-enforcement bodies.

These are not always the crimes that make the headlines, but they are the crimes that will shape the future of law enforcement in the modern era of electronic commerce and global networks.

My career as an expert witness, though, started with the nastiest of modern computer crimes: child pornography.

1. **Whisper Who Dares**

King's Bench Walk is a terrace of fine Georgian houses along the eastern side of the Inner Temple gardens in London. Close to the elegant façade of the Royal Courts of Justice across the Strand to the north and the broad Thames to the south, the houses in the terrace have served for centuries as the chambers for the lawyers arguing cases in the Royal Courts. Once true residences, they have long since been converted into impressive offices, the black doors decorated with brass panels that announce the lists of counsel who work from their upper floors.

Early in the spring of 1996 I was there at the invitation of one of those counsel, who had asked me to help in the defence of what was to prove a fascinating case. Although it was not my first taste of involvement in computer crime, this was to become the first opportunity that would take me and my work into court itself. And it was to be a case that would force me to question a lot of my assumptions about computer crime and the judicial response to it.

I had met the counsel, Nick Lockett, in February on a train from London to Edinburgh where we were both speakers at a government-sponsored conference on computer crime. Over supper I had told Nick of my work in computer security. Specifically, I had told him that after a youth that had included hacking computers I now specialized in analysing computer-hacking incidents on behalf of the victims and the police.

Nick is an exuberant, voluble man, passionately committed to his job and passionately interested in the law as it applies to computer technology. If I were asked to picture a barrister, Nick would be pretty close to the image I would have: round glasses perched on the end of his nose, hair just beginning to thin, and an intense, penetrating gaze that weighs your words and waits for your mistakes. Though I didn't know it then, he was to become a good friend, and he was to dog my career as an expert witness; our professional paths were to cross many times in the coming years.

Throughout the four-hour trip to Edinburgh he was determined to collect as much detail as he could on precisely how hackers hack and how a hacked computer system would look to someone analysing it after the event. And as I had gone deeper into the finer details of the analysis process he had become ever more interested. Nick was, he explained, representing a client who had been charged with an offence involving a computer, and Nick was convinced of his innocence. He was determined to persuade me to help by showing that his client's computer could have been hacked into by someone wanting to plant evidence.

As he outlined the case he was considering, it became obvious to me that it would be a fascinating challenge, though I was more than a little uncomfortable with the fact that Nick's client, Chris, was charged with being a paedophile.

Chris was a young postgraduate student. A dedicated and imaginative researcher, his interest was in the psychology of homosexual paedophiles: Chris had declared an interest in finding a treatment regime that could be applied to these individuals within prison or secure mental hospitals, either to cure them completely or to allow a better understanding of what might make them harm children in the future.

To achieve that objective, Chris needed to know more about the mental lives of such people. The mechanism he had chosen to study that mentality was 'Internet-mediated interviews': Chris had apparently shown in his third-year undergraduate project that people were more likely to be open and communicative over the Internet's anonymous medium than ever they would be in face-to-face interviews. He wanted now to extend this in his postgraduate work, and use it to establish and verify a model of paedophile psychology that he proposed. If it could be made to work, he believed that it could help in the understanding, and therefore in the treatment and safe rehabilitation, of paedophiles.

The basis of his work was the observation that many child abusers have taken to using the Internet to locate and to approach vulnerable children in online chatrooms, a distasteful procedure called 'grooming'.

There is a wide range of different types of chatroom area on the Internet – from web pages to dedicated communication servers – but all allow individuals to connect to them, to give whatever details about themselves that they wish, and then to exchange immediate, typed messages with one another. Perfect for rapid, anonymous communication. Many chatroom areas are dedicated to particular interest groups – music, fashion, sport, hobbies and so forth. Most are primarily for adults but there are many that are set up specifically to be of interest to children. Unfortunately but perhaps inevitably, these chat areas attract paedophiles interested in establishing contact with children, usually with a view to enticing them to meet up with them. The paedophiles who use these mechanisms are gifted at persuading the other users that they are children, and are often all too capable of gaining the real children's trust and co-operation. In too many cases, unsupervised children using these facilities have been persuaded to meet the 'child's uncle'. The result has been an abused, and sometimes even a murdered, victim.

As well as these child-oriented chatrooms, many of the paedophiles were known to use the Internet in small groups to share pictures and tactical advice with one another, either through email or through their own, more private chatroom communities. Chris had, apparently, managed to locate and gain the trust of just such a group.

Nick then explained the core of his client's problem. In order to gain the paedophiles' trust, Chris had had to present himself to them as a fellow-paedophile, and had then found himself receiving child-pornography images from those that he wanted simply to interview online. According to Nick, Chris had been shocked and appalled, and had immediately encrypted those picture files without having viewed the actual images. Worse, though, Chris had had to send some pictures to the paedophiles in order to assure them that he was 'one of them'. These pictures had been collected, according to Chris, from ordinary, shop-bought postcards and clippings from family magazines. They showed, for example, a group of boys playing beside the sea or swimming in a river. They were not, Nick believed, paedophile images even though Chris had obviously intended them to be accepted as such by the child abusers he had contacted.

Unfortunately for Chris, several of those with whom he was in contact were already under FBI investigation in America. When they were arrested the evidence on their computers had led the police to Chris in late July 1995. The FBI had contacted the UK's National Criminal Intelligence Service in London, with an 'intelligence package' giving Chris's details. The local police force had been alerted and had subsequently raided the university. Chris, who had a part-time job working nights at a local service station, was arrested just after 7 a.m. when he returned to his flat. The police had inspected Chris's files on the Psychology Department's computer and discovered the logs, correspondence and picture files, which they believed showed Chris to have received, viewed and distributed indecent pictures.

Although there were several hundred picture files in the material recovered, so as not to exhaust or alienate a jury with having to inspect all of them, the prosecution had chosen some 'specimen charges': the police had selected a collection of Chris's pictures and charged him on the basis of just those. For some of them, he was charged with 'making and possession'; for others, 'possession with the intent to distribute'. These are standard prosecution tactics in computer paedophile cases, and would become increasingly familiar to me as I worked on the police side for subsequent cases. In the UK, it is an offence to 'make' an indecent picture of a child: the intention of the law was to make it illegal to take original photographs of child abuse. Computers, however, create copies of files when they are downloaded, sent or received as electronic mail, or even moved from folder to folder on the computer. Under the letter of the law, these activities are also considered to be 'making' the indecent image and attract a much stiffer penalty than mere possession would.

The prosecution thinking was that Chris had copied some of the image files from his email collection onto other folders and even floppy disks that he kept at his flat. As such, for those specific pictures he could be said to have created an indecent image. For other pictures, the police were relying on several emails that Chris had sent to the American paedophiles.

In addition to his work at the university, Chris was also a scoutmaster for a local troop of Boy Scouts. He had, it seemed, promised to provide the American paedophiles with some pictures of the boys in this troop. Sure enough, a collection of pictures, dated shortly after that email had been sent, were discovered by the police. In that collection there were some pictures of children with whom Chris worked – though none of a sexual nature – alongside some of the nude boys swimming and playing, which Chris said had come from postcards.

After listening to Nick's explanation, I felt that the defence team had an uphill battle on their hands. Chris was indeed in possession of paedophile pictures, and he had indeed 'made' copies of those images; he had presented himself as being a paedophile, and had sent pictures of children to people he knew to be paedophiles. At best he had been naïve; at worst he was using his research to disguise a true interest in child sex. There seemed little that I could do to help in the situation.

But Nick was characteristically buoyant, confident that there were two particular areas that I could address. First of all, he was sure that the police had not handled the computer evidence correctly and that it might therefore be possible to have it ruled as inadmissible. Second, he believed that it might be possible to show that someone else – a 'hacker', for example – could have been responsible for the computer files and records that the police claimed referred to Chris's activity. Nick fervently believed that Chris had been set up by someone else. In fact, he explained heatedly, Chris was certain that he was being framed by someone on the university system-administration staff, though he had no explanation for why that should be the case.

Nick summarized the prosecution and defence arguments for me. The police position was straightforward: Chris was a paedophile, in possession of paedophile images; he discussed his interests with other paedophiles, swapping pictures and describing his exploits – real or imagined – with the children in his Scout group, to whom he felt a sexual attraction. The prosecution believed that they had clear and unquestionable evidence to prove his storage and distribution of paedophile material, and equally clear evidence of his sexual interest in children.

The defence position was equally straightforward. Chris was an innocent researcher, trapped by an accidental professional association with genuine paedophiles; his discussions and descriptions – indeed, his whole persona on the Internet – were a carefully constructed presentation to allow him to carry out important research. He had not, in fact, ever looked at the pictures that had been sent to him. Moreover, Nick was con-fident that I would be able to prove that someone other than his client – whether a system manager or not – could have been responsible for the images and related files recovered. In particular, Nick wanted me to show that a hacker would have been able to access his client's files undetected.

The most important point for Nick was this: if I could find a way of showing that Chris's files had or could be artificially created then that would be enough to cast doubt on the police case and Chris would receive the benefit of that doubt.

At first I was more than a little uncertain about that. But over the months of investigation that were to follow – and with every additional twist in a complicated story – it would come to seem ever more likely that in Chris we had an innocent man being framed digitally for one of the nastiest of modern crimes.

Although all of Chris's contacts had been in the US, he was being charged in the UK under the 1978 Protection of Children Act and the 1988 Criminal Justice Act, the two laws that make indecent pictures of children illegal in this country; there are broadly similar laws enacted in nearly every other country. The Protection of Children Act makes it an offence to 'make, distribute, publish, or show with the intention to distribute' indecent pictures of children; and the Criminal Justice Act makes it an offence simply to be in possession of paedophile pictures, whether having an intent to distribute or not. The laws reflect the fact that a picture of a child being sexually abused is a record of *real* child abuse, and that allowing someone to possess or to distribute such pictures would be to encourage or condone that abuse. Even in the US, with a constitution that protects freedom of expression and where at least some pornography can be excused as having 'artistic merit', child pornography is beyond the pale.

Unlike the situation with pornography involving adults, the pictures of children do not have to be obscene to be illegal. That is, they don't have to be proved as 'tending to deprave or to corrupt', but simply as being 'indecent': they merely have to have the effect of making normal people feel uncomfortable. It's a particularly broad definition that has unfortunately led to parents being prosecuted simply for having had naked pictures of their own children cavorting on the beach or in the bath.

I had been introduced to the phenomenon of Internet paedophilia when it was still a relatively new problem, on a visit to the West Midlands Police Obscene Publications Unit in Birmingham in February 1995. At the time I was working as a computer-security consultant to the Inland Revenue at Somerset House in London, as part of a research effort into the protocols for handling computer evidence. This was work that directly led to the nearly universally accepted mechanisms used world-wide by police and other investigators today.

I was visiting Birmingham because a few months earlier Detective Inspector Dave Davis of the West Midlands Police had had a breakthrough in an operation named 'Starburst', at the time the largest operation against computer pornography carried out in the UK. In fact, that operation is still resulting in groups of paedophiles being arrested right up to the present time.

A short, thick-set man who reminded me of Bob Hoskins, Davis had the air of a detective technically out of his depth but angrily determined to master the issues. Over the years that followed, not only did he manage to master the computer technology involved, Davis made an international reputation for himself as one of the leading lights world-wide in Internet crime investigations.

In a cramped but private evidence-viewing room, Davis had described the compromises and methods that he had had to invent, as he had shown us some partially blacked-out copies of the less extreme images seized. He had left me with a number of important impressions. First, that the paedophile images represent a record of a child having been abused, so that the police's mission was not simply to prosecute the person with the picture but to try and rescue the child and to catch those responsible for the abuse itself. Second, that the people collecting the computer images were imaginative in the way that they hid them: that they use encryption, misleading file names, aliases and the like. And third, that these people tended to arrange the pictures into very precise, hierarchical structures, evidence of well-ordered minds.

At the time, I was struck by the parallels to work that I had already undertaken studying computer hackers and the way that they protect the tools they use and the files they might copy. It seemed to me then that analysing computer paedophilia and the Internet habits of paedophiles – a task that Davis was sure would only grow in importance, given the associations he had uncovered from the Starburst work – would be technically close to work that I was already involved in, and that it would be particularly worthwhile. Because of this, even with my reservations about Chris's claims, when I was presented with the opportunity to work in that area I had found myself agreeing to help Nick with his case.

Nick had cheerfully waved me on my way from King's Bench Walk after our first case conference, with a sealed cardboard box holding a CD-ROM and three black lever-arch files stuffed with evidence and relevant material. Alarmed at the prospect of being stopped by the police with a carton of paedophile material and only a letter from Nick appointing me as defence expert for protection, I had hurried back to my office.

I didn't meet Chris personally until the case came to court several months later. However, in reading through the email, stories and notes in the first of the lever-arch files the day after that first case conference, I felt as though I had read his diary. There's something vaguely distasteful yet undeniably fascinating in looking so deeply into someone else's thoughts and feelings – particularly when that person might well be a paedophile – and I felt that I had come to know Chris well through that reading. Interestingly, though I wasn't sure that I particularly *liked* him, there was nothing in the writing to make me *loathe* him. He seemed to be a perfectly normal student, just like any others I had ever met or taught. The description of his research ideas struck me as rather vague and woolly, but then I was judging them as a computer scientist and a mathematician, rather than a psychologist: for all I knew, that was precisely how important psychology research was framed and presented. His email records showed that he had a number of girlfriends, an equal number of male friends, and an older woman who seemed – from reading between the lines – rather to dote on him. If one believed that he *was* a paedophile, some of his writing about his Scout activities could be interpreted as suspect; but, if one believed that he was *not*, then the interpretation could be entirely innocent.

The second file held the computer material that the police had taken as the basis of their prosecution case, and obviously it was the main area on which I had to concentrate. Here, there were rather more explicit email messages, which I presumed had been sent to the paedophiles with whom Chris was communicating for his research. I disliked these from the moment I saw them, not simply because of their contents. Admittedly, the messages were objectionable but of course there was no way of knowing whether the things said in them were true or not: Chris's defence position was that he had been playing a part; these messages could easily have been a part of that pretence.

What upset me was the name that he used in them: Christopher Robin. As a child, my parents' favourite lullaby for my brothers and I had been 'Little boy kneels, at the foot of the bed . . .', the one that ends, 'Hush, hush, whisper who dares; Christopher Robin is saying his prayers.' Until I was able to read it for myself I had always thought that my Dad had been singing, 'Little boy Neil's . . .' I had felt that it was *my* song, and so the 'Christopher Robin' name was a very personal – and I admit it, very irrational – link to my own childhood.

Paedophiles wreck children's lives, but my own childhood was perfect, with loving, stable parents and freedom within boundaries. I had certainly never been abused and didn't then know of anyone who had. In an unconscious way, Chris's use of that name became symbolic for me and made me determined that in the future I would work primarily for the prosecution in such cases. If Chris *was* a paedophile as claimed, then I did not want later to say that I had had a hand in keeping him out of prison and off the Paedophile Register. I wanted to keep 'Christopher Robin' as a name of childhood innocence and not of abuse.

For now, though, having made a commitment to Nick, I had to push that feeling to the back of my mind and concentrate on the material to hand. Chris was 'innocent until proven guilty'; that had to be my touchstone.

One or two emails seemed to be responses to earlier

messages from Chris in which he had apparently provided some pictures of his Cub Scouts to a paedophile at an American university, and even a handful of pictures of his own younger brother. This of course was an important element of the prosecution case, but as Nick had explained it to me – and as the material in the third file would make clear – Chris was adamant that he had *never* sent illegal material to any third party. The defence position, from which I had to proceed, was that, though he had sent some pictures, these had all been 'public-domain' photographs that had already been used in advertising campaigns or on postcards, and which he therefore felt would not be considered illegal.

Chris was also adamant that whilst he had indeed received material from some paedophiles, he had not known what to do with the pictures, had had no interest in them, and had simply encrypted the picture files without looking at the images they contained. This assertion was unfortunately undermined somewhat by material in the second file. The police had obtained a list of the commands that they said had been typed into the university computer by Chris in the early hours of the morning before his arrest. These commands included ones to view picture files that were in Chris's directories on the computer.

The police had also produced a detailed list of the files and directories on the system that belonged to Chris. They had shown in this list that the majority of the picture files were indeed encrypted, and that all of his picture files had been arranged in a carefully indexed hierarchy of reference directories. I was immediately reminded of some of Dave Davis's comments about paedophile behaviour: that they would encrypt their image files and arrange them in well-sorted hierarchies. Chris fitted that profile. Was that, I wondered, because Chris was a careful researcher, or because he was a paedophile who was using the research as a cover story?

The 'researcher' argument was undermined by a statement from Chris's academic supervisor, in which it was stressed that the university would never sanction a junior postgraduate student to obtain or to store any potentially illegal material, and that Chris had not in fact sought permission. The supervisor emphasized that projects had to follow a published Code of Ethics, and that he himself had never approved Chris's research – nor, in fact, had he ever had this aspect of it explained to him. The university was clearly washing its collective hands of Chris.

And finally, there was a statement from one of the American paedophiles whom the FBI had arrested and charged. His witness statement said that he had indeed received child pornography from Chris and that in return for immunity from prosecution he was prepared to come to England to testify.

It did not look good for 'Christopher Robin' at that point. It was obvious that the police had a pretty good case – and certainly one that was persuasive to me as I read the material through the afternoon of that first day.

However, it was not that clear-cut. One element in particular intrigued me: the commands that police said were entered into the computer by Chris the night before his arrest. That list was stored in a small 'history file' in his part of the university computer, with a new line of text entered into the file for each command typed. By reading the commands recorded in this history file, the police believed that they could show precisely what Chris had done on the university's computer.

Every time a new line of text was written into the file, the file would of course change, and the date and time of that last change was recorded on the file information. This is what is called a 'time stamp': a crucial feature of computer forensics. The last modification time for the history file would indicate when the last command was written to it.

Interestingly, this time was in the early hours of the morning, when the university computer terminal room was locked and no students were able to gain access to the computer. And at a time when Chris could prove that he was on the night shift at the service station where he was working to earn extra money. It simply would not have been possible for Chris to have been both at the service station *and* active on the computer at the university.

This, of course, explained Nick's interest in whether or not the computer could have been hacked. If I could show that these commands could have been entered by another user, then so too could many of the other commands; and if I could show *this*, then I could demonstrate that Chris might not have been solely responsible for the contents of his workspace on the computer. The paedophile images might have been put there by somebody else. Proving that the computer could have been hacked would therefore be sufficient to prove that Chris could be innocent.

Putting Chris's own material to one side for a moment, I read quickly through the outline case that had been prepared by the prosecution. The police contention, according to the Crown Prosecution Service lawyers, was that Chris had been able to access the university computer from his work, using a small computer that was in the office behind where he operated the night-service till. Since Chris was there alone on the night shift for an eight-hour period, that would have been plausible; but Chris insisted he did not, and that, since the computer was in fact locked in an office, he *could* not.

And because the police hadn't taken a copy of that machine (i.e. copied its files before anyone could tamper with it), it was hard for me to see how they thought they could prove it. Somebody – Nick, I presumed – had scrawled 'Abuse of process?!' in smudged ink in the margin beside that observation. I didn't know precisely what it meant, but it sounded accurate: if the police were wanting to rely on an argument built around the use of a particular computer, then that computer *must* be presented in evidence somehow.

And when I looked at the list of commands in the history file there was a tiny shadow of doubt that flitted across my mind. There was nothing I could put my finger on then, but there was certainly something about that file that deserved more attention later. Years before, when I had hacked computers I had learned to trust my intuition. Even if I could not say at that moment precisely why, I would still be certain that there was something about a stray fact or feature that could be used to break a system's security. I had that feeling now, reading the history-file list: there was something that didn't quite fit; there was something to it that I could use.

I stared at it for a long time, trying – just as I used to do – to force the stray thought to crystallize. The file was a list of a hundred commands, one per line, with a seemingly random large number preceding each command on the line. The number was ten digits long, starting '08'. The police expert had said that he didn't know what the number represented and that he thought it was simply a randomly produced reference number associated with the command, or a process-identification number used by the operating system.

I was positive that there was something more that could come of it, but wasn't sure what at that point; and the harder I tried to push the thought, the more elusive it became. Like any scientist I hate to rely on intuition: scientists prefer to rely on methods and processes, on repeatable, reliable mechanisms. But also like any scientist, I do use intuition to guide those methods and to gauge what are the 'right' directions in which to proceed. Unfortunately, unlike repeatable mechanisms, intuition cannot be timetabled. Though I was confident that I would eventually work out what was bothering me, right there and then I could not.

It was beginning to grow dark in the office at the end of that first day when I decided to leave the puzzle of the history file for later and turned instead to the images that had been seized from Chris's files.

The pictures Chris had collected were as nasty a set of pornography as one could fear to encounter. There were pictures of young boys together; pictures of adult men abusing tiny children, or watching as two or more boys writhed together on the bed, eyes dead and disengaged from what they were doing or was being done to them. There were pictures of children being hurt, being restrained, being frightened.

I didn't *want* to view the image files. Generally, I have found that it isn't necessary to see the pictures themselves; it is usually sufficient to examine the date and time stamps, file names and locations. In this analysis, though, I needed to compare images that had been given different file names within Chris's collection of images, so as to establish whether individual pictures had been copied, moved or renamed by him – or indeed, by any hacker intruding into his files.

Scrolling through the images on my office computer, door closed and screen turned away from the window, was a deeply disturbing and worrying experience. What concerned me most about the images was uncertainty as to the effect that they would have on me. By the time I came to work on this, my first paedophile case, I had been married for some ten years and my wife and I had just started a family. We had two happy little daughters and I found it incomprehensible that anyone could consider them as sexual beings. But it scared me to think that perhaps, through exposure to the child pornography, *I* might find myself viewing them in that light. I had no idea what might turn someone 'normal' into an abuser, so my fear was that these pictures could act as a trigger upon me.

For weeks and months after this first exercise of examining and analysing the picture files recovered from Chris's work-space I felt uncomfortable. I found it hard to cuddle or kiss my girls; I found it hard to look at them as they got dressed and I found it impossible to steel myself to bathe them. Worried about the effects of that collection of horrible images, I sacrificed a normal family relationship as a loving father for a period, until the insanity of what I was putting myself through gradually came home to me. I realized that the images were not going to have any effect on me other than severe distaste, and gradually I began to feel that it was safe and proper for me to hold, watch and enjoy my own children.

Although I knew that I was breaking into a new and exciting area of work, and a new chapter in my activity in computer crime, I was immensely disturbed by the effect it was having on my life and my peace of mind. I was committed to doing my best to help someone whom I had to consider innocent until proven guilty. But the first shock of my encounter with that type of material meant that, by the time I had finished ploughing my way through Chris's collection of pornography, I would have quite happily locked the lad up and thrown the key in the nearest canal.

Were it not for that niggling intuition about the history file, then even with my commitment to Nick I would have still been much happier to walk away. But that niggling intuition was to prove the key to the case.

It was just under a year and a half before I made my way to the crown court in the English Midlands town where Chris had studied and been arrested.

In those months I had had an exciting time: I had managed to uncover additional evidence to show that the university computer had, in all probability, been hacked; and even who it was that had hacked into his files. I could not show that Chris had *not* deliberately obtained and distributed picture files, but I was certain that I could show that only the 'hacker' had definitely *viewed* the picture files. And I felt confident that I could prove that the police had seriously mishandled the collection of the computer evidence. I could show that they had relied on methods that ran counter to the 'best practice' laid down by the evidence protocols I had worked on at the Inland Revenue and for the police in the years before meeting Nick.

I had briefed Nick and the rest of the defence team – the senior barrister and the solicitor, both child-abuse specialists from Manchester – some half-dozen times on the operation and principles of computers, to the point where I was reasonably confident that they would be able to make short work of a prosecution case full of holes. So although it seemed to have taken a lifetime to get to this point, I was feeling very confident as I drove up the sunny, early-morning motorway in autumn 1997; I was sure that I had done a good job, and I was looking forward finally to meeting Chris himself after all this time.

I had pushed to the back of my mind two important things: I had quickly moved to looking at the case as involving abstract technical arguments, rather than grotesque pictures of children suffering; and Chris himself had become equally abstract in my mind. If I thought about him at all, it was as a parody of a paedophile: a cross between a Benny Hill-style pervert and a character from a Grimms' fairy tale.

I was pleasantly surprised when I met him in the coffee shop at the court. He was young, smartly suited and with a boyishly charming air about him: good-looking, clean-shaven and with a dark, almost gypsy complexion and short-cut wavy hair; a long way from the popular image of a pervert and child abuser. He came across as articulate and bright, though intense. He was also quite obviously worried about what would happen once the case started, and equally concerned about the coverage that the case had already received in the local papers. Mud sticks, and even without proof – or even the beginning of the case – it sounded as though Chris was suffering from the fallout from the accusation. But sitting across a coffee table from him, I couldn't see him as anything other than an innocent: a student whose project had gone horribly wrong, and who was being made to suffer for it.

Nick and the rest of the defence team had agreed that the prosecution's technical expert and I would be allowed to sit on the legal benches throughout the trial. This was a feature of being a computer expert witness that I soon came to relish, seeing increasingly interesting cases up close. In this case, the computer evidence was so central to the arguments that my opposite number and I would be required to advise counsel on an almost constant basis as they questioned the university system-management staff and the police responsible for handling the evidence.

And the defence team certainly intended to do what we could to attack that computer evidence, given the miserable litany of mistakes and clumsy evidence-handling that I had uncovered over the past year.

First, Chris had accessed the university computer from one of a small set of personal computers in a terminal room; these had not been copied and preserved, so as to show evidence of what he had actually done.

Second, the police had preserved Chris's files, but in a way that didn't preserve the time stamps on the file, and which also altered the time stamps on the directories holding the files. For me, this was important evidence that had been lost, and also a good indication that the police had been clumsy and careless with at least this part of the work. If this had been done carelessly then what else might have been overlooked?

Third, the police had obtained a copy of Chris's 'history file' as it had appeared on the day of his arrest. The history file was the list of the last hundred commands entered into the computer by a particular user: a short-term snapshot of what the police presumed was his activity, but one that could not possibly go back over a great length of time. I was confident that the university would have kept back-up tapes for several months, since it was accepted practice to do so in case files were accidentally deleted and needed to be restored. The police had not thought to request those back-up tapes and so they had simply sat in the tape store at the university until I had asked for them and, with the police expert in tow, gone to obtain copies during the summer holidays. That meant that we now had several months' worth of commands registered against Chris's account to analyse; and they did not show him viewing paedophile pictures or, in any explicit manner, show him distributing pictures.

The most interesting thing that we could show, though, was related to the apparently random numbers associated with each command in the several dozen history files that we had collected.

Although my formal practical experience is in computer science, at heart I consider myself a mathematician – and mathematicians cannot ignore numbers. The numbers in the history file had bothered me ever since I had first seen them. The police expert's opinion was that they were random numbers. They were *not* random, of that I was sure: for one thing, the numbers increased; each number was larger than the preceding one, though by a varying amount. That *must* be important.

And the nature of the ten-digit-long number niggled away at

my subconscious. I had seen numbers like that before, though I couldn't remember where and when.

It took an innocent question from my daughter in the summer holidays to pull the memory out of hiding. She asked me how many seconds I'd been alive for, and when I had done the sums I realized that I had a ten-digit number, starting '11'. Had I been born in January 1970, by mid-1995 I would have had a ten-digit number starting '08', and *that* was what the 'random' number was reminding me about. It was a count of the number of seconds that the computer's operating system had been alive; it was a time stamp.

The university computer ran an operating system called 'UNIX', a particularly popular operating system in universities since it was initially offered free of charge in the late 1970s and early 1980s. Developed by Bell Labs, a part of the giant AT&T organization in America, UNIX had to have some way of internally representing the time of day. To do this, it had a counter which increased every second. The zero value for this clock, known as the 'epoch' date, was midnight on 1 January 1970.

Some rough calculations with the known time-stamp value for the history file convinced me that I was right. The numbers in the history file were the time stamps, represented in seconds, for when the specified command had actually been typed into the computer.

This was a tremendously exciting breakthrough, especially given that I had so many history files now to consider, going back several months before Chris had been arrested. I knew that the final time stamp in the history file must equate to the time at which the history file was last modified; and from the police evidence I knew what that was. This meant that I could attach 'real-world' times and dates to all of the recorded commands. And *that* meant that I could divide the commands into recognizable sessions (periods of use), allowing me to analyse the behaviour of the user of Chris's account. I could work out when he logged on and logged off, and I could see the usual pattern of behaviour on the computer.

When I did this analysis, I was in for a huge surprise. The

commands did indeed break down into distinct sessions, each with characteristic patterns. Chris – or rather, the user represented to the system as Chris – accessed his account at regular intervals and did routine things. He read his mail, moved files around, and deleted things. He performed 'housekeeping' commands; the sort of commands one would expect of a relatively inexpert user familiar with only the mundane aspects of computer use.

I had each session on a separate sheet of paper, and these sheets spread out on the lounge carpet one evening a few weeks before the trial, when I realized that the final session – the one that the police were relying on – was wholly different in character from any of the others. In this last session – running through the early hours of the morning before Chris was arrested, when he claimed to be working at the service station – the user had entered some unusual commands.

As I read them I became more and more excited, almost jumping around the room. The commands were not the commands of our client, familiar with the ordered hierarchy of his file system; they were the commands of someone exploring the file system. They were the commands of an *intruder*: a hacker *had* gained access to Chris's account; it seemed that Nick had been right all along.

In the early hours of the morning, an intruder had carefully explored his file system; and I could see that intruder displaying at least one known paedophile image file. This action, the police asserted, proved that Chris had lied and showed that he *had* viewed the paedophile images. The more I looked at the commands, the less likely that seemed. The series of commands showed the user listing a directory, before looking at each file in that directory; once each file had been examined, the user moved into subsidiary directories, repeating the process. He tested files before opening them, looking to see the nature of the file before it was displayed. This was not the action of Chris, who would have known the contents of his files. This was the activity of someone coming to the files for the first time, and exploring them methodically and deliberately. Who was it?

Was this a hacker who had used some trick to get access to the computer? Or was this a fellow-student of Chris's, who had guessed his password? Or was it perhaps one of the system administrators? More crucially, could this invalidate the police's evidence, since it could no longer be proved to have been Chris's own activity?

And then another exciting aspect of the command list became apparent to me: from the nature of the commands, I could deduce *precisely* who it was. Although I knew it would disappoint Nick, who liked the idea of a hacker on whom all Chris's problems could be blamed, I believed that I could rule out the prospect of an external hacker or a fellow-student. A 'true' hacker would have accessed the system from the outside, gaining access and 'escalating' his privileges to that of the most authoritative user of the computer: the 'super user' who logs in with the name of 'Root' and who has access to everything on the computer. This person is usually a system manager, but given the power that the super user wields it is an obvious target for the hacker.

If the commands had been entered by a hacker breaking in and escalating his privileges on the system, they would have been recorded in a different manner in the history file; indeed, they would not have been written into that file at all. The only way for the commands to have been recorded against our client's account history file would have been for the computer to have believed that the user was Chris. This would have required the user to have been logged in as Chris from the beginning, or to have been the super user and then to have changed their user identification into Chris's at a later time. Based on years of analysing the way that hackers operate, I simply could not believe that a mischievous or malicious hacker would have even considered doing that. An external hacker would have executed the commands in Chris's work-space, but stayed as the super user. They would have then had no limitations on what they could have achieved.

Some other indications helped me to see that the user had not, in fact, logged in as Chris initially. A user who logs in executes a specific login profile program that creates the operating environment in which they run all subsequent commands. By looking at the way in which the commands recorded in the final history-file session were specified, I could tell that our client's login profile had not been active at the time. From this, I could say that the user who had recorded those commands had logged in as a super user, had changed their identification into that of Chris, and had then clumsily explored and inspected the paedophile images in his file system.

And there were other interesting factors. One of the commands – specifically, a command to view the paedophile image – had apparently failed. The mystery intruder had typed the viewing command, and then almost immediately typed a command that told the computer what type of terminal they were using. I was confident that this was because the computer had not known what type of terminal to display the picture on and had given an error message.

Fortunately for us, in telling the computer what *type* of terminal, the user in fact gave the *name* of the terminal: a computer known to be in the university system administrators' room, inaccessible to a student even during the day, let alone in the middle of the night. I was completely confident from this that the commands had been typed by a system administrator, who had methodically examined Chris's files. And that these were the very commands that the police were accusing Chris of having typed. Astounding though it sounded, it appeared as though Chris was indeed being framed by a system administrator at the university, just as he had claimed all along. But which administrator? I realized that I could answer even this question with a high degree of confidence.

The UNIX operating system had been available free of charge to universities since the late 1970s, but it had gone through several variations in that time. Initially, the software had been developed by Bell Labs on the east coast of America in the early 1970s; this was the first distribution of the operating system in the period up to the early 1980s, and the nature of the commands it used was very distinctive. After that time, the main thrust of development had moved to the University of California at Berkeley, and this west-coast version of UNIX had a distinctive, but different, pattern of commands.

In that final meeting before the trial, I explained this to Nick and the rest of the defence team as being a 'dialect': east-coast or west-coast. Most system administrators 'speak' a west-coast dialect when they are managing UNIX systems, simply because that is the version that the overwhelming majority of them were trained on. Only those system administrators from my own late-1970s/early-1980s generation habitually 'speak' the east-coast dialect. But whoever had entered the commands into Chris's account in the early morning had used commands and a style that was so familiar to me that it had taken me several minutes to appreciate that it *was* so distinctive and to appreciate the implications of that.

It meant that whoever had typed those commands had in all probability been a university system administrator some time before 1985. That ruled out all but one of the university's computer-administration staff. The eldest and most senior of them had, for some unfathomable reason, framed Chris for a paedophile offence. We had our man, and our man was *not* 'Christopher Robin'.

The crown court was a modern, red-brick building. From the outside, it reminded me of a car park attached to an inner-city shopping centre; but inside it had the quiet reserve of a university library, with an underlying air of nervous anticipation.

Court sits at 10.30 and usually rises at about 4, with a one-hour break for lunch. Counsel – the defence and prosecution barristers – have a dressing room in a private part of the building, where they hide away to do their deals and fit their wigs and black robes. Lawyers from the Crown Prosecution Service have their own offices; the police have their own rooms; members of the jury have a reception area and a host of court officials to make them tea and keep them away from the public. Prosecution witnesses have their own, comfortable waiting rooms. But defence teams, defence witnesses, the press and the general public are left to fend for themselves. On that first morning at court we retreated to the self-service canteen on the top floor.

I enjoyed describing what I'd found in the history files and the deductions that I'd made. I felt like a digital detective, a modern-day Sherlock Holmes explaining my observations and the inescapable conclusions that I'd drawn from them. Chris's eyes lit up, convinced that this would help show that he was innocent; Nick, who had been certain that his account on the computer could have been hacked, felt vindicated; and the senior barrister – Ms Kushner – grinned like a Cheshire cat before bustling off to pass my written report to her opposite number.

It was a tremendous feeling. There was much patting of backs, rubbing of hands, and eager anticipation of several days' sport in the courtroom. And then Nick casually mentioned a new aspect of the charges. Chris had also been accused of a 'contact offence' against one of the Cub Scouts; he'd followed that child home and had an angry confrontation with the boy's father, who had accused him of molesting the boy. While awaiting trial on charges of possessing and distributing paedophilia, Chris had exposed himself to a charge of actual child abuse.

The young, eager, respectable-looking defendant – the defendant I thought I had gone a long way towards getting off from the computer-related charges – suddenly seemed now not to be an innocent research student trapped by someone else. I was being forced to appreciate that he was possibly a genuine paedophile, who had obtained paedophile pictures and had perhaps abused boys in his care.

I suddenly felt confused, angry and tremendously foolish. My clever-clever analysis work was completely valid, but I felt as though I was being cheated.

My opinion of Chris had altered so many times and so quickly that I was now feeling dizzy. When Nick had first described him and the case, I had felt sure that Chris deserved assistance; viewing the pictures and feeling my reaction to them, I had been equally sure that he deserved to be locked away. Having established that someone else had accessed his account – particularly in the early hours of the morning and in such an illicit manner – I was then convinced that Chris was innocent; more, I was convinced that he had been framed. And now, I was equally sure that he was not.

Out of self-defence I decided to stop having an opinion about his guilt or innocence. Our client became a source of computer evidence for me and no longer an individual in whom I had a personal interest.

The courtroom itself was light and airy, with modern tables and green-cushioned, foldaway seats. There was no obvious gallery and no obvious dock for the defendant to sit in, just a low wall that separated a small seating area from the rest of the court. Chris was shown in there by a shirt-sleeved security guard, who watched it all with the bored expression of one who had seen more than his share of scared defendants.

The jury was what I would come to think of as 'the usual crowd': two young men in jeans and casual jackets; three young women, dressed as for the office; four older women, dressed as for the bingo; and the rest were middle-aged or elderly men, reminding me of a bowling club. A 'middle England' collection, which Nick considered with a worried expression, sure that the defence would find little sympathy for Chris there.

As the prosecution opened their case and the collection of recovered and decrypted image files was displayed to the jury in the opening address, their shocked expressions and openly hostile glances at Chris made me feel increasingly uncomfortable. The prosecution counsel – a prim, scholarly figure – read emails aloud, lingering over the more provocative phrases. He called the jury's attention to the most nauseating of the pictures and described a devious, perverted predator placed in charge of young boys and relishing the exposure to their nakedness and intimacy.

It did not make pleasant listening, and when I looked over my shoulder at Chris – his eyes shielded, his head bowed – it was all too apparent that the QC's words were stingingly effective.

For the defence, though, Ms Kushner was equally effective;

perhaps even more so, given that the young and handsome Chris looked like anything but a predator and pervert. She herself had a matronly 'hockey sticks and ponies' air about her: a no-nonsense joviality, but a sharp wit underneath it. I was deeply impressed with her from the moment we met. She had made clear that she knew nothing about computers, but would listen, question and remember all that I told her. And she had.

In response to the prosecution's opening statements, Ms Kushner painted the picture of a researcher doing good despite hostility on the part of society to the subject matter of his research. She emphasized the purely hearsay nature of the evidence against Chris: how it was primarily built on the accusation of the American paedophile, who had agreed to testify only in return for immunity and could not therefore, she claimed, be trusted. And she gave a taster of the arguments that were to come regarding the nature of the computer evidence.

I thought we were probably evenly matched at the end of the opening statements, and certainly Chris was looking less pale when Ms Kushner sat back down.

Over the days that followed, the defence team's tactics were fairly straightforward. I guided Ms Kushner in questioning the prosecution expert and other computer evidence witnesses, so as to draw out all the points I wanted to make about the computer evidence. This, she explained, was in order to limit the expression of complicated computer material to the prosecution witnesses. Since she was certain the jury would be confused by that evidence, she wanted that confusion to be blamed upon the prosecution and not her defence witnesses. I must admit to having been disappointed at not having the prospect of my own time in the limelight; until, that is, I saw just how hard-edged the examination and cross-examination of the witnesses was.

The first few witnesses on the opening day were non-contentious: police officers who had arrested Chris as he'd returned from the night shift at the service station and then interviewed him. Their evidence was simple and short, and ran over the first day or so of the case. The real drama started when the prosecution computer expert was called to the stand on the second day to begin the lengthy process of outlining what he had uncovered.

Almost immediately I realized that there was a problem. I had described the operation of the computer – the way files were stored, pictures moved, email handled, etc. – using terms that I believed Ms Kushner and the rest of the team would understand. I had given them the correct terms for things, like 'time stamps', 'back-up tapes', 'encrypted archive'; but I had also tried to explain the computer's activities to them using terms like 'locked file cabinet', 'fingerprint' and so forth. The prosecution expert was also trying to simplify the concepts involved but had chosen a different way of representing the computer. The result was confusion. When the prosecution counsel examined the expert the answers flowed quickly and easily, as was to be expected: they had quite obviously rehearsed the way that things would be explained. But when Ms Kushner tried, the result was a set of questions whose meaning *we* all understood but the expert did not. All parties got steadily more flustered; and inevitably that ended up with the prosecution expert looking bad in front of the jury, and the court struggling to understand the concepts being explained.

Nick, Ms Kushner and Chris were pleased, but I felt like a scoundrel. I had liked the prosecution expert; but I hadn't agreed with him a form of words that would be used by both of us to explain the most fundamental concepts to the court. The computer evidence was being misunderstood and he had ended up looking incompetent. I vowed that that was not something that would ever happen to me, and so far I've managed to avoid it.

It was on the third day of the trial – and the second day of the prosecution computer expert's evidence – that Ms Kushner dropped the bombshell regarding the history-file discrepancies.

The prosecution expert had already seen a copy of the summary report that I had given to Ms Kushner and could find nothing to disagree with in it. From the witness box and under oath he had to agree that there was a major problem with the evidence. He agreed that in all likelihood a university system manager was responsible for the commands that he, on behalf of the police, had ascribed to Chris. Ms Kushner was also able to make him agree that *all* of the computer evidence recovered from the university system could have been placed there by a system manager wishing to implicate Chris. While asserting that there was no particular reason to suppose that this *had* happened, the expert was forced to agree that if it had then the evidence he had seen would have been wholly consistent with it.

These were precisely the points that we wanted to establish: points that would, according to Nick's explanation at our first meeting in London, be sufficient to cast doubt on the prosecution case and allow Chris to walk free. Although I had my own doubts about Chris, the defence case was looking stronger by the minute.

But naturally the prosecution wanted to establish whether my deductions about the system administrator were correct. The easiest way to do this was to put each of the half-dozen administrators under oath and then to ask them.

There was no pleasure to be had in watching the parade of nervous system administrators as one by one they filed in and took their oaths. Their confusion was palpable as they were asked whether they had been in the building on the night in question, whether they recognized the commands and whether they were responsible for them. Since I knew which of the half-dozen was the only one who could possibly fit the profile, I let my mind wander, looking over some of the other evidence that had been collected.

I had looked through Chris's email many times. There are two things of interest in an email message: the text of the message itself, and the 'extended headers' that describe it. I'd read and analysed the text, looking for linguistic patterns and for any obvious differences between Chris's 'normal' email and the 'Christopher Robin' messages. I hadn't found anything crucial or interesting there. I'd also inspected the headers in great detail, tracking the messages through all the intermediate computers responsible for their transmission and looking to see whether or not they could have been intercepted and altered. Again, I had found nothing of interest.

But as I listened with half an ear to the procession of puzzled administrators, I realized that I had never considered the emails as *files* in their own right.

Just like the commands in the history file, the email messages have a time stamp: several time stamps, in fact, recording when they were written, when they were transmitted and when they were received. These time stamps are also included as part of the series of headers at the top of each email message. As a message passes from computer to computer, each one stamps it with the date and time and the name of the computer. This is rather like franking impressions and handling details applied to a letter as it passes between two large companies.

When the email message arrives at its ultimate destination it is then copied into a large file that acts as the user's 'inbox': the mail storage space that is handled by the email reader program. As the message is copied into the email inbox it changes that inbox file, so the file date and time stamps for the inbox are changed to represent the date and time at which the email message is received.

Again just as with the history file, the time stamp on the inbox file should be the same as the final time stamp on the last message written into the inbox. Unfortunately, it wasn't.

I began to feel sick. Not only was the time stamp not close to the correct – or at least a consistent – value, it was in fact a whole day out. Why should that be? The minute and second figures looked to be correct, but the hour and day values were wrong. And then I realized why: the computer was operating in the wrong time zone. Instead of being set for Greenwich Mean Time, the computer clock at the university had been set to Pacific Daylight Time. It was as though the computer was operating on the assumption that it was in Seattle or San Francisco, not the Midlands of England.

But could that be possible? Would a mainframe computer used and relied upon by hundreds of academics and students, and managed by a team of some half-dozen system administrators, be allowed to have a clock that was nine hours wrong? Surely someone would notice and complain?

Then I remembered that I had a statement in the lever-arch file from one of the system staff stating that the university computer was working correctly. The clock simply could not have been wrong. So what was the explanation? And what did it mean for my carefully constructed argument? What did it mean for the *police*'s computer evidence?

I was distracted, though, because at this point the senior system administrator was sworn in and an excited Nick nudged me hard in the ribs. This was the man who I had deduced had typed the commands. The next few minutes promised to be dramatic.

Formally, the system administrators were *prosecution* witnesses, so the prosecution had to call them and then immediately offer them to Ms Kushner for cross-examination. She led this final 'victim' through the same series of questions as the others, with the same negative results. When she'd exhausted those stock questions, though, instead of the curt 'No more questions' that each of the others had been dismissed with, she picked up another page of questions which Nick and I had prepared for her. From the corner of my eye I could see that the jury were leaning forward intently now to listen more closely.

She asked the hapless man where and when he had learned about UNIX, and on what type of computer; she established that he was most familiar with what I had coached her to call the 'east-coast dialect'. He was, of course, confused by the term, but quickly grasped what she meant and agreed. She established that the workstation quoted in the list of commands was one that he had access to; again, he agreed. She took him through the commands, getting him to explain how they must have been typed by an administrator at that workstation and that ascribing them to her client was unfair. Yet again, he agreed.

But he would *not* agree that he had been there at 3 a.m. the night before Chris was arrested and that the commands were ones he had typed.

Short of calling the man a liar, Ms Kushner had done as much as she could with the questions; and she had certainly cast doubt on the prosecution's case.

But I was still very worried about the time-zone question. If the computer *had* somehow been running on Seattle time, then the commands were not entered at 3 a.m. on the night before Chris was arrested but at midday on the day of his 7 a.m. arrest. If that was the case, then the commands were entered *after* the arrest but had still formed a part of the police case. This struck me as pretty unfair. It would mean that the police hadn't effectively 'frozen' the scene of crime and had polluted it themselves. That is the most heinous sin in the canon of forensic science, whose guiding principle is 'First, do no harm.'

The prosecution computer expert and the Crown Prosecution Service lawyers called for time to try and establish what had happened, and the defence agreed that the prosecution expert and I should work together to try and form an understanding. Over the next few days, the full disaster of how the police computer evidence had been collected, handled and mishandled became increasingly evident.

After having arrested Chris, we learned, the police had asked the senior system administrator at the university to help them to inspect and produce evidence from Chris's files on the computer. The administrator had done so, shortly before lunch on the day of Chris's arrest but in a way that he later admitted was clumsy and which left the history-file commands on the account. Just as I had deduced, he had logged in to the computer as 'Root' – the most privileged user – but had then changed his login identity to Chris by using a command that only 'Root' has access to. He hadn't realized that this meant that every command he subsequently typed was being recorded into the history file in Chris's account.

With Chris's identity, the administrator had worked through

the files, inspecting and displaying picture files. In doing this, he had overwritten the date and time stamps and effectively destroyed crucial evidence. He had not, however, set up his own workstation correctly and had had to pause and reset it before displaying the files. All of these commands were what I had encountered in the history file, and all of them were interpreted by the police and by the prosecution expert witness as being evidence of Chris's activities.

After having examined the files – thereby introducing erroneous commands *and* altering the access time stamps on Chris's files – the administrator had made a back-up of Chris's files from the university computer. The back-up had been sealed and witnessed, then been taken by the police and passed to their computer expert. To be able to inspect the contents – and to be able to give me and the defence team a copy – the prosecution expert needed to get the back-up contents onto an inspection computer system. And this is where the crucial series of mistakes occurred. Instead of copying the back-up onto a UNIX system, just like the computer it had been taken from, the police expert instead set up a new and pristine Windows system on a personal computer and copied the back-up onto that. He then created copy CDs of the files and it was from these that we had worked.

When I'd received the CDs, I'd obviously asked whether it was possible for me to have a copy of the original computer, since this process had retained the time stamps on the in-dividual files but had had to recreate the directories and had therefore lost the original time stamps on directories. I had been told that both defence and prosecution were going to work from these CDs, and because of that I didn't need to worry about the copying mechanism. A lesson learned: *nowadays* I would know not to accept that reassurance; then, I did not realize how crucial this aspect was going to prove.

The time zone on the copy computer – the Windows system – was set to the default value: Seattle time, the headquarters of Microsoft. As a result, all of the file date stamps were represented as though they were in Seattle; midday on the day of Chris's arrest became 3 a.m. on the night before it. Prosecution *and* defence had therefore been working with invalid dates – a horrendous error when one is creating arguments that involve crucial points of time. It had led the police to accuse Chris of having accessed the university computer from a personal computer in the service station; and it had led me into accusing a wholly innocent system administrator of having hacked into our client's files surreptitiously in the middle of the night. He was vindicated in court when the police expert revealed this catalogue of confusion.

The fact remained, though, that the police were producing in evidence a collection of computer files that had been inspected and altered by a prosecution witness, were relying on a manu-factured list of commands to prove that Chris had accessed the paedophile material, and were admitting to having misled the court dreadfully with regard to the nature and accuracy of the computer material.

The prosecution agreed to withdraw all of the erroneous material, and an accurate copy of the computer evidence was resubmitted. The history file was withdrawn, but even after that the prosecution still had a strong case for Chris to answer: he was still in possession of paedophile images; he was still on record promising to provide images to other paedophiles; and there was still the contact offence to answer.

As Nick had hoped we could, I had shown that the evidence did indeed contain indications of someone else having accessed the files. Unfortunately, that had been limited to the period after Chris's arrest. I had done a lot but not quite enough.

It took two trials to find Chris guilty of most of the paedophile charges laid against him. The first jury, obviously confused by the muddled story of poorly handled, poorly presented and hastily withdrawn computer evidence, were unable to form a verdict and were dismissed by the judge. A second trial a few weeks later in Birmingham saw a much better prepared and presented prosecution case regarding the computer material. In the defence team, we felt as though all our firepower had been spent on a valid argument based on badly preserved evidence; and I personally felt that a year and a half of my life had been wasted on evidence that was invalid from the very beginning.

The prosecution stuck with the basics. The defendant was in possession of indecent photographs of children, and this is an offence under the Criminal Justice Act. Chris's name and address were put on the register of known paedophiles and he served nearly two very unpleasant years in prison.

I was uncertain how I felt about that. Throughout the long period of work leading up to the trial, and through the trial itself, my opinion of Chris had altered so many times and in such a wild manner that I no longer really knew what I felt. On a personal level, the lad seemed eminently likeable, though I was certainly not seeing him at his best. But if he *was* a paedophile then he represented all that I would most fear for my children.

I suspect that he had probably found himself embroiled in a situation that escalated quickly out of his control. His project seemed to me to have been genuinely conceived and he did seem to have attempted to do work on it. But then he found himself on the receiving end of unexpected material. And though he may very well have been playing a part that exercised his personal tastes, he had got quickly out of his depth. Even with all of that, though, I could still not completely bring myself to regard him as a child abuser. Perhaps the only personal lesson that I could take away from the exercise, therefore, was this: stereotypes are not reality.

Professionally, the most important lesson that I learned was not to become interested in the guilt or innocence – or even the morality – of the individuals involved. I learned to consider the people as being computer users: the source of the material that I was interested in. My role, I came to understand, was sharply delineated: I was there because of an expertise in *computers*, not because of any expertise in *people*. Twelve citizens, and only those twelve citizens, have a right, a duty, and the ability to determine the defendant's guilt or innocence. My job was to ensure that, when computers were involved, those twelve were presented with a clear, appropriate and well-considered description of the computer evidence.

I vowed that I would never again ask myself what I thought or felt about the defendant in any case I worked on. I simply used the computer to cast the brightest light I could on what had been done, based on practical experience as a computer security specialist.

And that, of course, is the most important aspect of being a computer expert witness: to guide the court in appreciating the often arcane yet important aspects of the computer science involved in a particular collection of evidence, but then to leave it to the courts to make the decisions.

Over the years that followed this first appearance, I learned my craft as an expert witness. My colleagues and I are there to ensure that a judgement is based on a valid and independent statement of the technology involved, rather than a partisan expression that has been biased – consciously or unconsciously – towards one or other parties. We are there to help a court to establish whether technology that judges and juries can barely understand should be trusted, and whether assertions made by witnesses are realistic in the context of that technology.

But that role carries with it a heavy duty. Because of this requirement to explain, expert witnesses are allowed to express not only the facts involved in a case but also have the unique privilege of being permitted to deliver their *opinions*. We also have the equally unique privilege of being allowed to discuss elements of a case with one another, so as to find agreed features and agreed ways of expressing the relevant facts. As expert witnesses we have to work hard to ensure that our evidence is not only *heard* but also *understood*: we are teachers as well as witnesses. And we are further privileged, in that we are allowed to hear – and indeed, often to comment upon – evidence delivered by other witnesses. We are even allowed to correct misunderstandings on the part of counsel or the judge, often being recalled to the stand to give clarification or explanation in the middle of another witness's testimony.

As computer expert witnesses, my colleagues and I have three principal tasks within any given case. First of all, we must formulate a description of the computer and of any elements of its operation that are important in the context of the case. We cannot assume that the judge or any of the jury members has any prior experience with the technology, and we must ensure that the description is even-handed and accurate.

The second most important task for the computer expert witness is to help counsel to understand the nature of the computer evidence and how it supports or belies the defendant's assertions regarding their activities. We do this through initial witness statements and expert reports; through rebuttals of any elements of the opposition's expert's evidence with which we do not agree; and through case conferences, at which we are allowed – indeed, encouraged – to explain technical aspects as thoroughly as necessary and as clearly as possible.

And the third most important task is then actually to appear in court and try to address the often clumsily worded questions of counsel for the prosecution or defence, in the face of hostility from the defendant (and even from the judge and jury members if the case is particularly complex or particularly horrifying). Every expert witness has to be something of a teacher, but few teachers face such an ill-prepared 'class' with such challenging material. But then again, few teachers see such a varied and interesting range of topics.

In practice, most cases involving at least some element of computer evidence feature computer expert witnesses, drawn from a small group of individuals known to the police or to the lawyers involved. Because they are supposed to be independent, and because they are supposed to have agreed much beforehand, and because much of the technology is well understood by the experts if not by the court, disputes between computer expert witnesses should be rare. They *should* be, but in practice they are all too common, from minor episodes of good-natured sniping to full-fledged public arguments between experts who have a history of disagreement.

Complicated technology and ill-informed courts; highly

strung and argumentative experts frequently pitted against one another; and a range of challenging and criminally important types of case: this is the world of computer forensics in the era of high-technology crimes, a world into which I stumbled completely by accident.

2. Beginnings

I had come to be a computer expert witness from a background in computer security; and to computer security, like most, from computer-*hacking*. But I had come to computer-hacking from a love of mathematics and of English.

I had been of the first generation of schoolchildren to see computers as something other than room-sized monstrosities lovingly tended by white-coated supplicants. My school had bought a desktop-size Research Machines personal computer while I was still in the fifth form. From the first moment I was allowed to use it I saw that I understood it, could manipulate and subvert it, and that in programming I had the perfect opportunity to control something. And more importantly, I had the chance to apply mathematics and English together.

In English – and particularly in poetry – the *precise* word or phrase is something worth striving for; indeed, it's the whole point of writing. In maths, description precedes analysis and leads to understanding and the opportunity to extend and develop additional insights. I loved them both, but in my school in the mid-1970s children were expected to make an early and binding decision whether to go down the arts route, including English but not maths; or the science route, including maths but not English. I would have to discard one or other of my favourites.

I had chosen mathematics: a toss of a coin, biased slightly by the thought that I could earn more from science than from the arts. But in programming, I saw that my maths was necessary to understand what I wanted to achieve with a piece of software, and my English was necessary to express the intention to a point of precision even more accurate than in poetry. *And* I could earn a lot of money. I was hooked.

But if writing new programs was appealing, *subverting* existing programs – 'hacking' the computer – was totally irresistible.

When I started hacking computer systems, in the prehistory of the Internet back in 1980, the landscape was completely different from the modern world. Then, computers were easy to locate, easy to access, and easy to gain complete control of. They were not well monitored, but neither did they do particularly interesting things. Now, we have computers that are well secured, with complex passwords, hidden behind the protection of dedicated 'firewall' security systems. Now, they are hard to locate, hard to access and difficult to gain complete control of. But they are enormously more interesting to hack; and, because they process money, enormously more attractive to computer criminals.

This was in the years before simple hacking tricks were made widely available on the World Wide Web. Indeed, this was not only in the years before the Web, this was in the years when what would become the Internet in the UK was nothing more than a crude interconnection of a few dozen systems, mostly only accessible via slow telephone connections. The magic-wand tricks of today's hackers were many years in the future. Hacking computers – or rather, cracking their security measures – involved understanding the relationships between different programs and the operating system; it meant long hours of tedious exploration, for little reward other than the flush of success when it worked.

I learned how to hack the computers in the university where I studied mathematics, but from there I began to explore the wider world of other systems that these were connected to. I hacked into computers in universities around the world, even managing once to get control over a telescope in Hawaii.

Hackers played games: capturing control of hacked systems from one another; collecting 'totems', or pieces of information from different computer systems in different time zones; we encircled the world with ever more complex interconnections of hacked systems. These were days of essentially innocent computer intrusion: the clumsy network of slow telephone connections and transatlantic links was a playground containing any number of easily accessible systems. There *were* computers operated by the banks and the stock markets, of course, and my friends and I joked about hacking them and stealing millions. But they were so far beyond our ability at that time that they were safe; or rather, *we* were safe, since we would surely have got into huge amounts of trouble if we'd tried.

The early years of hacking were dominated by a handful of simple tricks: most obviously, hackers would try to guess, deduce or steal passwords to a system. We would look over people's shoulders as they typed in their password and try to work out what they had typed; we would try to introduce new files where they shouldn't be, or look for ways of making programs do the wrong thing. It was about creativity, imagination and determination; it was, above all else, something that we *assumed was possible*.

That assumption is perhaps the most important element. The best way to understand the mentality of a hacker – no less so today than it was then – is to think about playing a computer game: one of those puzzle-solving adventure games, for example. You are stuck, perhaps in a room within the game. The door to the room is locked but you know that you are expected to get through it to continue the game. You have collected all the items that are available and have read all the scrolls or secret messages or whatever in the game. You're stuck but you know that there *must* be a way through the door, or the game is wrong. You try everything you can think of: complex combinations of commands, or strange and outrageous things, perhaps even loading the game program into a text editor to see if you can see any recognizable sequences of characters. Perhaps you become frustrated and angry, or perhaps you simply ask a friend for their help, or get a crib sheet from the Internet. The key point is this: you *know* that there must be a way through the door, so you keep on looking.

Hackers think exactly like that about computer systems. They have faith in the fact that even the most apparently secure computer system *must* have a way into it. So they will keep on looking, keep on trying, keep on playing until the secret trick becomes apparent to them.

The landscape of computers and hacking has changed in the twenty-odd years since I started hacking, of course. The computers are different, and now there are a lot of these crib sheets for gaining access to even the best-protected systems. But some things never change, and the most fundamental thing is the belief that it is always possible.

I enjoyed the challenge of gaining mastery over the computer systems I could access, but towards the end of the 1980s the activities that I and my friends had been doing for fun became positively illegal. Though there were several factors that drove this, perhaps the single most important was the result of the unsuccessful prosecution of Steve Gold and Rob Shiffreen.

Gold and Shiffreen were journalists on a 1985 press tour of the BT Prestel computer centre in London when they spotted a printed sheet on the noticeboard along one of the corridors. It was from the system administrator, to advise staff that he would be on annual leave. Unfortunately, the sheet gave details of the supervisor login accounts 'in case anyone needs to do anything while I am away'. Naturally curious, neither man could ignore the information. Over subsequent weeks the pair were able to get access to extensive parts of the Prestel system including, most worryingly, the Duke of Edinburgh's email account.

Engineers were able to track the pair and discover their telephone number, from which they were accessing the Prestel system over a simple, slow modem connection. They were arrested by Detective Inspector John Austin of the Metropolitan Police Fraud Squad. A former computer operator, DI Austen had been tasked with establishing a Computer Crime Unit for the Metropolitan Police. Until April 2001 – when the National High-Tech Crime Unit was established in London's Docklands – this was the premier computer-crime-handling body in the UK.

The arrest of Gold and Shiffreen established the value and reputation of the Computer Crime Unit, but there was an immediate problem: with what offence could the pair be charged?

A variety of attempts to prosecute computer intruders had been made before this time. They had involved a series of ridiculously inappropriate charges: of having stolen electricity; of having criminally damaged computer equipment by changing the magnetic properties of parts of the hard disk; even of having stolen information that was, in fact, still held by the system owners. Most of these charges failed.

The Crown Prosecution Service therefore chose to charge the pair with offences of fraud under the 1981 Forgery and Counterfeiting Act. The thinking was that they had 'lied' their way onto the computer by pretending to be someone else. The specific charge was of having created a 'false instrument' in using somebody else's username and password to access the computer system.

Though it was apparent that Gold and Shiffreen had indeed done something that should be considered illegal, no-one was quite sure what the specific offence was. They had lied, yes; but was lying to a *computer* really lying? And was that a criminal offence?

The prosecution argued vehemently that it was indeed an offence, and that Gold and Shiffreen were two dangerous computer bandits who should be punished. At first, the courts agreed and the pair were found guilty of fraud. Naturally they mounted an appeal.

For that appeal, the defence argued that the 'false instrument' could not and should not be used to apply to a computer. What, they demanded to know, *was* the false instrument that the prosecution claimed was used? A false instrument would more naturally be a forged cheque, for example, used to fool a bank into releasing funds. In this case, though, the prosecution asserted that the 'false instrument' was the computer's internal operating state, which had been 'falsely created' by Gold and Shiffreen; they had, in effect, forged the credentials of a valid user.

The defence put together a particularly clever counter-argument. They accepted that the false instrument could indeed be the internal operating state, but they asked what it was that the false instrument was acting *on*? They argued that the thing being fooled was in fact this internal operating state itself: the 'false instrument' was fooling itself – clearly nonsensical. Moreover, it was doing so for only the barest fraction of a second – hardly comparable to the fraudulent production of a cheque or transfer instruction. Finally, in fooling a computer, what was being defrauded was an object rather than a person or an organization, and the law had not been written with that in mind. For all of these reasons, the defence argued that the conviction should not be allowed to stand.

In 1986, the appeal court agreed, as did the House of Lords when the case was brought before them in 1988. Steve Gold and Rob Shiffreen were set free, the charges against them overturned.

In their ruling their lordships stressed that a judicial review was evidently required to address what was plainly a criminal activity which fell outside of the then state of the law: a so-called 'lacuna'. Unsurprisingly, the judicial review proposed a new law to cover illicit access to computers.

In the UK, the Computer Misuse Act 1990 is the law under which computer-hacking and virus-writing was made illegal, with fines and prison sentences for those convicted. For me, it meant that what had previously been a fun exercise in exploration now carried a real possibility of a criminal record. It was past time to reconsider my attitude to computer in-securities; they were no longer opportunities for exploration but for study and repair work. I became first a computer scientist and lecturer at York University, and then an industry consultant in computer security. I analysed systems that had been hacked, or helped to design and build systems that were as secure as possible for the military, the government and financial organizations. Later I established and helped to run my own computer-security company and was nominated as an external professor at the Royal Military College of Science in the UK. And I became a well-respected and trusted figure, working closely with the police to combat computer crime.

I also realized an important principle: hacking into computers was fun, but analysing and tracking those who were responsible for intrusions was even more entertaining. Instead of hacking the *computers*, I learned how much better it was to hack the *hackers*.

In my career, I have applied that understanding of how hackers think and operate in two different ways. First of all, in investigating computer crimes. My initial investigations were into computers that had been hacked by outsiders or manipulated by insiders. Working with the victims, I collected and processed the available evidence; working with the police, I helped to train them in understanding and acting upon that data. And I have now come to be asked to help train the prosecutors employed by the Crown Prosecution Service to take those cases forward to court.

Second, I copy what hackers can do. I test the security of computer systems by pretending to be a determined or a casual intruder, or a disgruntled employee – or, in one thrilling exercise, pretending to be an armed raider breaking into a secure computer centre. I have run tests to break encryption systems, to persuade employees to co-operate with me over the telephone, and to hack into systems as far away as Australia. By doing these tests – or, now, by running a team of well-trained, non-criminal hackers to do the tests – I have been able to work out precisely which elements of a company's computer infrastructure might be vulnerable to attack. And therefore what elements of the infrastructure need to have improved protection.

I help to catch computer criminals; I pretend to *be* a computer criminal; and I manage to *stop* computer criminals. I've helped to set up a small, specialist company to do all of those things for some of the largest and best-known companies in the world. It's a fun career.

3. **The Business Card Test**

Hong Kong in the middle of the summer: sticky, close and *very* hot.

I was there in July 1999, two years after the 'Christopher Robin' case. In those two years I had worked on a variety of different cases and a variety of different problems, but ultimately – with the dotcom boom sounding loudly around me – establishing my own company had seemed like a sensible thing to do. My London-based consulting company was only six weeks old when I went out to Hong Kong, keen to see whether there was a market there to justify an Asian subsidiary.

To meet potential clients, I had agreed to give a talk on computer security, and in particular to give a description of the approach and the mentality of computer hackers. I chose as my topic the question of business cards.

A business card might seem like a surprisingly old-fashioned thing to consider in the context of high-technology hacking and computer crime. But they give away a surprising amount of important information to the hacker. Take a look at a typical business card. You'll see that it gives the name of the employee and the company, its logo and the office address. It will also give their telephone number, perhaps a fax number and a switchboard number, usually at least an email address, and often a website.

Now look at it like a hacker would. A switchboard number and a direct telephone number are enough to allow a hacker to deduce the range of numbers that the company's switchboard supports. Often inside large companies some employees will connect an unauthorized computer to the telephone network through the modem with which all PCs are now produced. This might be to allow the employee access from home; it might be to allow legitimate access to some application for support purposes; or it might be to let the employee access the Internet without being monitored by the company. In a large enough organization – and this can be deduced from the size of the telephone range – this possibility becomes a near certainty and the hacker is encouraged to look for those connected modems.

The card gives a name and an email address. This not only tells the hacker about that specific person but it also gives an indication of the rule that the company uses to construct email names. It means that the hacker now has a way of guessing email names and perhaps also of inventing them. He can then look for newsgroup postings from employees, perhaps indicating what they're interested in. That might be enough for the hacker to be able to start a conversation with the employee and to get to know them; the first step in being able to *use* them.

The website is an obvious target for the hacker. He can guess this from the email address or be given it immediately on the business card. Again, this gives him a target to begin exploring. Logo, address and company name provide the hacker – if he has a scanner and word-processing software – with enough to construct a plausible copy of the company's headed notepaper. The hacker can potentially use this to remove websites, redirect email or even capture legitimate users' network traffic by writing to the Internet service provider (ISP) to request changes.

An important point to remember about information security is that a vulnerability to hacking does not start with the existence of a weakness or a hole in a computer; it starts with a hacker first becoming interested in hacking the computer in question. And that means that the first things to consider are the things that begin to attract hackers' attention: anything that hints at an easy way of deducing or discovering system-configuration information.

This doesn't mean that companies shouldn't give out business cards; but it does mean that they should be aware of what information it might give out to a hacker. I wanted the audience to begin to *think* like a hacker, and to use that perception to ensure that their applications, systems and networks were protected from the types of approach that they could expect.

It seemed to be a well-received presentation, though the audience of mainly middle-aged Chinese IT and business managers seemed very reserved compared to an equivalent UK or American audience. But amongst the Chinese faces there were one or two Westerners, and one in particular seemed keen to talk to me just before the coffee break. He was the head of audit for one of the largest corporations doing business on the Pacific Rim. He made his way to the front of the auditorium as I finished and, Oriental-style with two hands and all due solemnity (though he was Australian), he passed me his business card. He challenged me in front of the large audience to examine the security of his Internet-facing computer networks and to try and gain access to the sensitive file servers upon which his multi-billion-dollar international trading business relied. Having gained access, to complete the challenge my company would have to obtain some interesting, relevant but above all *secret* file of information and provide a copy of it back to him.

I was being asked to be an 'ethical hacker': someone who acts exactly as a criminal hacker would do, but in a controlled and *legal* way, performing an exercise known as a 'penetration test'. The idea is to establish just how secure or insecure a system or network is, not through analysis of specifications or system configuration, but rather through trying to break in.

It was a challenge to relish, though there was one potential problem with the situation: we would, he explained, only get paid if we succeeded, and his IT staff had promised him on their honour that we would fail. For a company that had only been trading for a few weeks it was an enormous gamble. If it succeeded, the audit manager promised us a steady income stream in testing all the subsidiary companies in his group; if it failed – and failed after such a public launch – then we could certainly forget about the Asian market and perhaps even find the UK market a greater problem.

I didn't hesitate: I accepted the challenge, and gambled the future of my business.

The test itself could be carried out from anywhere that I could get an Internet connection: from the hotel I was staying at in Hong Kong or from my own offices back in London. As it happened, the Australian audit manager and I decided to run the test from London.

Beginning with only the Australian's business card meant that we knew nothing about the types of computer they were running, the location of those computers, or even whether they used Chinese or Western characters. We knew nothing what-soever. In information-security circles this is called a 'black-box' test and is the closest we can get to the way that a real computer hacker would approach a completely unknown target network. By doing this, we can show the client company not only what a hacker would do and how successful they might be, but also whether the client would detect the attack and how quickly – if at all – their network-support and security staff would react.

For most organizations it's a frightening and eye-opening experience, but it was obvious from our conversations that the Australian was relishing the prospect of being able to thumb his nose at his IT staff, who had assured him that the computers were impregnable. But for us it meant that we had to work from a standing start to attain some form of intrusion in just four days if we were to be paid. It was a tall order and I must admit to having been nervous when we started.

I began the test with a shamefully simple trick. The business card obviously gave me the address of the company's website.

I examined the web pages, and in doing this I was able to locate a number of other email addresses for people within the client company. Amongst these was the contact person for recruitment in Hong Kong, listed in the 'Situations Vacant' section of the website.

For a computer hacker a recruitment contact is a particularly useful target. They receive CV files – usually as Microsoft Word documents – which they happily open and inspect. One possibility for me in hacking the company's network would be to include a so-called 'Trojan Horse' application inside an apparently legitimate CV document.

A Trojan Horse is a program that looks entirely safe and legitimate but actually – just like the wooden horse the Greeks used against Troy – allows an attacker past the defences and inside the company network. Most corporate networks are protected by security-screening computers called 'firewalls'. These examine the commands and connections from computers outside the network to those on the inside and make sure that hackers cannot easily gain access. Typically, however, whilst these firewalls protect for connections from the outside to the inside, they do not protect for connections from the inside to the outside. Because of this, a so-called 'back connection' from an infected workstation on the inside to a hacker's computer on the outside can usually let a hacker gain access. And the easiest way to achieve this is by means of a Trojan Horse program, either transmitted as part of a computer virus or disguised and embedded within a document. I hoped the latter wasn't necessary, since any decent anti-virus program on the target workstation would detect the intrusion of a known Trojan Horse. This would mean that I would have to create a new one for myself. I didn't want to have to go to those lengths but it was worth knowing whether the option was available to me.

Having discovered the recruitment contact, I sent a simple email requesting careers information. The details of the request were contained within a Word document: I wanted to check that documents were indeed opened by the contact. They were, and I received a reply. This meant two things: first of all, that I could expect to persuade the contact to open a file attached to an email message. I had a chance therefore of getting them to execute a Trojan Horse program. Secondly, it meant that I now had an email from inside the company's computer network. And *that* meant that I could examine the 'extended headers' associated with the email transmission.

When you look at email normally, you will see that it says who it's from, who it's to, what it's about and a date; these lines are called the 'headers'. Hidden away in the message are a set of further lines – called the 'extended headers' – that are used by the mail-administration staff to track message transmission in the event of a failure or a problem in the systems. These are vitally important for computer forensics because they allow the messages to be analysed very precisely.

For example, there are two time stamps initially associated with a mail message. The first is part of the message-identification number and denotes the time at which the writer started to create the message. The second time stamp is placed on the message when it is first transmitted from the writer's own computer to the network's mail-processing system. The difference between these two times shows how long it took the writer to create the message. This can tell us a lot about the writer.

Other information stamps on the email include the system names and network addresses for the computers that transmit the message, including the name and address of the computer that the writer was sitting at when they created it. This is a gold-mine of useful information, both for catching the authors of blackmail or threatening email messages, and for gaining information that can be used to breach security on a system.

You can see these extra lines by having your email reading program list 'full' or 'advanced' header information. Doing this you can deduce the range of internal addresses used, the way that systems are named by the company, and the speed with which their network works. This is a lot of information that shouldn't really be available outside the company.

All of these elements were present in the extended headers

that I received from the recruitment contact. I discovered the name of the email gateway into the company and the address of the *network* gateway that connected the company to the Internet. I discovered the name and internal address of the computer from which the message had been sent. And I discovered the name and even the revision and installation details of the email-handling package used within the company.

Perhaps more importantly than all this, I had learned one thing of vital interest to any computer hacker: the client company concerned had little or no idea about how important it was to protect network-sensitive information. They would be high on the target list of any hacker interested in gaining access to a powerful computer network in the Pacific Rim.

I had started the exercise nervous as to whether we would be able to succeed – and so be paid – in the time available to us. But after just a couple of hours I had already begun to relax. Although the money wasn't yet in the bag, I was growing increasingly confident that we would be able to thumb our noses at the company's network managers. And more importantly, that we would be paid for the privilege. I was starting to enjoy myself.

So far the internal computer used by the recruitment contact was inaccessible to me. The email and Internet gateways, however, were easily accessible and formed a viable initial target. I got a sheet of A4 paper and stuck it on the wall. I drew two boxes on it, one for each computer, and wrote the name and 'Internet address' beside them. A computer on the Internet is like a house on a street. It has an address and it has several ways that it can be accessed: doors, windows, cellars, holes, etc. The computer's address is called its 'IP number'. IP is 'Internet protocol' and is the basic mechanism that is used on the Internet for sending data from computer to computer. In IP the data is split up into small connections called 'packets'. These are sent from one computer to another via any intermediate computers. To ensure that the destination computer can be found, each computer has an IP address: a number, similar in many ways to a telephone number but made up of four values between 0 and 255: 123.234.62.10, for example.

To begin hacking a target computer the hacker needs to know these IP addresses, and we had discovered them very quickly. It wasn't yet coffee time on the first day of the test but I already had my starting point. Before trying to hack them, though, I wanted to know even more about the company's networks.

When a company gets an Internet connection it has to register the names and Internet addresses of the computers that will access it directly. That database is publicly available and when I looked at it I found around a hundred computers that belonged to the company. That was more than a little startling: Internet service providers will tend to have hundreds of addresses, simply because they need that many for their business; ordinary companies usually have a handful, such as their website, their email server, their main access gateway and maybe one or two others. Although individual PCs within the company might also have access to the Internet, this will usually be via some intermediate computer called a 'proxy': the internal addresses will usually be hidden behind the single proxy address. In this case, though, it seemed that *every* internal PC was registered directly onto the Internet rather than through a proxy. It meant that our victim company was an unusual one. The odds on my little gamble seemed to be shortening by the minute. I was beginning to feel ever more confident.

It could be that the company had *registered* all those addresses but was not actually *using* more than the usual handful. The next step that a hacker would take is to see which of those computers were connected to the Internet. There is a program that will do this by bouncing a short Internet message to the computer. If it is connected, the computer will reply; if it isn't, or if something like a firewall is protecting it, then it won't. The idea is a little like a submarine using radar to see what kind of echoes it receives; and indeed, the program that does this task is actually called Ping.

I found that almost all of the hundred or so computers were present. Our victim company really *was* an unusual one. A huge number of computers was accessible over the Internet, and it seemed as though no firewall protection was acting to prevent those systems from being seen. We were trying to copy precisely what a 'real' hacker would do and feel about the exercise. At this point I made a note that the hacker would be wildly excited. I tore down the A4 sheet of paper and replaced it with an A2 sheet from a flipchart. I had a lot of computers to examine.

It could be that there were even more computers than these. Amongst the registration information held in the public Internet databases are details of several systems called 'name servers'. These provide the translation from the computer's 'name' to the computer's Internet address, rather like an online telephone directory. For example, a computer might be called 'mail.acme.com' with Internet address 123.234.62.10. The name server provides that association. A hacking tool called 'Dig' is available to query those name servers and to prompt them into delivering information on all the computers within a given network that can be accessed from the Internet. If the name servers had not been secured then this would give me even more target information.

Sure enough, running the Dig program gave me an even more comprehensive list of systems; the Australian audit manager had been right to doubt his IT staff. It looked as though his company's IT security was well below par; I could almost start spending his money already.

The next thing that a careful hacker would do is examine each of the computers in turn to see what they are and what they do, rather like a professional burglar examining houses to see which is worth breaking into. To achieve this the hacker will use one of the most powerful general tools that have been developed for testing computers: a 'port scanner'.

The access routes into a computer are called 'ports'. Each computer on the Internet has a maximum of around 65,000 ports, most of which are not used. (These are called 'closed ports'.) An *open* port corresponds to a particular program running on the computer and using the Internet connection, and most computers will have only a handful of these. The specific types of ports available and programs running on them characterize the computer and provide the hacker with all the information they need in order to break in. A port scanner acts a little like the burglar as he looks around the outside of a house, looking to see what windows and doors there are and whether any of them might be open or easily forced.

One of the earliest such programs was called SATAN, developed by an IT security specialist to evaluate his own machines. Like many such tools, in the hands of a security consultant it can be used to protect a computer but in the hands of a hacker to gain access. The author of SATAN knew this, but made the tool available to the wider world so as to encourage all system managers to consider the integrity of their systems.

This practice of making potentially damaging information or tools easily accessible to the hackers, with a view to encouraging system managers to protect their systems, is known as 'full disclosure'. Usually it emerges as a conflict between IT security experts and application or system developers when a new problem is encountered with a particular product. Hackers or *bona fide* researchers will discover a potential breach and will then develop a so-called 'proof-of-concept exploitation': a simple little program that uses the security vulnerability to gain access to a computer, thereby demonstrating that the vulnerability is a real one.

But what do they then do? In full disclosure the researchers will publish details of the security breach along with the proof-of-concept exploit, allowing system managers – but also hackers – to establish whether they are indeed vulnerable. It is to be hoped that the researchers will also have published a suggested way of resolving the issue – often called a 'fix' or, if imperfect, a 'work-around' – and this can be used to test that the hole has been repaired.

Alternatively, the researchers will keep the breach a secret, and will contact the developer of the application or system directly. This allows the developer to work on producing a solution for the problem before the researchers tell the wider world. Unfortunately, during this period the system managers of any vulnerable computers do not know that they are vulnerable. If a hacker has already deduced the existence of the security hole then they can exploit it with a degree of impunity.

It is a difficult circle to square. Usually, researchers who have developed a proof-of-concept exploit will wait for a short time before publishing it. During this period – usually a week or so – they will inform the developers of the problem. Microsoft, one of the developers with the worst track record for security problems, has tried to insist on a thirty-day period for this embargo; this looks unlikely to be successful.

However, because of this philosophy of full disclosure, a wide range of hacking tools is publicly available for use by hackers and security analysts alike. And one of the most important is the modern descendant of the original SATAN tool: the NMAP, or 'network map' tool, developed by a hacker known only as Fyodor. We use NMAP, as does almost every hacker and security professional in the world.

SATAN worked by attempting to open a full communication session with each of the 65,000 or so ports potentially accessible on a given computer. Naturally this sequence is easily detected by the computers targeted and is now usually not permitted. NMAP is more subtle than this: it connects to the ports in a random sequence, and it does so with lengthy delays between attempts. It also doesn't do a 'full' connection attempt. Instead, it performs what are called 'stealth' scans. One such type of stealthy connection request is to try to *close* each of the ports rather than to open them. If the port is already open – that is, with an application running on it – then the close request will receive an error message to indicate that the scanner doesn't have permission to close the port. If the port is in fact already closed then a different error message is sent back.

In this way, NMAP can work out which ports are open without obviously alerting the computer to the scan. Although the computer itself might not notice the scan, the whole purpose of the protecting firewall is to detect, prevent and raise the alarm when any form of scan – stealthy or obvious – is attempted. I decided that another small gamble was in order: instead of running this scan as slowly and as stealthily as possible – so as to have a chance of evading detection – I decided to be as loud and as obvious as I could. I was already beginning to form a low opinion of the company's network staff: I no longer wanted to thumb my nose at them, I wanted to rub their noses in how bad they were.

It was a gamble, of course: if they noticed the firewall's alerts they would do what they could to stop us, perhaps even by turning off their Internet connection. They would only have to do this for a few days and we would definitely lose the gamble. But I wasn't sure that there was, in fact, a firewall there at all to raise any such alerts. Nothing had stopped us from 'pinging' the systems; and on the network-tracing exercise there was nothing that was obviously a firewall. I was starting to think that there was *no* form of protection for this network at all. The Australian audit manager was perhaps not so much gambling as bluffing, not just with a pretty poor hand but with no cards whatsoever.

It was lunchtime on the first day of the test when we started the port-scanner program running on the complete range of computers we had discovered, loudly checking every system in turn. Even though it is doing something intellectually exciting, watching the scanner run is close to the most boring thing in the world, as it lists each computer in turn and then begins the slow but inexorable process of testing each of 65,000 possible ports on each computer that one is testing.

In the warmth of the tiny office rooms I was soon hypnotized watching the stream of numbers and tests scroll past on the computer screen – and so my staff and I did what all real hackers would do: we went across the road for a drink.

It seemed incomprehensible that such a large organization could be running without a firewall in place. The firewall forms the first line of defence for a network of computers belonging to any company, and is a computer that has two functions. First,

it receives Internet traffic on one side of itself, on its first network connection, and passes that traffic through to the internal
network on its other side, on a second network connection. It
therefore acts as a gateway from the outside, 'hostile' network
of the Internet, to the inside, sensitive network of the company.

The second thing that it does, though, is to examine and filter
the network traffic on the way. It looks to see whether the traffic
represents hostile activity on the part of a hacker, and if it does
then the firewall will refuse to pass the traffic inwards. It acts,
in other words, like a nightclub bouncer trying to keep out
troublemakers.

Like a nightclub bouncer, it has to be told about all the
possible ways into a particular computer – all the ports that are
open – and, indeed, all the computers that it is screening traffic
for. If a computer is added to the Internet connection without
the firewall being told, then it will not know about that computer and will not be able to protect it.

When I got back from the pub that afternoon, I saw that all
but one of the computers in the list of several hundred *were* protected by a firewall: for almost every request to examine a port
on every computer, the response was that it was inaccessible
because of the firewall. We had been wrong in our gamble, and
had run the risk of being locked out of the entire network.

It was a nasty moment. We had been guilty of the worst kind
of sin in these exercises: overconfidence. Nervous, I called the
audit manager to see whether any alerts had been raised, fingers
crossed and sweating even more than I had done in Hong Kong
a few weeks earlier. Laughing, and not in the least bit surprised,
the Australian told us that there had been no alerts raised whatsoever: the firewall protected the network but had not been set
up to raise any alarms, so as not to overload the network-
management staff. It was atrocious security practice and
seemed incredible but at least it meant we had managed to duck
that particular bullet. We were still in the game.

Even though we had been lucky in avoiding detection, we now
had to find a way through the firewall. That, of course, was disappointing. Or rather, for the malicious hacker that I was

pretending to be, that would be disappointing. For the Australian's company, it was a bit of good news.

And fortunately for us there *was* one computer that didn't seem to be protected. Naturally that attracted my interest; was this going to be our way in?

We began to examine that lone unprotected computer in more detail. When an operating system is first installed on a computer it is said to be 'out of the box': the configuration is a general-purpose one, particular to each given operating system and version. Having a simple, default configuration makes the manufacturer's life easy, but it also makes life easy for the hacker, because that default configuration is both easily guessable and usually very insecure.

The unprotected computer was an out-of-the-box UNIX system; clearly someone within the company had made a major error. An error like that is certain to act as a lure for a hacker: it represents a real and immensely exciting prospect of gaining easy access to a sensitive computer network.

Just as a real hacker would do, I made that unprotected, vulnerable UNIX machine my prime target.

Once a hacker has chosen his target, the next thing he will do is examine it as closely as possible, looking to see precisely how it works. To do this, the hackers use a process called 'banner-grabbing': for each port that is running an application, the hacker will use a simple program to connect to that port and try to elicit an error message. By default, all applications and services have error messages that are as helpful as possible. Amongst the bits of helpful information that they provide are the program name, version number and sometimes even the details of the operating system on which it is running. All hackers use this banner-grabbing trick to see which version of the application or service is actually present, so as to see whether the program is vulnerable to a known 'exploit', i.e. a trick to gain access.

We were in for our next surprise when we looked at this: unlike any computer system that I had seen in nearly twenty years, this computer was not only running vulnerable applications, it was also configured so as to give its name to anyone who asked. It was called 'Homer'.

I gleefully wrote up what a real hacker's feelings would be at this point: anticipation and excitement. Our client company was in a lot of trouble.

We decided to try and guess the password for the most privileged user – the 'Root' or super user – on that computer. Since it was clearly a mistake for such a vulnerable system to be visible on the Internet, I guessed – or hoped – that the system administrator might also have been so inexperienced that he would have chosen a simple root password. The simplest is no password at all; that didn't work. Next, I tried a password of 'Root'; that didn't work. Finally, I tried the name of the company; yet again, that didn't work.

It's surprising how many times simple tricks like those specific password guesses *do* work, since most systems come with some form of easily guessed default password like those. For example, Microsoft's popular database server has a privileged account called 'SA' that comes by default with no password at all. Only very few database admin-istrators know about the account and think to apply a password, meaning that an awful lot of websites have proved vulnerable.

The problem isn't limited to the computers themselves, either. The cables that link computers within networks are themselves controlled by sophisticated devices called 'routers'. These can be controlled remotely by network administrators, provided that the administrator knows the device password. The default password, known widely to the hackers, is the word 'public' or 'private'. Once a hacker has guessed the router pass-word, they have total control of the network and can read, delete or alter any of the data that might pass over it. Breaching security by means of such a trivial trick as password-guessing might seem unlikely but in practice it is all too commonly possible.

However, in this case the most trivial passwords hadn't been successful, so I decided to brainstorm some more possible passwords, based on a computer name of Homer: Ulysses? Iliad? Odyssey? Argonaut? . . . I made a long list of possible words, intending to write a simple program to produce multiple variations and spellings of each, and then present them to the computer one at a time. In passing, though, one of the salesmen working for the company called out from the other room: 'Simpson.'

I tried it. It worked.

With the simplest, oldest type of hacking trick in the canon we had gained root access to a computer on the network of one of the world's largest and wealthiest multinational companies. What is more, although we had yet to find an interesting file to present to the auditor, so as to win the gamble, it looked as though the Australian would be pleased with our efforts even if we were to have stopped at the end of that first day. He would be able to haul his IT staff over the coals for being so lax and overconfident; and once we had tracked down something interesting, we would get paid and have the opportunity of doing more work for the company. Never had I been so pleased with a cartoon character.

Obviously we couldn't just leave it at that: it wasn't even the end of the working day, and anyway none of us was in a rush to get home that night. I added the Homer system to my diagram on the wall, and we began trying to work out exactly where in the network the computer actually was.

From the email headers received from the recruitment contact, I knew the internal addresses of two computers: the one that the email was created on and the internal email server. Because I knew *some* addresses, I could guess a range of other addresses – and when we came to examine it, we found that Homer was on the same network as the email server that had sent us our message. We also discovered that it had connections to only one other computer and that it had only one user registered to access it. I presumed that this was the person who had set up and then forgotten about the computer, since it had apparently not been used for several months.

Unfortunately for the company, the user who had set it up had allowed it to have what is called a 'trust relationship' with his own computer. This is a convenient way to use several computers within a network, with no requirement to log into each one as it is needed. Instead, logging in to just one of the computers in a trust network automatically gives the user access to each of the other systems. Convenient in normal working conditions, but a disaster when one of the computers in the trust network is hacked into. In this case, it meant that, as Root on Homer, we were also Root on the other computer. I moved from Homer onto the owner's computer, and found that this had in turn trust relationships with several of the company servers.

We discovered the user was one of the most senior system managers in the company, with almost universal privileged access to the company's networks and most sensitive servers. The Australian audit manager really was right to have been concerned; their problems were even worse than we or he had thought.

Our wall diagram was growing by the moment, as I added the dozen or so systems that this user had just given us privileged access to. Inspecting each in turn, we learned that they were main servers in different countries, scattered around Europe and the Pacific Rim.

It was time to see just how much further this intrusion could be taken.

Like the overwhelming majority of corporate networks, this company's had a mixture of computers. There were several computers called 'servers'. A server is a computer that provides a centralized service for a large number of different users on the network. This can be to store data files, to hold important applications, or even to give access to the wider world through the Web or through email services. In this particular network, these servers were based on Microsoft's Windows NT operating system.

As well as these centralized servers, the network also contained smaller computers dedicated to individual users.

These are commonly called PCs or, for the more powerful versions, 'workstations'. There were two different types of workstation that we could find. The overwhelming majority were running Microsoft Windows and were being used by the ordinary members of staff to do word-processing, spreadsheets and simple accounting functions. The others were being used by the network and system-administration staff, and these were running a version of the UNIX operating system just like that installed on Homer.

We had control of a small collection of these UNIX workstations at the end of our first day. Our second day's objective was to extend that access – avoiding detection by the network-administration staff – to as many other UNIX systems as we could, and in parallel into the Microsoft components of the network. And when we had managed *that*, we were going to see what interesting trophy files we could discover for the audit manager to show to his IT management.

Even before that, though, we had to make sure that we had a guaranteed access route into the network. We had one access point in Homer, but no hacker likes to have only one way in: the network staff might discover it, and either block or monitor it. Even though we had won our gamble, I still didn't want to run the risk of detection; having been so cavalier with the firewall earlier, I was now determined to be as sensible and as careful as I knew how.

Our first job on the second day was therefore to open another access route. I decided that we would use a 'back connection'.

When we had used the port scanner on the previous day it had told us that there were open ports on several of the computers – for example, for email services – and that there were ports that were protected by the firewall. It had also, however, told us that there were ports on several of the computers that were closed. That is, the firewall was not blocking our attempts to connect to those ports, but there were no services running on the computers on those ports.

We had some routes that could 'tunnel' through the firewall

because it had been told to ignore them, since the computers the firewall was protecting were not using those particular ports. It was a little like a bouncer at a nightclub told not to bother watching a particular doorway because it was known to have been locked from the inside. But we were *already* inside, and so we could open that door confident that it was not being watched.

On two of the computers that we had control of – part of the trust network associated with the computer we accessed through Homer – we created a process called a 'listener'. This is a simple program that runs on a chosen port, waiting for a hacker to send it instructions. When it receives those instructions, it executes them exactly as though the hacker was already logged in to the computer. We added a password to the listener, so as to protect it from any other hackers that might discover it. Safe now in the assurance that we had several ways back into the network, we moved on to widening the scope of that intrusion.

Given that our initial intrusion had been by means of guessing a poorly chosen password, we decided that we would first attempt to extend our access through exploiting what was apparently a slack password policy within the organization. Users can be incredibly lazy people when it comes to choosing passwords. Not only can passwords often be easily guessed, but the overwhelming majority of users will also have the same password on all of the systems to which they have access – and system-management staff are no different. I guessed that, if I could discover the passwords used by the system-management staff on the UNIX systems we already had control over, then these same passwords would likely be used on the other systems that they operated. Had the organization had a good policy for password control then this wouldn't work; based on what we had seen up to this point, I was prepared to wager that they didn't.

We started by examining the passwords stored on the systems that we had already breached. Computers used by several people must have a way of storing the valid passwords so that they can be compared with the password typed into the system when a user tries to log in. To protect the password from casual discovery it is stored in an encrypted form. Unfortunately, there are hacking tools that can recover the original password from that encrypted form. To provide an extra level of protection, the file that contains the encrypted passwords is configured so that only the most privileged user of the system can read it. This did not cause us any difficulties: we *were* the most privileged user on that large range of computers.

We still had to be careful that we didn't encounter any of the network administrators themselves. For the next day and early evening, as we moved from system to system, we would continually run a small collection of monitoring applications on each computer, looking to see whether there was an administrator logged onto the machine and what it was that he was doing. This is called a 'meerkat': like the little ground-squirrels, a hacker periodically sticks his head up for a quick look around before getting back on with his work. The pattern of these meerkat checks is distinctive from hacker to hacker, one of the features that we would later observe in tracking real hackers at work.

In the case of this intrusion, though, we managed to remain unobserved for the whole period; it was as if we had the entire building to ourselves and could wander at will. I began to collect the password files from each of the UNIX systems available to us and discovered the next, alarming aspect of the company's security. All of the UNIX system accounts had three-letter usernames – their initials, I presumed – and in the majority of cases the password was either the same as the username or was the username reversed.

This was a truly staggering insecurity – a level of operational naïvety that I hadn't come across since beginning to learn how to hack UNIX systems at university in 1980. Back then, there had been relatively few hackers threatening the integrity of the essentially harmless systems accessible. But these systems, accessible so easily, were responsible for handling payment and credit transactions with values in the hundreds of millions of dollars.

It was literally unbelievable, but as I explored further and further it was ever more evident that the audit manager who had employed us was going to have a huge job on his hands to correct these faults.

Not all of the users had such simplistic passwords. Some had more complicated ones, and I began to use those accounts to gain access to the Microsoft network. I guessed that the UNIX network was managed simplistically but that the Microsoft network had slightly better controls. It seemed that I was correct, and the stronger passwords – though still breakable – had been forced on the individual users by the Microsoft administrators.

Using those passwords, we were soon able to access a range of Microsoft systems, though only as relatively unprivileged users of the computers. There seemed to be a strict segregation of duties between the UNIX administrators – every one of whom we could pretend to be – and the Microsoft administrators. We could not, in fact, find any of the names or workstations of this group, so we couldn't begin to guess or to capture their passwords, and attempts to guess the privileged-account passwords on the Microsoft servers all failed. To capture the level of control of the Microsoft network that we had of the UNIX network was clearly going to mean some detailed system-hacking, rather than the lucky password breaks that we had managed up until now.

The Microsoft systems were being well managed, but the majority of the system managers' attention was being directed towards the obviously accessible and vulnerable systems facing the Internet, rather than those within the corporate network. And it was on those internal systems that we were now focusing.

One of the reasons why Microsoft operating systems and applications are so popular is that they are – at least in comparison to the UNIX equivalents – easy to install and to configure. The out-of-the-box configuration options remove a lot of confusion in how to set up the system: as the installation program operates, the default options that it selects are usually sensible ones and most administrators will simply accept the defaults. This, though, results in generic configurations, in which elements of the operating systems that are not strictly required are in fact installed. The result can be file or application servers which also have the web-server components installed and accessible, even though no web services are required. These services can then be exploited by hackers. This was the case with several of the accessible servers within the company's internal network.

The greater bulk of the hacking tools available to attack Microsoft systems are directed at the most widely accessible types of systems: web servers. We were therefore faced with a large collection of potentially vulnerable servers, in which the default web services were accessible but wholly unmonitored and unprotected.

In the default configuration – the out-of-the-box state – the Web services are operated on the server as though they were being run by the most privileged user, called 'Administrator' in Microsoft NT. I also knew that there would be various test services available, including several that could be subverted so as to run *any* local application that we specified. What I wanted was the 'Security Accounts Manager' or SAM file – the Microsoft equivalent of the encrypted password files that we had already recovered from the UNIX networks.

Just as with the UNIX version, the SAM file is protected by the operating system, so that it cannot simply be read by a user, not even by the Administrator. To ensure that the contents of the file are never scrambled, there is an operating-system program to produce a back-up of the SAM file, though this can only be run by the Administrator. Because the web services were being run as though by the Administrator, and the test program could be subverted to run any system application, I could therefore use this to produce the SAM back-up file and to copy the back-up into a web page. And from there I could simply download to my own computer and decipher it.

We moved inexorably through the Microsoft network, capturing the Administrator passwords on each internal server – until after a short period of time we had total control of all of the systems. I could introduce new employees with their salaries paid directly to us; I could even alter the amount payable to my own company for the project. I could read all their email, access all their documents, inspect all their accounts. I could, at a keystroke, bring a multi-billion-dollar-value company with a century-long trading history, employing hundreds of thousands of people, to bankruptcy.

The test had started with nothing more than a business card. We had then uncovered a minute crack in their perimeter security, from which we had been able to gain mastery first of one complete network, then of the other . . . and finally of the whole company itself. It was an object lesson in one of the central tenets of computer security: the system managers have to protect *every* possible vulnerability, for the intruder need only discover *one*.

We now had to find that 'interesting file' that the audit manager had charged us with locating as a totem to indicate that our victory was complete. With total visibility and near-complete control of the environment, it was a matter of choice rather than necessity which file we presented. At leisure, with only the occasional meerkat check, I sifted through some of the systems that we had found. One had a huge folder marked, helpfully, 'Confidential' and containing the source code for the company's new website, due to be launched in a few weeks. And in there, in pride of place, was the new company logo, unseen by anyone other than the most senior managers and the company's design agency. We agreed that that was the perfect choice.

We wrote our report and bound it elegantly, as befitted a document to be delivered to an Asian company sensitive to such things. In pride of place, on the inside front cover, we put a copy of the new logo, the significance of which could not be overlooked by anyone reading the report. That the new logo was discovered before launch was embarrassing but not disastrous; the point that we wanted to make was that *any* item of information, valuable or not, could have been discovered by a hacker. The IT department's complacency could have cost the multinational dearly, and it was only good fortune that had protected them from even greater problems before our arrival.

The company were of course stunned by the results and by the relative ease with which we had attained them. We had won our gamble and gained a friend for life in the Far East. The Australian audit manager was thrilled with the results that just four days of effort had produced. We had done exactly what any hacker would have done and could tell him what would have needed to be done to have kept us from being so successful.

And that is the whole point of undertaking such tests: not to expose the company concerned to ridicule, but to allow them safely to see just how a real attacker would go about exposing them. For us, it was a fascinating exercise; it was also useful practice in what a real hacker would do and feel, which was soon to come in particularly useful when we were asked to help on an exercise in tracking a real hacker through the clues that he had left behind him.

4. **To Catch a Hacker**

1999 was the very height of dotcom mania, with a multitude of companies making apparent fortunes from little more than clever Internet domain names and with the stock market soaring to unsurpassed values on the promise of the 'new economy'. In the midst of this enthusiasm, one small company based just outside London was brought to the very edge of disaster by a computer hacker.

Worse, though the police and I were sure we had discovered exactly who that hacker was, we found that proving it was impossible – illustrating one of the most important gulfs in criminal investigations, between *knowing* something and being able to *prove* it in court.

This was both one of the most fascinating and the most frustrating cases that I ever had to work on. I was able to apply lessons learned from analysing hacker activity, from copying hackers in testing computer vulnerabilities and from studies of encrypted files. It involved working with some of the most challenging technologies and establishing some intricately conceived chains of logic; but ultimately it had to be marked down as a failure which didn't even get to court, and from which we could only learn.

The victim company was based about forty miles west of

London and provided an online IT recruitment service. It had been trading for about five years, first through regular postal services and then through email, marketing its services over the Web by means of a carefully collected and well-managed client database. That database *was* the value of the company, and in February 1999 – just as the company founders were preparing to sell out and retire as millionaires – it seemed that the database had been stolen. A hacker had broken into the company's computer network, taken a copy of the crucial client database and then apparently established a rival company to siphon off the business.

The first the directors knew of the intrusion was when they had been contacted by disgruntled clients who had demanded to know why their email address and other details had been provided to another company. Insisting that they hadn't, the directors had ordered an investigation of the computer systems. At midnight on the day that they had first been notified of the issue, the technical director had sat and watched as a hacker had logged onto their most sensitive systems and continued the task of stealing piece after piece of their most precious intellectual property.

Incensed, the technical director had killed the connection to the hacker, only to see them reappear a moment later. Again and again he had tried to lock the intruder out of the systems, only to see them repeatedly resurface. Finally, in impotent frustration, the director had had to kill the power to the company servers, confused and angry at the simple way in which the company's unique value had been stolen from beneath his nose.

I was told this story a few weeks later by the police officer handling the theft. Simon was a detective sergeant with Surrey Police and was one of a group of officers I had helped to train in computer-crime investigation the year before.

Even before setting up my own consulting company, I had worked closely with the UK's police staff college outside Basingstoke. Bramshill is a fine old Elizabethan house and grounds that were donated to the police force many years ago.

Until the national police training school moved to Wyboston, just north of London, in 2002 it was the premier staff college for training detectives and uniformed officers in computer-crime investigation.

I had gone there first at the request of the Metropolitan Police Computer Crime Unit, the unit established by John Austen and responsible for catching Gold and Schiffreen, and indirectly responsible for the introduction of the Computer Misuse Act. The detective inspector running that unit after John's retirement, Phil Swinburn, had seen me lecture on some aspects of tracking computer criminals and had asked me to repeat the presentation at Bramshill the following month. Simon had been in the audience for that second presentation and I remembered him well. A short, thick-set detective with fair hair and a bright, cheerful disposition, he had been entertaining to talk with over the coffee breaks and had asked some intelligent questions during the session itself.

Faced with his first major computer-crime incident since that course, Simon had cast around for anyone able to help his team to understand what had happened, and had decided that some of the tricks I had described to the course attendees might be of use in the investigation. Over the phone, he described the situation to me. Having described the company and its problem, Simon explained that the technical director had done a lot of good work himself in tracing the intruder. It seemed that the hacker had logged onto their computer from a system in mainland Europe.

The technical director had the numerical Internet address (IP address) for the connection, and had done his own research. The address was a computer used by a web-hosting company in the Low Countries, which provided services primarily to pornographic websites. It had also been hacked quite recently, by hackers from a group called Hacking for Girlies, who had left a series of messages on the web pages. These messages were written in a distinctive style, with various characters replaced by numbers or symbols: 5 to replace S, 4 to replace A, and so forth. The database hacker had left a similar message. Was it possible that they were the same person, or perhaps both members of HFG?

Unfortunately for the technical director, the trail had run cold at that point: the Dutch hosting company did not keep any form of logs and had no way of providing a further link from that point. Worse, once the hacking had been discovered, the technical manager for the hosting company had decided to reinstall its computer, reloading the operating system and applications from the original software-distribution CD. The result was that he had destroyed every bit of evidence that it might have held.

Simon and his officers had no prospect of tracking the hacker directly through that side of the link. Whilst that was obviously disappointing, they *did* have the other side of the link. They couldn't track the route of the victim's database file, as it had been transmitted from the hacked computer, but they knew where the database file had ended up: with the rival company that had sent emails to the victim's existing clients.

A detective working for Simon examined the extended headers on a sample of those emails and quickly discovered the domain name of the company that had sent them. On the Internet, the domain name is the readable form of the IP address and is most usually related to the company name. A company called Acme, for example, might have a domain name of 'acme.com', or perhaps 'acme.co.uk'. For email or for web-browsing, human users would give the domain name; for the computers, however, this must be translated into the corresponding numerical IP address. The association between the domain name and the address is held in a database called a 'domain-name server' and is generated when the company first 'registers' the domain name with their Internet service provider (ISP). To register, a company must provide a variety of details, including contact names, addresses and telephone numbers, and these can obviously be traced.

From the domain name on the email, the detective therefore had two ways of tracing the company. First of all, he used the domain registration to get the contact information; and then he confirmed that it was correct through a search for the company details at Companies House in London. It turned out to be a small operation, run by a young man who also ran a one-person IT consulting company to do, amongst other things, system-security testing through 'ethical hacking'.

As far as the police were concerned, they had almost certainly caught their hacker: he had means, motive and opportunity to carry out the hacking. After swearing out a warrant, Simon and his team raided the man's house in a small town to the west of London, catching him by surprise while he was still active on the computer. He was arrested and his computer seized, and Simon interviewed him at length about what he had been doing.

The man denied hacking into the company. His story was that the database file had been provided to him by a stranger he had met in an Internet chatroom. As Simon explained over the phone in our initial discussion, it was the modern variation on the 'A bloke in the pub gave it to me' story that he had heard a thousand and one times before. The problem was proving that the man he had arrested had in fact obtained the file as a result of hacking, and had been the hacker on the night in February.

And so Simon had called me, since I had shown him and his colleagues on the training course some effective techniques to use in the analysis of computer-hacking activities and the identification of individual hackers themselves. I agreed to look at the system they had seized from the young man and tell them what I could learn from it.

I thought it would only take a day or so; I was very wrong.

One of the greatest problems facing any computer-evidence analyst is the sheer quantity of information that is available. Computers can hold a *lot* of data, and even files that have been deleted are still in fact present somewhere – even if just as relics – on the computer's disk drive.

This last point is particularly important in computer forensics and arises because computers are remarkably lazy devices; they are programmed to do the bare minimum of work to satisfy a user's request. This means that files the user might have believed they had removed are, in fact, still available to investigators.

Though different operating systems handle things slightly differently, the data is usually arranged on the hard disk into 'clusters' or 'blocks' that are read or written as an entire unit. A cluster might contain around 500 or 1,000 characters. To find the correct cluster on the disk, the computer keeps a record of the file's name and of its location. A file is held within a 'folder'; physically, the folder is a list of file names, together with the location on the disk where an information block for the file is to be found. That information block contains the time stamps that are so important for computer forensics, and it also contains a pointer to the first cluster in the file; that cluster has the file's contents plus a pointer to the second cluster, and so on in a chain through the disk.

When a file is deleted, two things happen: first, a 'Deleted' marker is placed in the directory file beside the file name, over-writing just the first character of the file's name. The rest of the file name is retained, allowing a forensic engineer to re-construct it. Second, the information block is marked as 'Deleted', simply through a flag being reset from 'True' to 'False'. Again, the information block and the actual file-content blocks connected to it are still present on the disk, until they need to be reused by other, new files as they grow larger and demand more space on the disk.

Because so much of the original, deleted file is still physically present on the hard disk, with clever software those files can be read and even reconstructed if only small parts of the original file have been overwritten by newer files. This means that when examining a computer's contents, *all* of the disk has to be examined, and that can be an unimaginably large amount of information to be considered. For example, a single floppy disk can hold just less than a million and a half charac-ters – enough to hold a 500-page book, or to be printed on a pile of A4 paper around two inches deep. The main disks on computers are many times larger than this: a typical disk drive might be around *ten thousand* times larger than a floppy disk – a pile of paper tall enough to interfere with flight paths if it were to be printed out and which would require several lifetimes of solid reading if it were to be examined.

The contents of the computer that Simon and his team had seized had been copied onto CDs by the Police Forensic Science Service. Unfortunately, the computer had not been a small one. In fact, it had had three disk drives present in it, meaning a truly staggering amount of data to be examined. It was complicated further by the fact that the system had not been a simple one. Most computers usually run a single operating system – Windows, for example – but this one had been con-figured to run one of two possible systems: Windows 95, and a popular version of UNIX called LINUX. Of the three disk drives, two were used for the Windows files and one for the LINUX.

Doing any kind of searching of the computer contents was going to be a long, slow task complicated by the different types of files in the two operating systems. There was then yet another complication: when we came to inspect the files on the system we saw that a large number of them had been protected using an encryption tool called PGP.

Encryption is a way of disguising the meaning of some data or message. It is the electronic equivalent of sealing informa-tion in a box so that it can only be read and understood by someone having the appropriate key. In encryption, the 'box' is the algorithm or method by which the data is manipulated, and the 'key' is some large number that is used to control the operation of that algorithm.

Provided that the key is kept secret and the algorithm is sufficiently complex, encryption can give a great deal of security to information. It is used to protect email messages, to ensure that credit-card details are not visible as they are passed over the Internet and even to disguise the entire contents of computer disks. Encryption is central to information security and has been central to my life in countering computer crime. I have worked on exercises to test or to break encryption systems used by banks, and even to help define the very word 'encryption' in a landmark legal case.

(The case was on behalf of a cable-TV company, which wanted to stop pirates from gaining access to its transmissions. In order to do this, the company had needed to prove in court that its transmissions were encrypted and therefore protected under the Copyright Act. Unfortunately, the act doesn't define the word 'encryption', and we quickly discovered that nor does any other UK act. It wasn't defined in any records of Parliament or in any other rulings, so I had to go to court and create a definition of my own. We defined it as a 'process of transforming the meaning of information so as to make it unintelligible'; and since we won the case that is the legal definition in the UK until such time as that ruling may be extended.)

PGP stands for 'Pretty Good Privacy', and this is precisely what it provides. Although not as secure as full military encryption, it does provide a very effective defence for most purposes. The software had been developed in 1991 by an American cryptographer called Phil Zimmerman. It's a powerful utility, and a complicated one. At least, the version being used by our hacker was a complicated version. It involves not one but three different kinds of encryption.

First of all, the file to be protected is encrypted using a standard program called IDEA – the International Data Encryption Algorithm – with a key that is generated automatically by the PGP application. IDEA was developed on behalf of the US government and is known to be very hard to break; the only reliable way is to try each and every possible set of numbers for the encryption key, a process known as 'brute force'. This encryption is therefore a very strong 'box' that protects the file in a way that is, for all practical purposes, completely secure. By choosing a long enough key – over 1,000 digits, for example – a fair fraction of the lifetime of the universe would be necessary to try each possible key in turn.

This then leaves the problem of making sure that the person who you want to be able to decrypt the file has a copy of the key that was randomly generated. You need to be able to give them the key, as well as the file encrypted with that key. To solve this problem the key itself must also be encrypted – put in its own 'box' to be passed to the user – but not in the same way as the file. If it was done in the same way, the 'box' would have to contain its own key, making unlocking it impossible. Or it would have to be put in a second, different box – meaning that the key for this second box would have to be transferred, and so on *ad infinitum*. An alternative is required.

For military purposes – or for banks, the diplomatic service, or any situation where all the correspondents are known in advance – the secret key can be physically transported by armed guards to its destination. Obviously, this isn't possible for those using encryption over the Internet to pass secure messages to people in different countries whom they might never meet in real life. The issue of how to achieve this is termed the 'key exchange problem' and it was solved using a clever mechanism that was developed by three American cryptographers, Rivest, Shamir and Adelman. Their initials give us the name of the scheme: RSA.

Where the IDEA algorithm uses the same key to encrypt and to decrypt, RSA has two distinct key values: the first encrypts, the second decrypts. The two keys are mirror images of one another but are completely different: one cannot be deduced from the other. This is called 'asymmetric encryption'. The first key is made public, allowing anyone to encrypt a message to a particular person; the second key is kept private, so that only its holder can decrypt the message. This is generally referred to as 'public-key cryptography' and is the basis of the PGP application – and indeed of almost all Internet encryption schemes used for passing credit-card and other personal details to online retailers and banks.

In the Pretty Good Privacy application, the symmetric encryption key produced by the application automatically – and used to encrypt the file – is therefore itself encrypted using the public key for the person the file is to be sent to. This is a box that can only be opened by the private key corresponding to this public key; it is completely tamper-proof. The symmetric key and the file, both of them now encrypted in separate 'boxes', can then be put together in an email message, for example, and transmitted to the recipient.

The recipient needs only to use his private key to recover the original encryption key, and then to use that recovered key to decrypt the file itself; in effect, opening one box with his private key, so as to obtain the key necessary to open the other box. Inside that final box is the message.

It is necessary though for the users of these schemes to protect their private key, in case someone should get a copy of it and read the messages illicitly. This private key therefore needs to be stored in yet another 'box', this time on the user's computer. This is the third encryption, which needs the user to enter a word or phrase known only to them so as to unlock that most secret of boxes. This complicated word or phrase is called the 'pass phrase' for the PGP encryption. Provided that the user keeps their pass phrase secret, their private key will also be secret, and any messages or files encrypted for them will be secret.

PGP – and any other system like it – is only as secure as the components that it is built from. RSA and IDEA are both considered very secure; the weak point in this scheme – as with most information security – is in how the user applies it, in particular their choice of pass phrase and how secret they can keep it.

Knowing that the only way of accessing the encrypted material was through using the pass phrase, Simon had asked the suspect to give it to him during his initial interview. The young man said that he'd forgotten it, a claim that frankly defied belief given that he was marketing himself as a security specialist. What was more, from the time stamps on the files that had been encrypted, we could see that some at least had been accessed only a few hours before the police had arrested him. If he'd truly forgotten the pass phrase then it couldn't have been very long ago. It seemed obvious that the suspect was not telling the truth.

Surprisingly, there is no compulsion to give one's pass phrase to the police. Evidence is seized by the police in the UK under a warrant that is authorized by the Police and Criminal Evidence Act of 1984, PACE. This had envisaged the need to seize computer evidence, and it required suspects to provide the police with computer material that they could 'take away' in a 'readable' form.

Unfortunately, 'readable' is not the same as 'intelligible'. Files encrypted with applications such as Pretty Good Privacy can indeed be 'read': the file can be printed out as a wholly unintelligible stream of printable characters. The meaning, of course, is entirely lost – that being the whole point of encryption.

Our suspect had therefore satisfied the letter of the law in allowing the police to take and copy his computer in a way that allowed them to read the contents of the files. To avoid this problem in future, a new law was passed in 2000 allowing the police to prosecute a suspect who does not surrender his pass phrase under warrant. Called the Regulation of Investigatory Powers Act, this law has been roundly criticized by civil-rights campaigners as being too stringent and far-reaching. In many ways it is, but with respect to encrypted material it only provides criminal law with powers that have been present in *civil* law for a number of years: the civil evidence production orders do not have the confusion between 'readable' and 'intelligible'; it has long been the case that encrypted material has had to be decrypted in civil cases.

This case, unfortunately, predated the introduction of the new act, and was being brought under criminal law by the police rather than under civil law by the victim company. It meant that we needed a way of decrypting those files if we were ever to understand them.

Simon hadn't been put off when the hacker had claimed to have forgotten the pass phrase. In interview, he and his team of detectives had offered to help the suspect to remember: was it a single word or a number of words? Was it a common phrase?

Was it in English? Trying to maintain a façade of helpfulness, the hacker had offered that the pass phrase was probably constructed from typical pass*words* that he used.

Of course, he could have been lying, but it gave us a starting point. A pass phrase – notwithstanding the hacker's claim to have forgotten it – must be *memorable*: as it's the only way of recovering protected files, it's important for the user to be able to recall it. Also, it has to be easy to type, so that the user doesn't make mistakes. These two factors usually mean that although a pass phrase *can* be the entire graveside speech from *Hamlet*, it is usually much shorter. Equally, a quote from the speech is both memorable and likely.

We had a useful program that we'd written to trial different pass phrases in a brute-force form of attack. It was a fairly quick application and we had a very fast computer on which we could run it. We also already had a truly enormous file of common pass phrases, based on advertising jingles, nursery rhymes and snippets of Shakespeare, Monty Python, *The Hitchhiker's Guide to the Galaxy*, *Star Trek* and the Bible. We had no reason to suppose that our hacker's pass phrase was in the list, but equally no reason to assume it wasn't. Checking with this fixed file – referred to as a 'dictionary' in information-security circles – was the first and most obvious thing to attempt.

We set the brute-force program running last thing on the Friday evening before going home for the weekend and let it run for the fifty or so hours that were needed to exhaust the pre-prepared dictionary list. I wasn't surprised on the Monday morning when we found that the program had finished without success.

We next turned to the suspect's comment that the pass phrase was perhaps constructed from pass*words* that he commonly used. It seemed plausible but I have to admit I felt it unlikely that he had been telling the truth. But still we had to examine the possibility. It took an hour or so to extract every password that was used in the hacker's computer – for his Internet service provider access on the dial-up connection he used, his several email accounts, the various users of the LINUX system, and so forth.

When this was done, I had a list of fifteen or so simple character sequences based on words that he commonly used. A simple program then combined selections from these fifteen, along with common linking words and symbols in all possible ways. It produced literally millions of potential pass phrases, which again required the better part of two days to exhaust.

Again, we failed to find the pass phrase. And again, I was not surprised. This time, though, we could provide a full report for the police: the suspect had *definitely* lied to them about the nature of the pass phrase.

The most obvious of the ways to subvert the encryption protection had been exhausted, and so we were left with only the most painfully protracted version of the brute-force attack. Often, a password or a pass phrase, since it has to be processed by the computer, will end up being copied onto the disk, even if just as a scrap of text in amongst a lot of other, irrelevant data. Also, the pass phrase is by definition made up of words that are known to the user; these words might well be used elsewhere as well, in documents on the computer or even in diaries or note-books that might be recovered from their house. The user might even have written the pass phrase down somewhere in case they forgot it. In my first paedophile case, for example, with the psychology student who had called himself 'Christopher Robin', I learned that he had recorded his pass phrase in a self-developed code and that he had written this on a scrap of paper which he had hidden in a box of diskettes. Unfortunately for him, the code he had used was broken by a determined police officer and the pass phrase had been recovered; hence, the police had gained access to his encrypted files without needing his help.

Remembering this, I went through every scrap of paper that had been recovered from the suspect's address, making detailed notes of any and every character sequence. Diary entries, phrases from saved letters, names and addresses – as many things as we could find were all typed into a potential phrase list. Then I started with the computer, and used a simple program to extract every recognizable word that occurred any-where on the three disks.

I had hoped that we might have found some hint at the pass phrase in the suspect's diaries or unencrypted files, but there was nothing of that sort. I was left with the far from satisfactory option of creating an extended brute-force attack, which I was certain would not be successful.

Combining the collections produced an immense list of possible words, which would have required a pile of paper several storeys high if it were ever to have been printed out. But we were not finished: now we had to combine these words together, just as we had with the earlier password list, to create possible pass phrases. Then, each of these had to be tested to see if it was the valid pass phrase. It would have required many decades on even the most powerful of super-computers to have completed this list; obviously, with our limited resources, we had no chance of getting the pass phrase other than through the most astounding stroke of good fortune. The objective, though, was in fact *not* to try and find the pass phrase through this long-winded approach, but rather to be able to demonstrate in court that we had tried. I could prove – to a high degree of certainty – that the suspect had lied to the investigating officers about the format of the pass phrase, and I could show that the pass phrase had last been used only a few hours before the suspect had claimed that he could not remember it. I hoped that this would add weight to any criminal prosecution that might be brought, showing that the suspect had been obstructive and should not therefore expect any leniency from the court.

In the mean time there were other, more interesting things that we could do with the computer evidence.

Leaving to one side the contents of the encrypted files, there was still a massive quantity of data to be examined on the seized computer's disks. I needed a way of organizing our work, so that we weren't faced with the impossible task of ploughing through all the raw information.

The most obvious solution was first to consider the files that had been created or last altered during the period of the hacking incident itself. We knew from the summary report prepared by the Forensic Science Service that the clock on the seized computer was accurate – or at least that it had been accurate at the time the engineers had examined it – and so this should give us a realistic view of what might have happened on the computer at the time.

Again, we were in for a surprise. It was apparent that the computer had indeed been used during the night of the hacking; in fact, that was something we were already sure of, since the police had telephone records showing that the computer had been connected to the Internet throughout that time. However, the files that we had were evidence of normal Internet-browsing and of a chat session that lasted almost the entire period when the hacking was supposed to have taken place. Worse for the police case, it was obvious from the content of the chat log file that it had been the suspect's girlfriend who had been using the computer at the time.

I was dumbfounded, as were Simon and his detectives when I phoned them and told them of the problem. The match of the dial-up session to the hacking session couldn't have been co-incidental, could it? Could the log file and the web records have been falsified?

I tried hard to work out a way that they could have been. It would certainly be *possible* for the suspected hacker to have falsified the file records simply by taking a file with some other time stamp and somehow resetting it to a different value. But that, I knew, would leave a trace. To be copied onto the disk, a file is divided into smaller blocks of characters, called clusters: a computer's disk can be thought of as one very large array of these clusters. When a file is created and copied onto the disk, the clusters are not selected by the operating system software at random. Other clusters adjacent to a particular file's own clusters will have been assigned to files created at roughly the same time. Those to one side of the file's clusters would belong to files that were created immediately before that one; those to the other side, those created immediately afterwards. A file that has had its creation time falsified would stand out like a sore thumb.

To check this, I picked my way carefully over the copy of the disk using some specialist inspection software, looking for every cluster of every file related to the period of the hacking session. They were all in the sequence that I would have expected if the information was wholly genuine. It *was* still possible that the hacker might have been able to fake this, but he would have needed the sort of software and equipment that I was using to examine the disk. We were confident that he did not have that, since there were no copies found on his computers or in his possession, nor any indication that it might have been used.

It seemed beyond doubt that the computer had indeed been used for normal web-browsing and for an extensive chat session by the suspect's girlfriend at the time the police were alleging it had been used to hack the victim's computer. It was simply not possible that the computer seized by the police could have had any involvement whatsoever with the hacking. Did he have *another* computer somewhere?

I phoned Simon and asked the question, but he was adamant that every possible hiding place had been examined, and that there was simply no way that our suspect had access to a second computer at his home address. I was completely stumped.

An even more confusing fact, though, was that the computer did hold three encrypted files, with time stamps that showed that they had been created at the very end of the hacking session. Moreover, the names of those files – even though we couldn't see their contents – made us very suspicious that they contained the material copied from the victim's computer. The files were the same name, and of the correct size, as the stolen database material. It seemed unlikely that it could be a coincidence.

I was also worried about the suspect. I found a lot of hacking tools on the system as I examined it, but all were related to hacking Microsoft systems; the victim computer had been a

UNIX system, as had the intermediate computer. Both were hacked using a tool that I couldn't find any trace or mention of on the hacker's system – not in existing files, nor in any fragmented form in the deleted files. It *could* be that the UNIX tool was hidden in a PGP file, but if so then why were the Microsoft tools not hidden?

It seemed almost impossible to make a case that the victim had been hacked by the user of this computer: he didn't have the necessary skills or the necessary tools. The more I looked at what *was* on the computer, and the more I got to know about the suspect from looking at these contents, his email and other work, the more certain I became that he wasn't the hacker of the victim database computer. This person was undoubtedly a hacker, but not the sort of hacker observed on the victim computer. I had his own logs of hacking activity, showing him breaking into a range of computer systems. But all of these had been Microsoft systems, and none of the logs matched the pattern of behaviour that the victim company's technical director had observed.

It was obvious, though, that Simon's suspect was somehow *associated* with the person who had hacked it, since he apparently had a copy of the pilfered information created at exactly the time that the hacking session had finished. There seemed only one possible answer. Again, I phoned Simon and told him that I was one hundred per cent certain that there was a second hacker involved. Either this second person had hacked the victim company of his own accord and had then provided the encrypted detail to Simon's suspect; or the pair of them had worked together, at some other location, while the original suspect's girlfriend had been using his computer alone.

Although Simon knew little at that time about computers, he did know a lot about common-sense investigation techniques. Based on the contents of the computer, the obvious next question to ask was whether we could establish any 'associates' for the hacker. Did he have regular correspondents? Did he have contact information to other people? What sorts of people?

As Simon expressed it, although his first suspect was not *the* hacker, he was undoubtedly *a* hacker; it was likely that his friends would also be hackers and that one of them might well be the person they wanted.

We began the process of digging deeper into the computer. There was one obvious place to begin looking for the friend, and that was in our suspect's email. There was also an additional, non-obvious place that we could consider, directly related to the victim computer files that were found on the suspect's computer.

These files were still encrypted in a way that we couldn't read, but we *could* examine the nature of the encryption applied. In particular, we could see which private keys were required to be able to open the files. Our suspect's key was, obviously, one of them, but the file had also been encrypted so that it could be opened by a *second* private key. This second person was, we guessed, either the person who had carried out the hacking, or some unknown third party who had carried it out. Either way, finding this second person became a priority for us. They had either hacked the system themselves, or were somehow associated with the person who had. Just like following the trail of those who had handled stolen jewellery that might turn up at an antiques shop, we had to follow the trail of people who had had contact with this file. But all we had was the person's public key reference, a username based on their email address; in effect, a nickname rather than an actual name.

With a *name*, though, we could run a much more efficient search of the computer disks available to us. The quantity of data on the computers – the miles-high piles of paper that they represent – makes undirected searching physically impossible: the digital version of the microscopic needle in a massive array of haystacks. But *directed* searching – for a name or a known file – can be done rapidly and automatically. All I had to do was launch a simple search program to scan the entire mass of data. It took only moments to locate dozens of fragments and files that referred to the friend. There were text files containing notes; email messages between the pair of them; and, most interestingly, messages to others in which our initial suspect praised the hacking skills and exploits of this individual. There was even a contract between them, in which our second suspect had agreed to undertake security-consulting work for the first.

The more I read, the more convinced I became that this must be the hacker we were hunting. But we were no nearer finding a true name for the individual. Just as I was beginning to think in terms of schemes to make contact with the hacker – by sending some email to them, perhaps offering a job or asking their advice on a technical question – I realized that one of the email messages gave me a vital clue as to their identity.

In one of the email messages, our mystery hacker had been singing the praises of a university course that he had enrolled on to learn about computer security and computer crime. He gave the complete syllabus for the course, and I read it with a growing sense of familiarity. The previous year I had helped to teach and run an M.Sc. in computer security at the University of Glamorgan. The course that the hacker was describing could only have been that one.

In all probability, the anonymous hacker – now our prime suspect – had been one of the faces watching and listening to me the year before.

I thought that my phone was going to break from his noisy reaction when I called Simon and his team – for the third time in as many hours – to tell them what I had found. First of all, they had believed that they had a rock-solid suspect for the offence, whom I had snatched away from them; now, I was giving them an even more rock-solid suspect in return. They were ecstatic.

I was now certain that their original suspect could not – or at least, could not on his own – have hacked the victim computer. I was pretty confident that our new suspect was a much more likely bet, and I was *very* confident that we would be able to find his real identity from records at Glamorgan. Even though we only had the hacker's nickname – what is called a 'handle' – it was more than possible that the other, full-time lecturers at the university would be able to tell me it, since they would have gained much more familiarity with the students throughout the year than I could have done from one single day of lecturing there.

We still had a problem to face: the law giving privacy to individuals. In the UK, personal data is covered by the 1998 Data Protection Act. This sets out controls and limitations on how information relating to identifiable individuals can be collected, processed and stored. Without permission, personal data cannot be divulged, even to the police or those working on their behalf. Therefore I couldn't simply ask the organizer of the Glamorgan course, Dr Andy Blythe, to tell us the name.

Fortunately, the 1998 law *does* provide a mechanism for data controllers – those running a database, for example – to release information to law-enforcement officers. To do this, the controller must have a so-called Section 29 Statement, signed by a senior police officer, to show that the data is required in the course of a specific criminal investigation. This meant that I had to sit patiently while Simon approached his senior officer to have the form completed and faxed over to Dr Blythe. It seemed to take an age, my computer technician and I sitting and chatting desultorily in my office, waiting for the phone to ring. When it did, I was immensely excited: not only did Dr Blythe recognize the nickname, he was entirely unsurprised when I told him the context and the situation. The student had, it seemed, been dropped from the course, so I hadn't in fact taught him the previous year. Interestingly, he had been dropped because the Metropolitan Police had charged him with another computer-crime offence, relating to a mobile-phone fraud that he was apparently involved with.

We were confident, as I carefully wrote down the name and address, that we now had the real hacker Simon and his team were looking for. I felt that we were perhaps getting close to completing the exercise, though I had no idea quite how many confusing and distressing twists and turns this case had left to run.

*

We didn't have long to wait before we received a copy of this new suspect's computer. He had been found guilty of the mobile-phone fraud charges and been given community service along with a suspended jail sentence. A 'suspended' sentence is where a convict is not put in prison provided that they promise to behave; it meant that he was not sent to jail on the condition that he did not come under suspicion for computer-related offences during the period of the sentence. For Simon and his team, this meant that getting a warrant to seize his computer on these fresh charges was simplicity itself.

Two computers were found at his address and both were once more copied onto CD-ROMs by the police forensic specialists. Yet again, the bulk of the data was protected by encryption, and yet again the suspect had refused to provide his pass phrase. But that was where the similarity between our original and our latest suspect ended: this hacker was of an altogether different grade from our first.

Simon's first suspect did indeed hack computers, but in an amateur fashion. His main trick seemed to be to scan the Internet looking for home computers connected to the Internet and infected by a popular Trojan Horse program through a virus. These programs modify the operating system on the infected computers so as to allow a hacker to access and control them, and therefore to copy crucial passwords or pass phrases for their own use. Our first suspect seemed to spend a lot of his time attempting to infect PCs and looking for PCs that had already been infected.

As hacking goes, this is fairly unadventurous stuff. By contrast, this new suspect was a skilled, proactive hacker. Although the bulk of his computer data was very well protected by encryption, there were unprotected areas of his disk. In these, we found logs of him hacking into around a dozen very prestigious organizations throughout the world: mobile-phone networks, banks, media companies and large Internet service providers.

These records were 'script logs': a transcript of every command and its output for a period of time from when the hacker started his hacking attack on a given target to when it was turned off. I could follow every command, every mistyping; I could see him forgetting things, and making notes of things; and I could see him pausing to chat online with other hackers, some of whom he helped and co-operated with.

Back in that first paedophile case that I had worked on for Nick Lockett I had examined records of commands typed into the university computer, some of them by the student, Chris, and some by the system manager. Looking over the records in the hacking case gave me a similar feeling of being the unseen watcher, but this was even stranger. What I was reading were records of crimes in action, like watching a bank robbery on a CCTV recording. It was an odd but very exciting feeling, though slightly disturbing given what this new hacker had been doing. The records showed him destroying or infecting valuable company databases; they showed him stealing and distributing credit-card numbers; they showed him defrauding companies; and they even showed him stalking and abusing people online.

In particular, I was able to look over his shoulder as he hacked network after network with a consistent efficiency. More interestingly still, it was done with a consistent pattern that was almost indistinguishable from the pattern observed on the victim's computer system.

I was now confident that we had our man at last. It was alarming, though, to see the range of targets that he had succeeded in breaking into. Because I was in effect seeing what he was seeing as he had hacked them, I could easily work out what I myself would have done in each circumstance. I could work out what he knew and what he didn't know how to do. He was alarmingly good; much better than I had ever been as a hacker, perhaps on a par with some of the more expert hackers I now employ within my specialist penetration-testing team. He was the real thing, and studying his form so closely was more than a little exciting.

I spent a day going carefully over the records of his hacking activities. We needed to know whether he had indeed been responsible for the hacking of the database files; second, we had the unpleasant task of telling the police about some of the picture files that we had found on his computer.

An interesting aspect of English law is that there are very few kinds of picture that it is illegal to possess. Pornography is controlled by the Obscene Publications Act. Something is 'obscene' if it would 'deprave or corrupt' those who see it, which encompasses some particularly nasty types of pictures. But the act outlaws the publication, not the possession. It's lawful to have copies of all manner of images, provided that you don't copy, publish or distribute them; and also, provided that you don't import them through a customs post. Only paedophile pictures – indecent pictures of children, as defined by the Protection of Children Act – are illegal to possess.

Viewing picture after picture on our new suspect's computer, I rather wished it was possible to rewrite the law there and then. The computer contained thousands of sadomasochistic pictures, along with pictures taken at morgues and at accident and murder scenes. There were pictures of horrific and explicit tortures, including piercing and immolation; there were pictures of criminals being castrated and of kidnap victims being mutilated. Even though I had already been exposed to material like this, it was a deeply disturbing collection. It was made worse when we looked through transcripts that he had recorded of his chat sessions and it became obvious that he was quite seriously fascinated by the subject of sadomasochism and regularly practised on girlfriends, willing or otherwise.

This, of course, was the material that was *not* protected by the encryption system. I was astonished to realize that there might well be even more, even worse material in the three-quarters of the disk that we couldn't access. I felt that we were really getting to know this latest suspect, as a hacker and as a person. I could honestly say that I didn't particularly like him or relish the prospect of getting to know him better through his work.

Unsurprisingly, in such a huge collection of obscene pictures, there was a set of images that we were confident would be considered to be of children. So at the very least we felt that we would be able to provide the police with some charges to bring against the suspect, even if he didn't prove to have had any association with hacking the database for his friend to use.

That was looking increasingly like it was going to be the case. We could find no material on the suspect's computer related to the hacking; worse, we couldn't even find files whose time stamps were remotely close to the hacking period. Either our suspect had not been involved, or he had been involved and those files were in the encrypted portion. Or, a third possibility, there was another computer that he had used.

Without a means of breaking the encryption, we would not be able to tell whether there were files stored in the protected portions of the disk. Given the incredibly close match between the observed hacking on the victim computer and the patterns that we could see this new hacker working to, it would seem to beggar belief that he was not involved somehow. That meant we had to consider the notion that there was indeed another computer somewhere.

As additional evidence that such a second computer must exist, I had managed to uncover a text file in which this hacker had made a note of his PGP pass phrase. This was unusual to say the least. Hackers would normally guard such a phrase with all the care appropriate to such a sensitive piece of information, as indeed our earlier suspect had. But instead, this unusually competent hacker had made a clear text note of it. I was immediately suspicious. To me, it seemed obvious that he must have had some other, even better way of protecting the encrypted material. And indeed he had. Although we had his pass phrase, and although we had a large collection of encrypted files, nowhere was there a copy of the Pretty Good Privacy program itself on his system. The pass phrase alone was useless without the corresponding file containing the encrypted private key, and that was nowhere to be found. Worse, not only was there no indication of the file containing the private key, there was no record in the computer's automatic records of it having ever been present on the computer.

According to the hacker's computer, the PGP application had never been installed or used. Yet I knew that the hacker used the encryption application, since files encrypted with his key were all over his and our first suspect's computers. He must have had a second computer that the police hadn't been able to find.

This was beginning to feel more than a little melodramatic, and Simon and his team were astonished when I called them in to present what I had found. They had thought they had the hacker easily caught, but we had shown them it was someone else; they had thought they had got all the computers, but we now showed them there was at least one that they must have missed.

Simon was naturally disappointed and confused, but at least we could give him some indication of where to look for that computer: both our first and our second suspects had an email service that was accessible through the same domain. That domain also had a website – which seemed to be run on the same computer as the email service – and when I looked at it, I saw that this computer carried web pages for a group of around half a dozen different hackers. When I looked closely at the hackers involved, they included some that I knew the Metropolitan Police Computer Crime Unit were already interested in for other offences.

A few months before the hacking incident that Simon was investigating, officers from the Computer Crime Unit had been investigating a series of attacks against government computer networks in the UK and America. The hacking had even gone so far as to gain access to the ground stations controlling the orbit of satellites that were considered military assets. In other incidents, hackers in this group had broken into the network of one of the world's largest credit-card operators. They had collected a mass of information from the hacked computers and had used this to try to blackmail the company for many millions of pounds. This was not a group of amateur – or 'script-kid' – hackers; this was a gang of professional computer criminals, and Simon's new suspect was clearly a 'player'.

What was exciting was that this case gave us an excuse to seize and examine the computer being used by the collection of professional hackers. We might uncover records of their activities, and perhaps even copies of the programs and tools used by the group. It was a delicious prospect, but first we had to discover where the computer holding the websites and email actually was.

Just as Simon's team had done with the domain name they had found on the very first set of email headers they had examined in this case, I started by examining the domain-registration details. The domain had been recorded by one of the hackers, though I could tell at a glance that it was fictitious: the postal address given for it was 24 Grosvenor Square, the American Embassy in London. We weren't going to locate the company quite as easily as Simon's team had tracked down that first hacker. However, the computer had to be connected to the Internet somehow, through an Internet service provider, and although the operators of the *computer* had lied about who and where they were, this company might not have done. We had to check.

As part of the domain-registration information, the Internet service provider for the web and email service has to be specified. Examining that told us that they were a small company based just to the south-west of London and that one of the hackers from the group was the technical contact for the ISP.

We had to be able to tell Simon and his team the exact location of the computer that they needed to seize. It might be in the building with the Internet service provider's computers, or it might be in a totally separate location. If we told Simon to raid one building and the target was elsewhere then there was the risk that the hackers would be able to irreversibly delete all the data from the computer before it could be seized. We had to get this bit right if the exercise was going to be worthwhile.

There is a clever tool, used by system managers and hackers

alike, that can help work out the location of a computer. It is called Traceroute, and it works by finding the address and transmission time between each of the computers and network components lying between the hacker and their target. Using this, we could tell that there was barely any time difference between the ISP's 'front-door' computer – their link to the rest of the Internet – and the target web and email server that we were searching for. Data packets flowing over a length of network cable cannot go any faster than the speed of light, and the time gap between the target and the front door was so short that we could be confident that the two were connected by a single cable that was short enough for it all to be within the same building.

We could give Simon a precise address for them to raid, confident that the target computer was in that building within a few metres of the Internet link computer. We could also tell him exactly how many other computers were in the building, by examining the ISP's connection records and performing the tracing exercise to each one of those. It turned out that there were about a dozen computers in the building, though we had no way of knowing which was physically the system that we needed the police to seize. They would have to mount an early-morning raid to arrest the directors and staff from the ISP company, before then being able to demand their assistance to locate and seize the specific computer that we needed.

With a team of local uniformed officers, Simon and two of his team mounted an early-morning observation of the offices, in a small town just outside the M25 south-west of London.

To a generation brought up on the near-perfect police operations of *Dixon of Dock Green*, *Z-Cars*, *Juliet Bravo* and the rest, the actual raid itself sounded more like *Keystone Cops* than British policing at its best. Shaking with suppressed laughter, Simon later described the morning to me.

Simon had observing officers surround the building, waiting for the owners – three Asian brothers – to arrive and unlock. As the three of them had strolled towards the corner doors, sipping their morning cups of Starbucks coffee, the message 'Stand by, stand by' had gone out over the radio. Unfortunately, two of the local officers – uniformed constables in civilian clothes for the raid – somehow misheard the warning as 'Go, go, go' and raced down the hill towards the three suddenly terrified men.

Simon later learned that the building was a former bank and had been raided by a confused and dim-witted gang of armed would-be robbers the year before. They had apparently held the three brothers at gunpoint, threatening to kill the eldest unless the safe was opened for them. They refused to believe that the building was no longer a bank, and that all the oversized safe room now held were cables and processor units as it was being rebuilt as an Internet service provider.

Fortunately for the owners, that first attack had ended peaceably enough when the gang had finally been persuaded that there was no handy pile of cash lying around. But it had obviously traumatized the three brothers so that, fearing a repeat, they had thrown their half-empty coffee cups at the sprinting police officers and dashed towards the building, fumbling manically for the two keys needed to let them in.

Seeing their colleagues break into a sprint and then apparently be attacked by their targets, the rest of Simon's observation crew had broken cover. The three cowering brothers had been surrounded by half a dozen burly men, and it was left to Simon to try and calm the situation. Eventually he managed to persuade the brothers to read the warrant and, relieved at not having to face a shotgun again, the eldest brother pointed mutely but eagerly at the computer in question.

Once more we were presented with a pile of CDs that police engineers had created from a seized computer. Once more we ploughed our way through them, looking for evidence linking our suspect to the database-hacking. And once more we failed to find anything incriminating for the night of the hacking incident. More confusingly, we also failed to locate the private key for the encryption application used by our suspected hacker.

It was a very disappointed group that collected in the tiny computer forensic laboratory at my offices at the end of that week, to review what we could and could not prove about the database-hacking. We knew it hadn't been done on our first suspect's computer and we believed that it wasn't done by him. We believed that the hacking might have been done by our second suspect, and there was definitely information to link him to the offence; moreover, the nature of the hacking observed was similar to the pattern of hacking that we saw from him in record after record of his activity. But we had no *evidence* to show that this second hacker was indeed responsible: his computer was protected by an encryption installation that he refused to discuss; and the server that we had seized had nothing regarding the database-hacking on it anywhere.

It seemed to us that we had reached the end of what we could do about the database-hacking, and that it was best for us to advise the police to go with whatever else they had, the paedophile material in particular.

It was a huge disappointment, and something of a failure. From being pleased and confident at my cleverness in tracking the second hacker, I had gone to the depths of depression in not being able to do more with it.

Many claim hacking and fraud are 'victimless' crimes; crimes against computers not against people, like robbery and violence. But the directors of the company targeted suffered enormously from the intrusion and from the way the value of their company was attacked. One of the directors suffered a virtual nervous breakdown from the strain and retired from the business.

Whilst we could do nothing about the database-hacking, the material that we had uncovered pointed unequivocally at a long and torrid list of other, even more important hacks on the part of the group we had uncovered.

At the time of writing, no prosecution has been brought against the hackers that I uncovered for Simon and his team, for a variety of reasons. Chief amongst these is the almost uniform reluctance on the part of all the hackers' victims to press charges, given the universal concern over bad publicity. Because of this, I can't give the names of the corporate victims nor even the precise nature of their businesses. One was involved in satellite TV broadcasting, another in mobile phones and another in banking; there were also charities and gaming operators on the list of victims that I prepared for the police over the course of several weeks from the end of 1999 to February 2000.

The list of obvious vulnerabilities exploited by the hackers would have made embarrassing reading for the company management and customers in each case, so in many ways I wasn't too surprised by their reluctance. But I was angry at the offhand way our efforts were dismissed by these corporate victims. Without victims willing to press charges and give evidence, the police are usually powerless to prosecute. They *can* bring charges, but these would be all but impossible to prove in the face of apathy or opposition on the part of the victims.

We had no choice but to accept their decision, but I'm not sure that justice, policing or the computer industry is best served by this stance. It is particularly cruel that the police, without these prosecutions, find it hard to justify the ex-penditure of time and resources on what should be recognized as major crimes.

Given the nature of the companies on the list of victims – and indeed, there were *no* minor companies in the collection of evidence – it was the Metropolitan Police Computer Crime Unit that handled discussions with them over whether to prosecute. Until the formation of the National High-Tech Crime Unit in April 2001, the Computer Crime Unit always took the lead in these major investigations.

The first meeting – with a mobile-phone company – was in February 2000 at the Computer Crime Unit offices, which were then in Richbell Place, close to Holborn in London. At the time, the unit was still run by the tall, cheerful Geordie Phil

Swinburn, who was later to be instrumental in establishing the National High-Tech Crime Unit, after he was supposed to be enjoying his retirement. The meeting was called by the officer whom Phil had appointed, Paul Cox.

When the two representatives of the mobile-phone company arrived, I began the long task of explaining what we had found, and what it meant. The hackers had gained access to the network through a system for which they obviously had a root password; how they had done this we never found out, though we had some idea that they might have obtained passwords for the system through having hacked into the engineering computers that serviced the phone company.

From this initial intrusion, the logs showed three hackers, all from the group we'd identified, exploring different parts of the network. They had introduced programs to collect further passwords and accessed just short of a dozen large, central servers that ran the phone company's entire operation. They had then copied a large number of programs and documents back onto their own computers.

As Paul and I talked the two phone-company representatives through what we had uncovered they nodded and made notes, agreeing that this was important. Occasionally one would murmur or whistle under his breath as some particularly clever aspect of what the hackers had done impressed them. These hackers had had extensive, unmonitored access to some sensitive systems involved in controlling a good portion of the mobile-phone network; more worryingly, it was a part of the mobile-phone system used for billing and call tracing activity (an element that was to prove particularly problematic in a later murder case that I was to work on). The two visitors made a careful note of every compromised machine, thanked Paul and me for our time when we'd finished, and then calmly got up to leave.

Paul was incensed, and I was shocked. But the two men had absolutely no intention of carrying forward a prosecution. They were adamant that it would be too damaging for the company's reputation, though they did ask if I could give them a copy of what we'd found. Before I could frame a polite answer, Paul butted in and told them, in pretty uncompromising terms, that the information was evidence *for a prosecution.* No prosecution, no information. The pair simply shrugged and went away.

It was the same story with every one of the victims. In each case Paul, with or without me, talked the system managers or information-security officers through the findings. In each case, they simply made a note of the subverted systems and went away to fix them.

I still believe they were in the wrong: prosecutions should have been brought. Yes, the intrusion was an embarrassment, but *everyone* running a complex network on the Internet is going to suffer from these attacks. By not bringing the attacks into the open, the nature of the techniques used by the hackers does not become public knowledge, and others end up suffering similar experiences.

Having seen the look on the faces of the victims in the database hack, I know how important that is.

I learned a great deal from the failure associated with this particular exercise. And since I used this as a core element of the training that I carried out for the National High-Tech Crime Unit when it was first established, in April 2001, the UK response to computer crime was informed by this failure as much as by success elsewhere.

We learned just how much difficulty a computer-crime investigation can face when the suspects use encryption applications effectively. We had always known that encryption would create problems, but in the past we had always managed to find some trivial mistake on the part of the user that we could exploit. As encryption becomes easier and more widely applied, this problem is going to get steadily more frequent. The lesson resulted in the National High-Tech Crime Unit being provided with expert technical assistance from the UK government's own code-breaking resources which support the intelligence services. Not all computer-crime cases that involve encryption warrant the application of such an expensive resource, but for those that threaten the national infrastructure – through terrorism, for example, or through damage to important utilities – then it is available.

The other important lesson was the need to bring industry – most particularly, telecommunications and Internet companies – more closely into computer-crime policing. Liaison groups between industry and the police have become increasingly forceful, and the pressure to report and to address computer crime effectively has never been greater.

Although this case has to be marked down as a failure, the impact on the policing of computer crime in the UK – and, through the dissemination of best practice, the rest of the world – cannot be underestimated.

For me and my company, this exercise provided a useful insight into what real hackers are capable of doing; a lesson that we soon needed to apply in real life to a particularly urgent problem.

5. **Bolting Stable Doors**

There were three of us, our heels loud on the tiled floor as we waited for our host to collect us from amongst the alabaster figurines and bronze statues in the client company's elegant reception area in a fashionable district of London.

The organization was a relatively new client. They were the holding company for a group of enormous concerns spread around the globe, controlling billions of pounds' worth of luxury-goods businesses, wholly owned by one, staggeringly rich individual. Despite its wealth, the holding company employed only around 150 people, and operated like a much smaller one; at least as far as its computer infrastructure was concerned. A few weeks earlier we had performed a vulnerability assessment on them and had gained control of most of their Internet-accessible web systems relatively simply, given the absence of even the most obvious of protective measures on their servers.

Since then we had issued urgent recommendations regarding the reconfiguration of their firewall, helped them to liaise with their Internet service provider, and a consultant working for me had developed an information-security policy that we hoped would address any subsequent problems. He was with me to explain how far he had got and what else might need to be done.

The third person with me in the waiting room was a salesman working for my company, who had said he felt certain that the organization now had another, even more pressing problem that they had hinted they wanted to discuss with us.

I was feeling content, sure that we were about to have a comfortable meeting with a happy client. The only discordant note had come as we had signed in, when the consultant – who had just spent two weeks on site – had glanced through the visitors' book, frowning over one particular name. That man was, he explained, another contractor and he was *trouble*, though he didn't want to expand on this in the reception area.

Our salesman had arranged the meeting with the information-systems director and a newly appointed security manager, who had been brought in specifically to take control of and manage the security aspects of the operation. We had been told that the new security manager would be handling the further implementation of our recommendations, one of which was for the head office here in London to take a greater degree of control over the network operation of the several subsidiaries around the world. I had not thought that to be a contentious suggestion, though the IS director had looked a little worried when first we had described what would need to be done, during the feedback session after the successful intrusion and vulnerability test.

The meeting was in a penthouse conference room at the very top of the building, with views out over the rooftops towards the huge wheel of the London Eye on the river. The atmosphere was strained, both men shifting uncomfortably and struggling at times to meet my eye as I talked about what still needed to be achieved. I detected a recent argument between or involving the pair of them, a sense of bruised sensitivities and of something that was – and that would remain – unspoken during the meeting.

It wasn't until we were getting our coats and preparing to leave that the pair, glancing for reassurance at one another, asked if it was possible to have a follow-up meeting at – they both emphasized – *our* offices. Puzzled, but keen to understand what their problem was, I agreed.

That second meeting was a day or so later and was an even more intense affair, held not in a penthouse but in our secure conference room in the lower-ground-floor offices at Buckingham Gate. To the sound of tourist footsteps heading towards the Palace and the endless parade of coaches above the sunken garden outside our window, the IS director explained that they were facing an immediate and deeply disturbing problem. In fact, the security manager interrupted to emphasize, it was more than a problem, it was a very real *danger*.

The IS director explained that the overwhelming majority of their computers and networks – and certainly all of their Internet access – were controlled and jealously guarded by one man, the contractor my consultant had labelled 'trouble'. This person was a firm favourite of the group owner – the incredibly wealthy man who controlled the company completely – but was considered a conniving and dangerous individual by everyone else in the organization. An alarm bell began to sound in the back of my mind.

The contractor had insisted on a meeting at the London office before our meeting there – hence the appearance of his name in the visitors' book. There, he had been aggressively adamant that he would *not* be relinquishing any control of the network, since no-one else had the capability to control it as he had. In the meeting, our contacts had the impression that the man had been reading private email belonging to the IS director and might even have read documents taken from their workstations. Worse, it seemed as though he might also have managed to hear words spoken in closed meetings that the pair of them had held with equipment suppliers. Not, they emphasized, the *gist* of the meetings, which might have been reported by a supplier, but the *exact* words used.

They felt positive that the man had had their offices bugged, their phones tapped and their computers accessed. Hence the strain of that earlier meeting and their insistence on using our offices, away from any risk of bugging.

My immediate reaction was disbelief. It seemed too much like a spy novel, though of course the company *did* control huge sums of money. It could be possible, bizarre though it sounded. I decided that I had to assume that it was all for real, and asked them to describe the individual to me – not what they thought he had *done*, but what he was like as a person.

An interesting picture emerged. The owner of the group – to whom the man reported directly – thought the contractor was a genius, and that he alone was able to make their arcane and cumbersome network actually work. Indeed, whenever he wasn't there, it seemed the network inexplicably failed until the man returned to fix it. The owner spoke highly of him and scoffed at complaints or adverse comments about the man, making sure that he was well rewarded and protected from criticism. By contrast, *every* other member of staff – from the receptionist and secretaries, through the managers, accountants, technical support staff and on up to the directors – disliked the man.

The picture the pair painted, my consultant nodding agreement at every point, was of a person who trampled over others, deliberately causing hurt and fostering disagreement, while gathering as much control of as much of the corporate network for himself as possible. A man who would not let others or their ambitions and feelings stand between him and a selfish objective.

That alarm bell was ringing louder and louder as they talked, and one word was lurking in my mind: 'sociopath'.

A sociopath is an individual who, though usually highly intelligent, doesn't feel or conform to the norms of a society. An extreme version would be a serial rapist or killer: remorseless, sophisticated and often very difficult to catch. But the more intelligent sociopath doesn't often need to resort to violence: they are able to apply manipulation and psychology to get what they want. One indication, I had read, was an individual who can make those people important to them like and trust them, whilst all others – about whom they have no feelings, and to whom they act carelessly and without remorse – distrust and dislike them almost instinctively. On the face of it, this seemed to be the type of person we were dealing with here, which would make him *very* dangerous if crossed.

There was, though, an alternative explanation. It could be that the individual was seeking ever more control of the network so as to manipulate and exploit it for gain. It could be that his anger over potentially losing control of some elements was fuelled by greed or by fear of discovery. In which case – given the sums of money that we already knew from our tests could be manipulated – he would be equally dangerous if crossed. He might even, I considered, be working for organized crime, given his callous attitude to others and his potential for getting access to the huge transactions routinely handled by the network.

I didn't like either explanation and nor did the IS director and the security manager, who both shook their heads in disbelief as I explained them. Though the ex-policemen from my computer-crime investigation team – whom I had asked to come and join the meeting – were in agreement with me, the IS director in particular wanted to believe that all they had to deal with was a troublesome contractor and not a truly dangerous individual. They wanted us to help them remove the individual from the company, and then to examine his computer so as to establish whether he had indeed been hacking into their systems.

It was easy to ask, but we all knew that it would be difficult in the extreme to achieve. Removing a criminal employee from an organization under the best of circumstances is difficult enough. Their accounts and passwords have to be deleted, their computers collected, termination agreements constructed and signed. It can all get messy in the best of circumstances, and this was a long way from being the best of circumstances, given the almost total control that the contractor would seem to have over the infrastructure and systems. There would be an enormous risk of him being able to regain access to and destroy sensitive data, or even leave behind him programs that would alter or destroy data after a certain period of time.

These programs are called 'logic bombs' and can be enormously difficult to detect. All the contractor would have to do is introduce a program that would periodically check to see whether he had accessed the systems for a given period of time. If he hadn't, the program could assume that the contractor had been dismissed, and could then overwrite vital data, alter business-critical applications, or even make the entire network fail irreversibly. The cost to the business would be impossible to estimate, but we could be certain that without its computer network it would struggle to survive.

This scenario might sound far-fetched, but it was one that we had had to address three times over the previous year, though admittedly not when the employee had been as difficult as this individual could prove to be. We had had to remove an IT director who had altered the most-privileged-user passwords without telling anyone. That man had demanded several hundred thousand pounds for the passwords, and we had been asked to try and find an alternative. We did, by hacking the systems and resetting the passwords ourselves, but it had not been easy. Because of that experience, we knew that it *could* be done, but only with a great deal of very carefully controlled, confidential effort.

I gathered my thoughts and began to outline what this particular client would need to do if it was to remain secure and operational during the transition period. Even as I explained, yet more aspects of the problem emerged. The contractor routinely worked from home, on the European mainland; he had also brought in a team of his friends to help run some of the key financial systems; and he had established private network connections for himself into many of the company's subsidiary operations so as to allow him to control them more easily. Guaranteeing that he was unable – directly or indirectly – to attack the company's infrastructure would be difficult, as would seizing control from him of any laptop or home-based equipment belonging to the company.

It looked like an immense job that would have to be incredibly well managed and to enjoy a great deal of good fortune, if we were to take control without allowing the suspect the opportunity to damage systems on his exit or to regain control of key systems afterwards from outside the organization.

First of all, we would need to form a complete picture of the network, including the access points that he was known to use, such as the dial-in and these private network connections. For these, we would have to work out what his legitimate accounts were – and be ready to reset their passwords – and discover all other privileged accounts to be reset. The information to allow us to do this would have to be collected covertly over a period of several days, outside normal working hours, if we were to avoid alerting him or his friends to what was being done.

Second, we would also need to consider all of the systems and networks that were not obviously under his control, and ensure that the Administrator accounts on these were also under our control, again by being prepared to reset the passwords. In particular, we needed to do this for the switches and routers that made the organisation's networks actually operate.

Third, we needed to examine the known remote dial-in access points to the network and lock him and his friends out. The only way I could see of doing this, though, was to lock *everyone* out and allow them back in under a controlled process.

Fourth, we would need to control access to the head-office systems from the subsidiary networks, to make sure that he could not come back into the computers through a trusted route.

Finally, we would have to travel to Europe to seize his computers from him, to allow us to examine them.

I described all this, encouraged and prompted by the former police officers on the team. I'd gone through precisely these aspects before, on banking and government computer networks, but never where it hadn't been possible to arrest or detain the suspect long enough for us to exercise the complete control we would need. That was the final part of my worries: what would our suspect be doing while we ran around resetting passwords and disabling network components? And what would his *friends* be doing if he were to realize what was going on?

We needed to ensure that he was out of contact and unable to access the systems or contact his friends for the several hours that might be necessary to reset the passwords and access rights on a large collection of computers.

We discussed those worries for around thirty minutes before the plan was established. Over the course of the next few weeks, we would ship a team in after hours to gain the information that we would need. At the end of the following week, the suspect would be taking a two-and-a-half-hour plane flight, so control of the network could be achieved while he was in the air and completely out of touch. It would be *very* tight, but we felt we should be able to do it in that time.

When he landed, the contractor would be met by one of my ex-police officers, who could then seize control of his laptop and, with a civil search warrant, go to his home in order to seize any company computer assets that might be there. Finally, our suspect would be presented with legal documents informing him that any attempt to access the company computer assets would be considered unlawful.

At the end of this activity, our penetration-testing team would be provided with the details of the network that were known to our suspect, and they would be invited to try and gain access. It wouldn't prove that we hadn't missed anything, but it might uncover anything we *had* missed.

The best-laid plans, of course, go quickly awry.

A major part of the plan involved not telling anyone – particularly the subject of the investigation – that there was an investigation taking place. Almost immediately, that element was thrown out of the window as it became apparent that not only might the contractor have had access to email and certain documents from the IS director's computer, but that he had a *complete copy* of that computer stored on his own workstation.

This was discovered when the security manager, returning from the meeting at our offices, had examined a back-up tape from one of the file servers used by the contractor. The entire contents of the contractor's desktop, email and 'My

Documents' folder had been replicated onto the server. There, in an innocuously named folder, was a complete replication of the IS director's own computer contents, including a variety of confidential and sensitive documents regarding the running of the organization. It must have been a deeply disturbing moment for the IS director, who was understandably furious. But what had been a mere suspicion now looked like a smoking gun.

The contractor was due to return to the company's London office the following day, and the security manager asked if we would attend their offices then and take a copy of his laptop in order to prove that the contractor had made the copy of the director's computer.

It was a delicate position. On the one hand, copying the laptop would certainly give us evidence to show that the contractor was up to no good, but it would also alert him, in the most obvious way, to the fact that his activities were known. We had no way of telling what his reaction to this would be, and I was anxious not to allow him the opportunity to damage the organization before we were ready to respond.

I counselled firmly against the measure, but the IS director was adamant. Reluctantly we agreed that two of our computer-crime investigators would attend the organization's offices with the security manager and would take a forensic copy – called an 'image' – of the laptop for us to investigate. In an attempt to alleviate his suspicions, we agreed to present the activity as a standard, head-office-wide audit of laptops and systems initiated by the new security manager. It wasn't the strongest of stories, but it was the best we could construct in the time available to us.

The next day, the contractor was settling down to begin work in a visitor's office when two of my team knocked and walked in. As the security manager explained the cover story to him, they quickly removed the laptop's hard-disk-drive unit and slipped it into a small caddy drawer on the side of a suitcase-sized, matt-black portable computer-imaging system. While the contractor fumed and tried to raise the organization's owner on the telephone to object to the intrusion, the imaging software needed only a few minutes to take a complete and forensically accurate copy of the laptop drive. It was so quick that they even had time to replace the drive unit back in the man's laptop before he had finished explaining to his patron what was happening.

Unfortunately, the pair couldn't simply leave immediately and return to the lab at Buckingham Gate. Instead, so as to support the cover story, they had to pretend to take copies of all of the other systems at the head office, a tedious session of make-believe that lasted for most of the morning.

Finally back at the office, we soon realized that we had struck gold. Even the most cursory examination of the laptop image was enough to convince everyone that their suspicions were correct. It was much worse than they had thought. Along with the copy of the IS director's computer, there was also a large number of other, even more sensitive documents including copies of material from the *owner*'s private files.

There was no direct indication of fraudulent behaviour – no records of illicit transactions, for example – but we all felt that here we had easily enough evidence to persuade the owner to stop protecting him. It was the IS director who made the call to the owner, and the response was immediate and unequivocal. The security manager was grinning as he came back into the room and gave us the thumbs-up and the instruction to proceed with the rest of our plans.

It took us four solid nights to examine each of the servers in the organization's global network, accessing them covertly out of hours by means of our own private network connection from the security manager's office in London.

Locating the Administrator accounts was simple enough, using a hacking trick and a standard Microsoft application. Usually, when you access a computer running Windows over a corporate network, it is necessary to log on to it: to give both a valid username and the appropriate password for that account. Bizarrely, Windows allows something called a 'null connection': instead of giving valid access credentials, you connect and give no credentials whatsoever. Access is granted, but only to a limited portion of the target computer. That limited portion, though, is sufficient for a standard Microsoft system-administration program to be able to collect details of the accounts active on the computer system, including usernames and the permission levels associated with each one. For all of the computer systems, there were accounts called 'Administrator' – with full administrative permissions – and on a large number there were other, differently named accounts that also had these full permissions. These, we decided, were probably the ones that our target was planning to use.

We had to gain access to each of these computers, over the company's computer network, and reset these passwords. And we had to do so without knowing what the passwords for the Administrator accounts actually were. The only way to do this was by hacking into the systems, one by one – a job that we were perfectly placed to do.

It was, in many ways, a similar exercise to ones we had done a hundred times before: access a network and worm our way from system to system, 'capturing the flag' on each one. There were some crucial differences, though. Usually, we try not to let the security team spot what we are doing; this time, we had the manager's full co-operation, so that was not a problem. However, normally it doesn't really matter if we are spotted by the system-administration staff during a test; this time, it would have been a disaster.

The team of penetration-testing engineers – my hacking crew – had to be more careful and more covert than ever before or since. They had to sneak into the office along with the cleaning staff at the end of a working day and set up a completely in-dependent, trusted, highly secure, dedicated link from the security manager's workstation back to our laboratory. Then they had to use this to gain control of each of the servers in turn, using a variety of the most covert tricks we could find.

Just as with many of the other internal penetration tests, most of the servers we encountered had not been 'hardened': they were in the default configuration that we call 'out of the box'.

They had many unnecessary services available that would have been removed had the system administrators realized that the computers were going to be attacked by determined hackers. But because the systems were considered to be internal, and therefore protected within the corporate network from external attack, they were vulnerable and were steadily and quickly conquered by the team.

During those four long night-time sessions the atmosphere in the basement penetration-testing laboratory was more tense than I can remember it having been before or since. An open-plan room, the lab has an underground feeling to it. And especially at night, when it is lit only by the glow of the multiple computer monitors on each engineer's desk, it has an intense atmosphere of controlled threat. Night after night, we ordered in a pile of pizza and beers, and to the thumping bass of loud music the team sweated their way from system to system, throwing instructions, insults and whoops of delight from group to group as they decoded each system's secrets in turn.

For each of the conquered systems, the objective was the same: to take a copy of the file of encrypted passwords, so that we could decode them and get *all* of the passwords used by our target subject. As full control was gained on each, the file was copied down onto our laboratory computers and loaded across our internal, highly protected network onto one ultra-fast computer. There the password-decrypting program was let loose to decipher each collection of passwords in turn.

It was eerie to watch on the system's over-sized monitor. For each collection of encrypted passwords – representing each one of the conquered servers – we had a window open on the monitor, giving the list of encrypted passwords. In each window, a flickering series of characters displayed every one of the hundreds of potential passwords that were being trialled by the software every minute. As it gained a 'hit', the list of encrypted passwords was gradually, inexorably replaced with the 'plain-text' version.

There was the feeling of steady inevitability about the

process. It was a joy to watch the team at work, and within just a few days we had total, unconstrained and wholly covert control of the organization's network.

Each of these server systems then had to be examined in turn. Always at the back of my mind was the worry about a logic bomb: a program that would execute and cause potentially irreversible damage to the stored data if it detected that our target subject was no longer able to gain access to a particular server. Defeating the contractor under those circumstances would have been at best a Pyrrhic victory. We wanted to do what we could to avoid that problem, so once each server was under our control I had the team make a record of the applications and data that it contained. With this, and with complete control of the servers, I was confident that, even if logic bombs had been installed, we could rapidly rebuild any damaged systems.

We were ready to wrest control of the network and servers away from the organization's potentially criminal system manager, though only time would tell whether we were ready for his reaction. I phoned the IS director and security manager and, with fingers firmly crossed, told them that we were ready to make our move.

There remained just one major concern: would our subject indeed catch his flight as planned, or had we done something throughout the course of the last few days that might have alerted him? We had done all we could to minimize the risk of making him aware – at least, as much as we could, after having so obviously taken a copy of his laptop the week before. But there had been no communication about the exercise through email, and only the smallest possible number of people in the organization knew what was happening. Conscious that our target might indeed have bugged offices or telephones – though I privately believed that to be unlikely – we had used codenames when discussing the tasks and had arranged to meet the IS director and the security manager outside the main buildings whenever it was necessary. Even the purchase order for our services described only generic 'security consulting' as the product. Finally, we had collected and reviewed the audit logs on each of the gateways and key servers, checking that no changes had been made and that there had been no illicit access other than our own.

We were fairly sure that we had the matter in hand, but there was still that nagging doubt to contend with, just as there must be with any such clandestine operation.

It was 9.30 on a Thursday morning when our subject was due to take his flight, and so on the last plane of the Wednesday night I despatched one of our former police officers to be there to meet our man at the airport in the morning. I also had someone watching and waiting at Heathrow to ensure that our subject did go through to the plane as planned. We were waiting anxiously back at our offices, ready for the phone call that would tell us we were safe to proceed with the takeover element of the operation, ready for that guaranteed three-hour window during which several dozen servers, a series of distinct networks, gateways and remote dial-in access points all had to be locked down and reconfigured.

The plane was delayed. Thirty minutes; fifty minutes; ninety minutes. My nerves were increasingly frayed with every notification from the airport. We had everything ready to roll but it seemed like fate was conspiring against us. Finally, nearly two hours later than it should have been, the plane was called, and we were told that our target was making his way from the executive club lounge to the departure gate.

It was time to swing into action. I had planned to do the lockdown in three distinct phases. We would defend the perimeter of the network; then the servers and business applications that our subject was known to have his own, private access to; and finally the rest of the servers and applications that the organization depended upon.

Locking down the perimeter was the easy bit. Our subject had just three known ways of accessing the network through the perimeter. First of all, he could dial in to the remote-access servers by using a normal modem connection. We were fairly sure – from the access logs we had copied and from what we had been told – that our man didn't ever use the network this way, but it was still an access mechanism that we wanted to restrict in case he decided to do so via another user account that we weren't aware of. I had one member of the team go through and reset all of the passwords, so that every user – legitimate or not – would have to have their accounts unlocked by the help-desk staff. I had the security manager contact the help desk and warn them to refer all callers regarding remote access directly to him.

The second access mechanism – which we already knew our target used – was through one or more of the private network links that the contractor had established. These are encrypted channels over the general Internet, which our man could access simply by connecting to the Internet and going to a specific web page. There he would have to give a valid username and pass-word, and if these were accepted then he would have a secure connection through to key servers on the internal network. Our immediate approach was to remove the target's access rights to this service by erasing his username details from the server. However, he might also have access through some other username, so we again locked out all users from the service, relying on the help desk to work with the security manager in filtering the reinstatement of individuals throughout the next few days.

Other than being a frantic race against time, this part of the exercise was straightforward. We had the first two parts of the job done before, I imagined, our man's plane had finished taxiing from the stand at Heathrow. The third access mechanism was altogether more problematic.

There was a range of computer services accessible over the Internet. There was a website, an email service and a file-transfer service, and a range of other servers running specific applications that needed to be accessed by companies within the group to manage their order-processing and accounts functions. Where we could happily lock our man out of the dial-in and private network services simply by locking everyone out, that was not practical in this third case, since too many others needed this access. Instead, we had to disable the email and file-transfer-access accounts that were known to be his – along with those accounts we had discovered to have administrative privileges that he might be able to use – and to change the Administrator passwords on the various service applications.

It was a time-consuming thing to do and could be, at best, only a partial set of counter-measures. There might well still be user accounts for which our man knew the password and from which he might be able to cause mischief. All we could rely on were the subsequent modifications we planned to introduce to those systems – in particular, our intention to provide an intrusion detection system to monitor them more closely, rather like putting a CCTV camera into a building that might be burgled.

Until then we would have to watch the systems directly and personally, by remaining logged in as 'Administrator' on each one and by close monitoring of all the processes running. And we would have to do this reliably from the time that our man was once more outside our control, when he was finally left alone at his house later that day.

One final thing needed to be done to the perimeter: the organization's Internet service provider had to be persuaded to remove our subject from the list of those authorized to make changes to the organization's website or Internet-access services.

By my estimation, our man's plane was just about over Paris by the time we had completed this part of the exercise. We had the outside as well defended as we could, but it was *still* possible that he might be able to get in. We needed to make sure that he couldn't get up to mischief if he did. The team turned its attention to the servers within the organization's internal network and began the laborious task of disabling suspicious accounts and introducing new passwords for each Administrator. The team worked their way steadily down the agreed list of servers, in the order that we had already decided was the most sensible.

In my mind's eye, I had a picture of our subject's plane

making its way inexorably across France, perhaps beginning now the long descent from thirty-odd thousand feet towards an unsought-for appointment with a former City of London firearms officer. Even with that pressure, I could do nothing to hurry the task. For each server, we had to delete our subject's account and change the password on the Administrator and similarly privileged accounts so as to control access. We couldn't simply change the passwords to a random value. We had agreed a list of new administrative passwords with the security manager, so for each change we had to check the new value against the list. When this had been done, we had to consider the applications on each of the servers and make sure that any accounts able to drastically affect the application's function were also locked down. Next, we had to take an update of the data stored on the server, in case it had changed since earlier in the week, so that we could rebuild the server rapidly if required.

Finally we took a few, tense minutes to watch over the server, in case some previously unseen logic bomb had been triggered by our activity and was ready to destroy the server and its contents.

Our man's flight must have been on its final approach when the last of the internal servers was locked down, and the members of the team looked across at me to see what we had to do next. To me, it seemed obvious: our next job was to try and hack the organization, just as I expected our subject to try and do when he discovered what had been done.

If the flight had been a tense one for us back in London, it was even worse for the pair waiting to meet our subject at his destination. The organization had asked the finance director to accompany the ex-policeman I had sent. For the finance director it was all a new and unpleasant experience, but for my investigator it was very much 'business as usual'. A former member of the police's renowned Tactical Support Group and a former marksman and sniper specialist, he had trained first as a detective and then as a scene-of-crime officer before deciding to specialize as a computer forensics investigator in the City of London's perpetually over-stretched Fraud Squad. If any background could have prepared him for the long and tedious wait at the airport, that was probably the one.

For all his experience, the pair had arrived at the airport an hour earlier than needed and had then had to endure – just as we in London had had to do – the two-hour delay to the flight. Nerves were fraying by the time the plane landed, and as a result they were probably more abrupt in intercepting the man than they had planned to be.

The finance director took the lead, identifying the subject as he cleared Customs and made his way into the arrivals hall at the airport. The director went to greet the astonished man and directed him to a coffee shop nearby, where he passed him a package of documents. These were the termination papers for the contractor's employment, along with an explanation that all access rights to the organization's computer infrastructure were immediately withdrawn.

At that, my ex-policeman reached to relieve the man of his laptop and company mobile phone. Describing the scene afterwards, my investigator said he felt sure the man would refuse, and might even cause a scene in the public coffee shop. Astonishingly, he did neither, simply passing the complete laptop bag across the table, along with the mobile phone, not yet even turned back on after the flight. It was hard to decide whether the man had nothing to hide or felt that he had hidden it too well to be found, or perhaps had even decided that it could no longer *be* hidden and so had simply given up.

The pair of them went with the subject to his home nearby, the ex-policeman travelling in the man's car while the finance director followed. There, they collected the two PCs that he was known to have, and reiterated that he no longer had access permission into the organization's network and that he would definitely be prosecuted if he tried to gain it.

Phoning me as they drove away, my investigator seemed astonished at just how easy it had been to collect the material and how unthreatening the supposed 'sociopath' had been in practice. All I could imagine was that we had probably missed something important, but there was nothing to do but congratulate him and tell him to hurry back with what he had recovered.

As it happened, what he had recovered was almost completely worthless. Although the laptop originally imaged at the London office was amongst the items recovered, its disk contents were wholly and completely different from the earlier image. Evidently, the man had swapped the disk drives – and that original was never discovered; the only copy was the one that we had made at the office. The new laptop disk drive, seized from him at the airport, and the computer contents from his home were, to all intents and purposes, completely new operating systems almost devoid of meaningful content. Evidently that earlier exercise in London had spooked him into destroying at least one disk drive and quite possibly more.

We were left with just the material from that first imaging and with the ever-present worry that, since he *had* been warned, he might well have done something underhand with the network.

As the days and weeks passed without incident, as the team monitoring the servers reported no intrusions, and as we gradually passed control over to the IS director's own staff, it seemed increasingly that we had won. We began to make preparations for the prosecution that we felt sure was going to come against the contractor for computer misuse. We waited and waited.

When the exercise had first been discussed, my senior computer-crime investigator – a former detective sergeant with the Met's Computer Crime Unit – had confidently predicted that, even if we did find anything, it would never see the inside of a court. It seemed that he was right: the organization was wanting quietly to forget all about the problems.

It was not unexpected; rare is the company that takes a computer-crime case to court, rather than simply dismissing the culprit. But the organization had one more, astonishing surprise up its sleeve. A few months later the consultant who was developing an information-security policy for the organization came back into my office. Aghast, he announced that the organization had not only not prosecuted the contractor, the owner had in fact reinstated him and put him in sole control of a sensitive and highly important network-development project.

We had, it seemed, won the battle but the contractor had won the war. He had used his influence over the owner to convince him that it had all been a misunderstanding and that he had been working with the owner's best interests at heart all along. He admitted being over-zealous in his monitoring of the network, and that was all that was said.

Today, the contractor continues to work for the organization, jealously preserving his increasing control over the network, and the staff continue to fume about the intrusions and problems of privacy. Improvements and alterations to the organization's global network are hampered and, most frustratingly, the contractor continues to enjoy the owner's confidence and trust.

It's hard to draw any concrete lessons from an experience such as this – other than the obvious one, that a well-managed and successful investigation is sometimes not sufficient in itself; that sometimes we win the battle but overlook the war. Personally, I felt I learned a great deal from the experience, not least that almost overwhelming difficulties are faced by even the most competent of information-security professionals when tackling real-world problems.

But there is still a strong sense of pride in being able to combine the best legitimate hacking skills with the best computer-investigation skills to resolve a problem. We did solve the immediate, specified problem for the company concerned. If they failed to take complete advantage of our skills and our experience then we surely could not be blamed for that.

6. In the Public Eye

Pete Warren is a freelance investigative journalist who had worked for the *Sunday Times'* Insight team, specializing in computer crime and technology-related issues. I'd got to know him in the mid-1990s when we had both attended a book launch at a restaurant off Leicester Square. After the event, a group of us had planned to go on for another drink, and he and I had spent a hilarious twenty minutes trying to find a cab that Pete – who had just written a savage article about MI5 – could be convinced was not being driven by a spy. Over too many glasses of beer, Pete tried to explain how his phones had been bugged, his children photographed and followed, and how he was now convinced that the bar staff were about to denounce him. Although at the time I thought that he was barking mad and paranoid to boot, Pete and I became firm friends – enough for me to try and describe some of the basic principles of computer forensics when he had asked to know what it was all about.

One notion in particular appealed to him: that the contents of deleted files can often be recovered from a disk drive. He was fascinated by the idea that it was far from easy to wipe files – be they paedophile images, text documents or whatever – from a computer; that it was almost always possible to locate some small fragment of crucial evidence from even the most carefully sanitized system. He was even more enthralled to learn that even if the whole operating system is reinstalled there would *still* be fragments left in place, unless a major exercise of overwriting and wiping those files had been performed.

This led to an interesting line of investigation: recycled or refurbished computers thrown out by large organizations. Was it possible for those computers still to contain crucial or even just mildly interesting snippets of data from their 'previous lives' within the company?

My immediate reaction was to say no. Any sensible company discarding computers – be they workstations or servers – would naturally turn to a secure destruction company and have them wipe the disks clean and provide a certificate of destruction. The services are not expensive and their guarantee is a particularly reliable one. In fact, I had spent some time a few months before Pete's question investigating and rating the services of these organizations for a client. I was sure that they were more than trustworthy.

But then that small worm of doubt surfaced. Yes, of course any 'sensible' company would do precisely that – but then again, no 'sensible' company would have obvious passwords, unprotected servers and unmonitored networks. I had already seen just how many companies failed to enact even the most straightforward of security measures. The world was evidently full of companies that were not 'sensible'.

I was forced to tell Pete that it was possible. I personally considered it unlikely that he would be able to track down any examples, and told him so. Those were words that he would later, gleefully, force me to eat.

Pete wasn't starting from an idle hope. He had already been told by a number of people working for some high-profile organizations that they believed the computers thrown out, sold on or given away had not been adequately deleted. Some organizations, for example, allow staff to buy 'end-of-life' workstations and Pete had been told that these had occasionally been found still to contain some data. His most obvious problem was just how to find computers discarded by the sorts of companies that he wanted to 'name and shame' without in-advertently giving away the details of those people who had told him in confidence about these lapses. He couldn't simply take computers that had been bought by employees, nor could he find a way of buying computers in similar circumstances. Computers that had been given away to charities were being *used* by their grateful recipients, who wouldn't jeopardize their good fortune by parading their sponsors' mistakes. He could patrol the streets, looking for computers that had been discarded in skips, but that was simply too hit-and-miss – and being a trained investigative journalist, Pete was simply too pro-fessional to rely on such an uncertain route to his story.

Pete decided to use a more reliable means of hunting his prey. Most, if not all, large companies have asset numbers and distinguishing labels fixed to expensive items such as computers. Pete assumed that any company so careless as to not delete data from end-of-life computers would probably also be careless with the labelling of the computers. All he had to do was lurk at car-boot sales and cheap computer markets, looking out for labelled computers. He assured me he already had fund-ing from *Channel 4 News* for the story; they would reimburse him for the few hundreds of pounds that the computers might cost him.

It all seemed a straightforward and easily achieved exercise, and I wished him luck, curious to know whether he would find anything. Pete had one further request: would I be prepared to image and examine the computers for him? Not expecting him to find anything interesting, I agreed. Had I known quite where that simple promise was going to take me, I might have been more careful.

As it happened, it was some five weeks between Pete's request and his arrival on my doorstep – easily long enough for me to forget all about why he should be standing there, grinning at me, surrounded by half a dozen desktop-size computer units that he had piled on the cobblestones outside our mews offices.

Between us, we carried the computers through to the

laboratory and stacked them carefully on the bench while Pete described the scrums of computer fairs and car-boot sales he had visited to locate them. Just as he had expected, finding computer units still with the companies' asset tags and owner-ship markings on them had made his life substantially easier. Now he wanted to know, and quickly, whether he had wasted the last month in the effort. The computers were all, he had been told, recently discarded by the companies as 'end-of-life' systems.

The first question that any computer forensic investigator needs to answer is: what am I supposed to be looking for?

As a former university lecturer, I love to teach and I had jumped at the opportunity when the police asked me to help train their computer forensic investigators. During those train-ing sessions, I had encouraged them not only to obtain the evidence reliably but then to try and frame 'closed questions' about the evidence. The answers to those questions can then be used to drive the rest of the investigation. In some cases, those closed questions are simple to produce. In a paedophile case we might simply ask whether the computer contains any indecent pictures of children. The computer forensic and investigation software includes a picture-gallery service, which can be used to collect all the pictures into one, easily examined group. Depending on the result of this first question, we might then frame further questions regarding websites, email, contacts and so forth. Fraud, hacking, murder, stalking and other awkward cases might be harder to frame questions for, but a careful approach at the beginning of the exercise can ensure that the investigator isn't bogged down impossibly in the mass of data that must be sifted through.

But in this case I was stymied. All Pete would say was that he wanted to know whether or not the computers contained data that should have been wiped. I had no obvious way of knowing quite *what* I should be looking for within the mass of data con-tained on the systems.

To begin with, I decided to concentrate on the purely mechanical tasks of capturing the computers' contents forensically, in a way that would allow us to examine the deleted files as well as any remaining 'live' ones. We used the exercise as a way of training members of my technical team in the process of recording and preserving suspect computers. Just as we would do with computers seized as part of an investigation, we completed the laboratory evidence logs, signing the computers in and recording the physical condition of each one.

Over a period of two days, I guided the technicians through the procedures for photographing and then opening the chassis cases, removing the hard-drive units and mounting them in the over-sized laboratory copying system – nicknamed 'Mycroft' – before running the imaging software. We went through the tedious but necessary process of preserving evidence copies on pristine hard-disk drives for storage in the safes, and on CD-ROMs that we could work with.

By the third day we had all six of the computer systems preserved and ready to be returned to Pete for him to sell at yet another car-boot sale, I presumed. Now the difficult decision of just *how* we were going to address his problem had to be faced.

I bounced the question around in my mind a few times, trying to see it in different ways. Pete wanted to know whether or not these computers still contained interesting data. It occurred to me that I could divide the question into two parts. First, did the computers still contain *any* data from when they had been used by the companies shown on the asset tags? Secondly, was that data likely to be of any interest to anyone who acquired the computers?

I could construct the timeline for the files stored on each of the computers and then look to see whether the file system contained any files that had been created more than, say, six months before. According to Pete's information about the computers, they had been only recently discarded by the various companies – financial organizations, for the most part, it seemed – and so half-year-old data files would suggest that they hadn't been cleaned at all.

That could be nothing more than a crude, first-cut approach

to choosing which computers we should concentrate on. It didn't take into account computers that *had* been wiped but ineffectually, for example. But it was a start.

The files and folders on a typical computer fall into two broad categories. First, there are the files and folders that are a part of the operating system and which are copied onto the main disk drive from the initial installation CD-ROM when the computer is first configured. These files tend not to change dramatically throughout the lifespan of a computer system, and form a kind of basic landscape against which the computer is actually used.

The second kind of files and folders are those that relate to the actual use of the computer by the owner. These files are the documents, email messages and Internet-related detritus that collect over the weeks, months and years of use.

In analysing the contents of files which existed from six months earlier, it was clear that the 'landscape' files – whose date and time stamps would reflect the time when they were created for the installation CD-ROM – would be irrelevant. For each of the six computers I produced the timeline listing of their file contents, looking through them for non-landscape files that would indicate that they had been used. I didn't expect to find anything and was mentally rehearsing what I would say on the phone to Pete when I called to tell him the results. Astonishingly, the second and fifth computers I looked at contained files that had quite clearly been created or accessed over the course of the last few months. Better still, in those two timelines there were *no* file-creation or access date and time stamps covering the last three weeks, when I imagined the computers had been thrown out by their respective companies, one a bank, the other an insurance company. Therefore I could be fairly sure that no-one had used the computers since they left their corporate owners. So maybe Pete was onto something.

I was still faced with that most basic of problems for the computer forensic investigator: how was I going to find the needles in the haystack of data that was being made available to me? Especially when I still had no clear idea what the 'needles' might look like. I needed a way of automatically sifting through the files to find those that might be relevant to my 'case'.

Then it struck me: maybe I should consider the computer data as *being* a part of a 'case'? Maybe I should assume some criminal or malicious or fraudulent activity had involved these computers, then use that view of the case to concoct my search terms, just as I would do in a real crime situation. This wouldn't be a comprehensive inspection of the computer contents, but it would be a start and might well produce some interesting material if there was anything there to be found.

For the insurance company, I decided that my 'case' would be that the computer still contained a collection of personal data – names and addresses of policy holders – and that there was therefore a breach of the Data Protection Act. For the bank, I decided on a similar Data Protection Act breach, this time concerning a leakage of bank-account details still held on the computer.

For the bank example, this gave me one obvious, easily understood search term: 'account' would generate interesting hits. For the insurance company, it was a little more difficult, but I decided that a word likely to appear in most address databases would be 'Street'.

By chance I ran the bank-account search first, leaving it to pick its slow way through the immense data file collected by the imaging tool while I went to make a cup of coffee. When I got back, I saw a long list of successful matches. The word 'account' appeared in a whole sequence of undeleted files that had been created or last altered when the computer was still within the bank's offices in the City of London. The computer had not been adequately wiped and did perhaps contain some relevant information to do with bank accounts. But what information might that be, and how interesting might Pete actually find it?

The next task was to step through the list of these hits. The image analysis program, Encase, presents a context for each hit of the search term. It gives the file details and it also shows the forty or so characters before and after the search term in the file.

One of these lines leaped out at me as I paged through the list: a copy of a letter giving details of charitable donations being paid from the bank account of a Sir Paul McCartney. Even with no journalistic training I could see this was likely to be of interest to Pete and his friends at *Channel 4 News*.

Encase allows the investigator to jump between different views of the computer evidence. From the search listing, I could shift the perspective so as to see the location of the document in the hierarchy of folders on the system. Using that, I could see that the first letter discussing Sir Paul's donations was one of several relating to him. Opening each letter in turn, the documents gave details of the payments – the amounts and the recipient – but also details of Sir Paul's account with the bank. There were account and sort-code details; information about the balance in the accounts after the donation; and even history of other payments.

There wasn't enough information in the files that I had found to enable one, for example, to defraud the bank or Sir Paul, though there *was* enough for it to be highly embarrassing. Worse, looking at the folders similar to this one, there was information about a large number of other, similarly generous customers. It seemed that the computer had been used by some-one within the bank's Personal Banking Division, providing services to the rich and famous.

Care must always be taken at this point of an investigation to avoid what we call the 'rabbit warren'. It is too easy, faced with interesting, enticing information, to be tempted into deeper investigations to satisfy curiosity rather than the objectives of the investigation itself, losing oneself in a rabbit warren of more complex searches. To make sure that doesn't happen, we train investigators to go back constantly to the specific questions they have been asked to address. In this case, I had been asked to establish whether or not any of the computers could be shown to have been disposed of without having been wiped, and whether they contained interesting information that should have been protected by being wiped. I had succeeded and had found that the answer to both questions was yes. It was time to stop.

I called Pete and told him that, if he was interested, I could tell him Sir Paul McCartney's bank account number.

It took Pete and his producer just fifty minutes to get to my office, demanding to see what I had found, insistent that the other computers could safely be ignored now we had such interesting material to play with. The producer was John McGee, a familiar face from *Channel 4 News*, who flipped between excited incomprehension at how we had found what we had found and a poor attempt to appear laid-back about the discovery.

We were *all* excited that something so interesting had been uncovered on a computer from a Sunday-morning car-boot sale. John was already trying to work out where he would site cameras and lights in our tiny forensic laboratory, while Pete was scribbling a rough script for what he was positive would go out on the 7 p.m. news that night.

I hadn't realized what I had let myself in for until the technical staff from Channel 4 started unloading equipment from the back of a large van a little while later. The lights were oppressively warm in the poorly ventilated laboratory room, and the camera had to be set up outside the door. Pete's questions were straightforward so that they would be understandable to a non-expert audience: What should companies do when they discard computers? What data might be recoverable? Would you need specialized equipment to discover what we had found? What *had* we found? How serious was this? Should we all be worried?

The interview itself was easy enough, though I was sweating and uncomfortable under the lights. Then John wanted to film me doing various technical things in the laboratory. They filmed me again and again typing at one of the computers and pointing out some of the interesting files on the screen. It seemed to take hours before they were satisfied that they had what they needed.

The programme itself was actually quite fun to watch. John McGee did the piece, introduced by Jon Snow about twenty minutes into the show. They had filmed a car-boot sale and the collection of computers; they had an interview with someone from a secure wiping company; and then they had me. It was the first time I'd been on TV and it was excruciating to see and hear myself – especially the way I had fumbled the connections on the disk drive as they had filmed me. The piece concluded with an abject apology from a spokesman for the bank and a brusque 'No comment' from Sir Paul's press agent.

For *Channel 4 News*, and for Pete himself, it was an altogether successful piece. For us, it was something of a success too, since the company got precious publicity from the peak-time transmission.

But then I began to wonder what the *bank*'s reaction was likely to be. They were a client of ours on the penetration-testing service; the security manager for their IT Department was a friend, with whom I'd worked quite closely a few years before; worst of all, my youngest brother was a senior project manager with them. Caught up in the excitement of the chase and the unusual activity of being filmed, I'd somehow not given any thought to their reaction. Now, with the time to think about it, I began to worry even more about what Pete might have got me into. The fallout began the following morning.

It started with a call from the bank's security manager – my friend – expressing his disappointment. The call was fielded by our managing director, who managed – after a lot of effort – to smooth ruffled feathers and save the account for us. Next was my brother, who told me about the ribbing he had had to endure over his morning coffee – for a programme he hadn't even been able to watch, since he'd worked late that night.

I was just beginning to relax when we received a call from the bank's lawyers, who had talked with *Channel 4 News* already and were asking us now to confirm our address so that they could send someone around to 'recover their data'. First, they wanted the computer that they had failed to wipe – though they were happy to give it back once it *had* been wiped; they had sold it, after all. Then they wanted the CD-ROMs that we had recorded and the copy disk drive we had made – but also, they said that they were going to seize Mycroft itself, so as to assure themselves that no trace of 'their data' could be found on our forensic equipment.

I explained that the computer was already back with Pete, presumably now somewhere in *Channel 4 News*'s offices; and that the copies that we had made were also in their possession, since John and Pete had taken them away with them the previous evening. I also stressed that there was no way I could agree to give access to Mycroft. To surrender the forensic analysis system was unthinkable. We simply could not allow that to happen, since it contained not only material relating to the investigation for Channel 4, but also material relating to nearly every other investigation that we had carried out.

When we do paedophile investigations we are extraordinarily careful to carry out the work in such a way as to ensure that any illegal pictures are copied – manually or automatically – onto one specific hard-disk drive that can be 'sanitized' at the end of the investigation, by running the data-wiping tools that we had accused the bank of overlooking. I wasn't worried, therefore, about inadvertently giving the bank's lawyers copies of illegal pictures. But I *was* worried about all the other types of investigations, where we don't have to be quite so careful about temporary files and copies of working documents. There was a very good chance that a lot of material relating to past or still-live cases would remain on Mycroft, a system that would normally have been locked away securely in the best-protected area of our offices. Had we let it out, *we* could have looked as foolish as the bank.

The legal tussle therefore began in earnest, with the *Channel 4 News* lawyers acting on our behalf. They explained that we were happy to provide all that was asked for, apart from the Mycroft system because it contained legally privileged information relating to other cases. The bank's lawyers objected, demanding at least access to the system. We refused, citing again the legally privileged nature of the computer. Back and forth the argument went – involving me, the MD and our legal advisers – until we finally reached a compromise.

The bank agreed that we could securely delete all relevant files on the system and that we could run a 'cleaning' program so as to overwrite all deleted file clusters and 'slack space' at the end of files with a random pattern. We had proved that the bank had not had the wit to clean the computers that it was selling on, and the bank in return had specified with great precision how we were to clean our own. It seemed fittingly ironic, and we did exactly as they asked, pleased to have come out of what might have been a very damaging situation more or less intact.

Pete, to his credit, looked suitably contrite when I told him about the problems, and promised to pay me back with a drink sometime. I'm still waiting for it.

7. **Gary Glitter's Laptop**

Where Pete Warren had put me firmly in the spotlight on national television, another Pete – DC Pete Lintern of Avon and Somerset Police – kept me in the back room, on a case that garnered significantly more publicity.

Avon and Somerset Police headquarters is in a modern campus-style group of buildings on the outskirts of Bristol, accessible along a narrow, steep road past the municipal tip. Not an auspicious area, I thought, trying to drive and follow the map that DC Lintern of the Fraud Squad had scribbled for me the week before. It was late evening when I arrived there and left the car in the sparsely populated car park above the main reception. A tall, fair-haired man with a West Country accent, Pete led me through the clean, echoing corridors of the new CID block and up a set of stairs to the open-plan office used by the Fraud Squad.

I was there to review the computer evidence in the case of Regina versus Paul Gadd – better known to the world as Gary Glitter.

The story is now a familiar one, though at the time it came as a huge shock to the world. Once more popular after years in the wilderness, the fifty-year-old star had always been dogged by rumours of sexual misbehaviour, though in most cases the stories had been dismissed as exaggeration or simple tabloid tales. Then he had handed in a laptop computer for repair at PC World in Bristol, and staff had found a collection of what were alleged to be paedophile images on the hard disk. They had reported this to the police and handed over the laptop, and Gadd had been arrested and pilloried in the press. Not all of the criticism had been directed at the pop star; some voices were raised against the staff at the shop, with suspicions that they had only inspected the laptop because of its association with a well-known figure. It was precisely because of this that Pete Lintern was asking me to become involved, concerned to ensure that they had considered every possible aspect of the case.

Ultimately, as is well known, Gadd was found guilty and the police case was found to have been well handled and carefully presented. Gadd served time in prison – not a pleasant experience for a sex offender, especially not one as widely recognized as Gadd – and then went abroad. In fact, as I write this, he has just been deported from his hideaway in Cambodia for alleged sex offences against young boys in that country. At the time I was asked to be involved, Avon and Somerset Police knew only that they had a high-profile case that had to be handled as correctly as possible, just as, at the time of writing, the American investigation into paedophile websites (called Operation Ore) is leading to a number of equally famous people being investigated.

Pete had approached me the week before, at a conference in Edinburgh. I had been asked there to give a talk to a police audience on the way in which defence computer expert witnesses approach the analysis of police-produced computer evidence. I presented the problems and issues that had been raised during the case of 'Christopher Robin' a few months earlier. With the luxury of a relatively expert audience, I had gone into great detail about all the possible defence approaches concerning paedophilia. I had discussed the increasingly popular 'hacking' defence: the claim that the material had been placed on the system by some other user or as a result of a hacking intrusion. And I had covered the so-called 'pop-up' defence: the claim that the paedophile pictures were not consciously accessed and downloaded but appeared as a result of an unasked-for pop-up window.

I had also outlined an approach to the analysis of paedophile and other computer-misuse offences that I had called the 'scene-of-habitation' analysis, developed in the aftermath of the 'Christopher Robin' case. The junior barrister in the case, Nick Lockett, had been adamant that Chris's picture collection had come about as a result of a computer intruder, and in fact at least some of the computer evidence had been produced by the university's system administrator.

That aspect of the case had raised an important question: *was* it possible to ascribe computer evidence to a specific person, even when they were masquerading as some other user? Or was it possible to be sure that computer evidence did *not* relate to a specific user, even though the computer records showed the association?

I realized that there was no definite answer but that there might be a way of adapting techniques used in other types of crime-scene analysis.

Every scene of crime is also a place that has been occupied and lived in legitimately. A murder room, for example, might be untidy. Did it become untidy as a result of the murderer's actions, deliberate or accidental. Is the arrangement of furniture, books and things intentional and therefore representative of the murderer? Or was it untidy before, in which case no interpretation of the murderer's actions and mentality can be made on the basis of the room?

I had first seen this described by the criminal psychologist Paul Britton, but I realized that this principle could also be applied to computers. Whilst a computer might indeed be used to store paedophile material, or to plan a series of robberies, or even to plan a sadistic murder, it is also used to hold information relating to perfectly legitimate activities. This could encompass things from the way that the user searches for particular topics – their preferred search engines and their level of sophistication – through to the way that they write email messages. Perhaps the most helpful aspect of the scene-of-habitation analysis is *textual* analysis. For example, a user might write abusive email, but they would also use the PC to write quite normal email. By analysing unconscious patterns in the normal writing, and by then looking for those patterns in the criminal writing, it may be possible to reinforce an assertion that the user was the author.

This principle could be applied to a wide variety of aspects of computer use: the websites deliberately chosen, the pattern of commands and of habitual usage, and so forth. All of them could be used to construct a detailed and effective picture of non-illicit computer use, and compared for matching aspects with the criminal activity.

In any forensic discipline, it's necessary to separate the criminal from the legitimate data. In the normal course of events, the legitimate data is put to one side, and the forensic scientist concentrates only on the important aspects of the criminal data, deriving evidence and analyses of activity from that. My approach, however, was first to analyse closely the patterns of behaviour and even of personality that could be derived from the *innocent* data. Through those, I would construct a detailed picture of what the subject routinely did – and only then turned to the criminal material. Armed with the features of the innocent material, it is possible to see whether common patterns of behaviour are present in both, and to try from that to ascribe identity and responsibility.

It was a technique that promised to be enormously useful, and the case of Paul Gadd a.k.a. Gary Glitter was the first opportunity I had had to use the method in a real criminal case.

Pete Lintern had approached me after the presentation in Edinburgh, and explained some of the background to the Gary Glitter case and some of the police concerns regarding it. It was a case that was attracting a lot of media attention and so they needed to be totally sure that they had done everything correctly. They had already appointed a computer expert witness, but what they wanted in addition was a comfort factor. They wanted to know that nothing had been missed, and they wanted some idea of what potential objections could be raised by a defence expert witness.

Pete wanted me to do that job for them, as an unpaid favour, with the promise that I wouldn't have to give evidence in court.

I'd known Pete off and on for the several years that I had had an involvement with the training of police officers in computer crime. I didn't know him well, just as one of a group of familiar faces in the fairly constant collection of police officers who attended the regular meetings and conferences held around the country. Although this is now changing – with the greater awareness of computer-security issues after 11 September 2001 and after the headlines surrounding computer-virus costs – there was a period when computer-crime-specialist detectives had to fight hard to continue in their role. Pete had been in that situation for Avon and Somerset, even though he was just about the only computer-evidence expert in the whole of the force. Perhaps because he was the only one fully knowledgeable of the computer issues about to be faced in the Gary Glitter case, he was more than a little eager to have a 'sanity check' of what he had done. I agreed to help him.

First of all, I decided to try and tackle the evidence as though I were the defence computer expert, looking to see what aspects might allow a challenge to be mounted. Second, I wanted to see whether there was anything that the scene-of-habitation analysis could bring to strengthen the prosecution case.

Computer evidence has to satisfy a number of precise requirements. Because the data is easily altered it is vitally important to show that it cannot have been changed, and that a range of controls and recording procedures are in place that cover the period *before* the computer evidence has been 'frozen'. This happens during imaging, when specialized equipment takes a perfect copy of the complete contents of the hard-disk drive from within a computer. Once the copy has been taken, it is retained on CD-ROM, where it is impossible for it to be changed. Before the copying process it is possible for the computer contents to be altered. It is this period that is of most interest to a defence computer expert witness.

Rather than immediately examining the evidence itself, I first went through the 'chain of evidence' for the computer material, showing the seizure and safe handling of the laptop from its collection at the shop through to its receipt at the Bristol forensic laboratory where I was sitting. There were statements from the staff at PC World, covering what they had done to the laptop; there were statements from the uniformed officers who had 'bagged and tagged' the unit, delivering it to an exhibits officer at the Central Bristol police station. The statements showed that the laptop had not been activated at all from when it had last been booted by the PC World staff shortly before they contacted the police – though the statements did illustrate that those staff had viewed some of the image files, thereby changing the last-access date stamps on a subset of the evidence collection.

While Pete played Minesweeper on a nearby workstation, I sat at his desk and read my way through the sheaf of witness statements. Assuming that each statement was truthful and would be attested to in court, it looked as though the laptop had been amazingly well handled in its progression from damaged piece of hardware at PC World through to suspect piece of equipment at Pete's laboratory.

The final collection of papers included Pete's own witness statement, along with the laboratory records showing the safe receipt of the sealed evidence bag containing the laptop. A laboratory reference sheet recorded Pete breaking the seal on the bag, removing the tiny hard-disk drive from the laptop – a process that I knew from bitter experience was often quite delicate – and then mounting that disk drive inside a 'caddy unit' so that it could be hosted within Pete's laboratory computer system. From there it was copied onto CD-ROM using a widely respected program accepted as valid and accurate in courts throughout the world.

Even on the most detailed inspection of the records, there seemed to be nothing amiss in Pete's laboratory process: he even recorded the measures he had taken to ensure that static electric shock could not have affected the disk drive during the removal of the unit itself, and the small error that he had observed in the laptop's internal clock.

I was fairly sure that a defence computer expert – someone playing the role that I had performed in the 'Christopher Robin' trial – would not be able to find anything to object to in the process of preserving the laptop contents.

Traditional forensic science has its fingerprint powder and its magnifying glass, its microscopes and its DNA swabs, its pathology table and its insect charts. Computer forensics has its imaging and analysis program, which serves the function of all of these.

The imaging part of the software reads the clusters or blocks of raw data from the disk: *all* of them, regardless of whether the blocks contain fragments of files, folders or deleted material, and regardless of whether the blocks are part of the operating system – or even the data blocks that tell the computer hardware how large the disk itself actually is. Forensic imaging applications take a complete copy of every last element of data stored on the hard drive and then record that in a series of large files that are copied – 'blown' – onto CD-ROM, so that the full state of the computer's permanent memory is preserved as if in amber.

The analysis part of the program then presents that raw disk data to the investigator in one of three different ways. The first is usually thought of as the 'explorer' mode. Just like Microsoft's Windows Explorer application, this mode shows the tree of folders in a panel to the left of the application screen. To the right, the contents of the current folder are presented as a list of files, along with the files' properties – size, date/time stamps, type, etc. – again just as in Windows Explorer. Two additional features, however, make this mode more powerful than the Windows Explorer view. First of all, a third panel at the bottom of the application screen shows the raw contents of the file or folder, exactly as it is stored on the hard drive. Secondly, the folder and file list includes all the files and folders that have been deleted by the user, allowing the investigator to see even the 'fossil' fragments of material that the user might have believed to have been removed.

Explorer-mode is useful for getting a feel for the computer in question. It shows the applications that the user has had installed; it shows the folders and structure that a user might have imposed on the computer. It allows an investigator to wander around the suspect computer in an easy, intuitive manner. Most investigators start with this mode in order to gain familiarity with the computer and with the suspect.

The other two modes are much more useful for the detailed, practical investigation. The second is 'list' mode: all the files and folders – deleted or not – can be listed, regardless of their location on the file-and-folder tree. This list of contents can be ordered according to a chosen set of criteria. The files can be ordered according to their date and time stamps, showing which files were last accessed or altered on the computer. (Most investigations have a 'timeline' associated with them: the order of dates and times at which particular events are presumed to have occurred. The ordering of all files by date and time allows the investigator to associate file changes with particular events.) Most investigators will move to the list-mode after having got a feel for the computer, and will then work from the timeline that the detectives investigating the case have determined as important.

The third mode is for even more detailed investigation: it is the 'raw' mode, showing the arrangement of the clusters or blocks themselves on the disk drive. The view is of a grid of blocks, with different colours to indicate different types of block: unused, files, folders, damaged, etc. When a block is selected – by clicking the mouse on it – then any other blocks associated with it, if it is a part of a file or folder, are also highlighted. This allows the investigator to see whether files have been edited and altered, and whether they are in the expected location. For example, if the date and time stamp on a particular file indicates that it was first created at a particular time, the blocks physically on the disk drive are most likely to be surrounded by blocks associated with other files created at about the same time. If they aren't, then this might well indicate that the files have been 'planted' there by somebody else. This is particularly important in a paedophile case, and even more important in this case, where it might be proposed that the PC World staff could have introduced the illicit material.

As well as these viewing modes, the analysis application allows the contents of files to be searched – for particular keywords or to locate all files containing pictures – and also allows the unused portions of files to be searched. When a file is written to one or more clusters, it is unlikely that the entire last block will be overwritten – not unless the file just happens to be precisely the size of a disk block. Because of this, a fragment of the last file to have used that block is likely to be in the unused – or 'slack' – space at the end of the file. The analysis application allows this to be searched, often letting the investigator uncover vital data such as scraps of incriminating letters or emails.

The computer forensic analysis applications are therefore enormously powerful tools for investigating computer systems and for allowing the investigator to see into the mind of the computer user as reflected in their writing and their work. They can show the patterns of habitual use, the things that the user has tried to hide, and the types of things they have sought out.

With Pete Lintern watching me closely, I started with the explorer-mode of the forensic application used by Avon and Somerset. It wasn't hard to see what had attracted the PC World staff's interest: three folders, not even hidden or encrypted, with names like 'My Gang' and containing picture files. It was a thousand miles from the careful structure and security described to me years before by Dave Davis in Birmingham; there was no doubt that these were paedophile images.

At that point, I wasn't particularly interested in exploring the *contents* of the picture files themselves; that could wait until I had a better feel for the structure of the computer. I continued browsing through the explorer-mode, looking to establish that he had an Internet account set up. He had, with a long list of similar paedophile pictures apparently downloaded from several 'Lolita-style' websites; there were records showing his having visited those sites a large number of times. He also had an email account and a simple office-automation application installed, apparently used to keep track of the details of his engagements up and down the country.

It was in many ways a typical laptop structure, representing a non-computer expert's use for predominantly pornographic browsing. The laptop seemed to have been used 90 per cent of the time for access to paedophile-interest websites and only 10 per cent of the time as a tool to support the 'Gary Glitter' business.

It took me about thirty minutes to complete that first phase of the exercise and then Pete and I broke to get a coffee and stretch our legs while he smoked. I had two questions that I wanted to answer immediately with the analysis tool. First of all, did the laptop contain paedophile material with which Paul Gadd could be prosecuted? That is, was it possible to show that the photographs discovered could satisfy the definition of 'indecent pictures of children'? Could I show that the possession of the picture files was deliberate?

Second, could I establish that it was indeed Paul Gadd himself who was responsible for the pictures appearing on his computer – rather than, say, the staff at PC World, or anyone else who might have had access to the laptop without his knowledge? It was this second question that I was hoping to apply the scene-of-habitation analysis to, but it was first necessary to establish that a charge really was there to be answered.

One of the many clever features of the forensic analysis application is its ability to collect *all* picture files on a suspect's computer into one, easily examined gallery. Pete had already done that – from which his own analysis had proceeded – but I wanted to repeat the exercise for myself, exactly as a defence computer expert would have done. On the sort of powerful workstation that Pete was using for the analysis application, it took only seconds to collate and arrange the gallery, and then I was able to step through the pictures, collecting into an evidence gallery all those that looked indecent.

There was a large group of these pictures, quite clearly illustrating sexual acts between adults and children, and between children. There was little doubt but that the vast majority of the picture collection amassed by Gadd was indeed illegal. Moreover, the gallery showed multiple copies of a large number of the picture files. I could see that the pictures appeared in the Temporary Internet Files location – showing that they had been viewed as a part of a web page – before then appearing in a second temporary file location, showing them downloaded from the Internet, and finally appearing in the folder collections that had first been detected by the PC World staff. After having made notes of around a dozen pictures that had followed that same programme of collection I was confident that I had reasonable proof of Internet paedophile behaviour.

The second question was whether it was indeed Paul Gadd who had placed the files on the laptop. The first thing to establish was whether or not the PC World staff could have made any alterations to the contents of the laptop. From Pete I had the timeline of the case, showing the period over which the laptop had been outside of Gadd's control up to the moment at which it had been seized by the police. Switching to the list-mode of the analysis application, it was easy to follow the date and time stamps on the listed files and folders so as to see the behaviour of the PC World engineers. I could see when they had booted the laptop and I could follow the file-access time stamps to see them inspecting 'My Gang' folders and a handful of the picture files within the folders. I could even see the specific picture-viewing application that they had used, since the last-access time on the program file also changed during this period.

Whilst each picture file showed that it had been *accessed* during this period of PC World inspection, the date and time stamp showing when the file had last *changed* was unaltered. Those stamps were for the time – several months earlier – when the user of the laptop had downloaded the files from the Internet. To corroborate that, I switched to the raw-mode, so as to examine the disk clusters representing the blocks of the image files. Those clusters were sandwiched between clusters from other, unaccessed files with date and time stamps that showed them to be in the correct sequence. Had the files been introduced at some later time, the clusters would have been placed at a different location on the hard drive. Even if the date and time stamps had somehow been altered to an appropriate value, this physical location would have betrayed the fact.

The physical evidence of the clusters on the hard-disk drive matched perfectly with the evidence of the laptop file-system arrangement of the files. I could be confident that the image files had not been introduced by staff at PC World – well, not unless they had access to sophisticated tools to allow the raw disk clusters to be altered and placed precisely on the physical disk drive itself, which seemed improbable in the extreme.

Once I had dismissed the possibility of the images having been introduced by the PC World staff, I went through each of the dozen or so picture files that I had selected for my mock exhibits, ensuring that each of them was physically in an appropriate place on the disk. I wanted to make sure that the question of later introduction of illegal material by other parties could also be dismissed.

It took about an hour, but at the end of it I was confident that the illegal picture files had all appeared on the laptop at roughly the correct time as shown by the creation date and time stamp associated with the picture file. There were no picture files that were not in the appropriate physical sequence on the laptop hard-disk drive.

The paedophile pictures had appeared on the laptop months before it had been handed in to PC World in Bristol for repair. But who had been responsible for downloading and collecting those pictures?

The laptop had had no password set: neither for the boot-up, according to Pete's own notes, nor for actually logging onto the system. *Anyone* who could get their hands on Gadd's laptop could be Paul Gadd as far as the laptop was concerned, and as far as any of us analysing the computer after the event was concerned. If I were the defence computer expert, that would be the point from which my analysis would proceed.

I envisaged that Gadd would have had staff, friends and lovers at his house from time to time, all having access to a greater or lesser extent to the room where he might keep his laptop. His telephone records showed when Gadd had accessed the Internet, and the police had established from his schedule and bookings diary that he was indeed at home at those times – but, of course, others might have been there as well. I had no idea whether that could be true but it was an obvious objection to raise with Pete over his case.

All of the material produced by Avon and Somerset Police said, 'Gadd did the following . . .' whereas it should have said, 'The user of the computer did the following . . .' and then established that the user of the computer was indeed Paul Gadd.

It was precisely to address these problems that I had worked on the scene-of-habitation analysis techniques. The first thing I wanted to do was to ignore the self-evidently illegal aspects of the laptop's use and to concentrate on the normal activity involved: difficult, given the limited way the laptop had been used, but not impossible.

I started by building a picture of the Internet use, looking at the date stamps on the access to entirely legal websites. Some of these related to venues that Gary Glitter had played at and tied in with email messages that were signed by Paul Gadd. Examining those email messages, I began to construct a detailed analysis of the way in which he wrote email and compared that to some of the letters and other documents also stored on the laptop, relating to his performing career, so as to confirm the stylistic patterns I was uncovering.

Like all writers of email and other documents, Gadd had particular forms of self-expression and particular blind spots about grammar. He wrote short sentences, for example, and misspelled certain words consistently; he used a comma where a semicolon should have appeared, but unlike most people used the apostrophe correctly. By collecting together all the written material that was not related to paedophilia and that would appear indisputably associated with Paul Gadd, I was able to complete a detailed picture of the way that the laptop had been used legally and to build a profile of Gadd's personality as he appeared on the computer.

With that in place, Pete and I then turned to the illegal elements of the laptop's use. We had a series of distinct sessions in which the laptop had been used on the Internet. Amongst sessions of legitimate use we had a large number of instances in which visits to the Lolita-style websites were intermingled. The time periods over which legal, then illegal, then legal websites were visited was often as short as a few minutes. There was also an email message sent by him to the operator of a paedophile website, in which the author gave Gadd's credit-card details and complained that he was having difficulty using the password and log-in details that had been supplied. The text was almost totally consistent with the writing style for Gadd that we had already established.

It seemed to me beyond reasonable doubt that the user of the laptop was indeed Paul Gadd, and that he had used the computer and Internet access predominantly in the pursuit and collection of paedophile material.

With the basics of the police case established – and with no apparent objections or problems that I could envisage the defence being able to raise – I decided to see whether or not the prosecution case could be strengthened in any way. Had Gadd himself taken any of the paedophile photographs? Had he sent them on to others? Had he received them from individuals whom we could trace?

I examined each of the pictures in the gallery of paedophile images that Pete and I had collected. None of them was in the format that would have shown them to have been digital camera shots saved onto the computer, or saved after having been scanned. All were of the compact format associated with images downloaded from the Web, and indeed, in all but a tiny number of cases we could recover the cached web page that the pictures had originally appeared within. It seemed likely that Gadd had not taken any of the pictures himself.

We then searched through the complete email record preserved on the laptop, looking for obvious paedophile correspondence. There was none: Gadd had neither sent nor received paedophile images by email, and he had had no other software installed on his laptop to allow the image files to be sent or received in any other way. It seemed likely that he had simply collected the paedophile pictures that had attracted his attention, storing them on the laptop in a way that was convenient for when he wanted to look at them. He was neither a creator nor a distributor of paedophile images, which was perhaps a blessing. He was simply a 'consumer' of child pornography, which is of course bad enough but not as bad as it might have been.

The impression that emerged from inspecting the laptop system was of a rather solitary man. His email was predominantly related to his tours, as were the few letters and other documents saved on the laptop. His Internet use was almost totally devoted to searching out the Lolita-style websites, and the majority of things stored on the laptop were those pictures. It almost seemed beyond comprehension that somebody could have been so foolish as to have allowed the laptop to have been examined by the staff at PC World – Gadd had in fact delivered the laptop himself, *asking* the staff to examine the disk for him! It was a long way from the more security-conscious and highly structured lives of the paedophiles I was more used to dealing with, but none the less, driving away from the Bristol Police headquarters a little before midnight that night, I was sure that the evidence was completely accurate.

During the trial a few months later, no attempt was made to challenge the computer evidence presented by the police. Paul Gadd was convicted for the possession of indecent photographs of children, and served a short prison sentence. Later, he left the country for Spain, after which he settled in Cambodia.

Obviously there is some satisfaction in having had a hand in convicting *any* paedophile, but especially one as high-profile as Gadd. After this case, I was involved in several dozen other, broadly similar exercises to investigate and prosecute Internet paedophiles. Now that I no longer become as personally disturbed by the images themselves – since I am doing what I can to prevent those images from going further and to remove the 'market' for those pictures – I feel enormous pride in these cases. There is a true delight to applying the computer forensic and scene-of-habitation analyses in such an important arena.

8. **Cyber-stalking**

The scene-of-habitation analysis isn't only used for such high-profile prosecutions as the Glitter case. We have also had some success in applying it elsewhere, and it has become an important contribution to the investigation of computer-related offences in the UK. One particularly useful place for this analysis method is in the increasingly common offence of online stalking.

Computer-crime cases usually arrive at my office in the form of a computer, a collection of CD-ROMs or tapes or diskettes, or at the very least a request to assist at a raid on some premises. This case arrived in a slim brown envelope, in the form of a small collection of email printouts.

It had been sent to me by an English detective, anxious to know whether there was anything that could be done to throw a light on a difficult and confusing case. It was an online love affair that had gone wrong, turning first into a case of online stalking, and then into a terrifying ordeal for the American victim. Eventually a solicitation to murder, with a 'bounty' for a young woman's death, had been posted on a website.

When I was first told of the case, I must confess to having shuddered slightly at the prospect. Like most modern Internet users, I have chatted, gossiped and even flirted online in the several communities of which I am a member. Mostly those users of the communities know where and how to draw a line between friendly banter and out-and-out pestering or abuse, but it is clear just how easy that line might be to step over.

I was fascinated to learn what had happened in this all-too-familiar scenario. The emails and printouts in the envelope told the story chronologically, and I settled down to read them through.

Brandy was an American woman in her mid-thirties who had joined an 'MSN community' in April 1999. Run by Microsoft, these communities provide a means for people to chat online and to swap pictures, ideas and emails. Brandy had joined a community interested in cookery, and had become friends with an Englishman called Paul.

From the printouts, it seemed that the friendship between the pair had progressed rapidly, moving from the online discussion groups to private email in a matter of days. Over a series of exchanges, they had gradually seemed to find each other more and more interesting, until they had begun to find one another positively attractive. The discussions had moved inexorably from polite exchanges, through flirting, to what we would have to describe as online sex. Brandy had even declared that, if she were ever to marry, Paul would be exactly the type of person she would go for. Not surprisingly, Paul had formed the impression that Brandy was single and that they had a chance of a life together. There was even discussion about setting up their own catering business together, and Paul began urging Brandy to come to the UK.

What Paul didn't know was that Brandy was in fact married to a non-commissioned officer in the US Army. Quite by chance Brandy's husband discovered the correspondence and challenged her with it. Her response was that she had never led Paul on, that he was 'just a friend' with whom she discussed catering and computers; that, in fact, Paul was becoming something of a nuisance. On hearing this, the soldier wrote an angry email to Paul, warning Paul to leave them alone.

At first, Paul's responses – preserved by Brandy and her

husband – were the expected bluster. He didn't believe that the man was Brandy's husband, since he had been all but told that she was single, and instead felt that Brandy was trying to dump him. Paul clearly felt hurt and betrayed, and believed that he was being lied to and that the problem was Brandy's hesitancy at commitment rather than the existence of a prior commitment to her husband.

It was hard for me to take the exchanges seriously at that point. The Internet is renowned as an environment in which people present themselves as they want to be, rather than as they are. The MSN communities, chat sessions and the rest are widely known as places of exaggeration, half-truth and outright lies. Anyone with experience of them would have simply shaken their heads and moved on. But Paul appeared to have been smitten, and in further emails continued to ignore messages from Brandy's husband while sending hurt and angry messages to her. Messages which appeared increasingly disturbing and threatening, and which showed that Paul was becoming more and more out of control.

In the later messages, he claimed to have employed private detectives to track Brandy down, and to have used various Internet-accessible search facilities to find out more about her and her husband. He had obtained their home phone number and begun to make threatening calls; he had maps of their house and had discovered where they both worked. He had approached their colleagues; and had even, in the most horrifying twist to this story, begun to take steps to try and have her killed.

For Brandy and her husband, it was becoming increasingly frightening, as an embarrassing exchange between a lonely housewife and an online pen-pal was turning inexorably into stalking and threats of violence. Then Paul raised the stakes further still, sending Brandy an email containing the address of a website that he had set up.

The website had pictures of Brandy, along with a description of her husband and details of their home, their movements and their habits. It had a long description of the 'crime' that Brandy had committed in leading Paul on and then betraying his trust, and an impassioned warning that she was not to be trusted. Most terrifyingly of all, it offered a sizeable amount of money along with detailed descriptions of how it would be paid to anyone willing to assault and murder Brandy, either alone or with her husband.

The angry emails had been bad enough, but a publicly accessible web page containing specific details and death threats was a terrifying prospect. The pair took the material they had collected to the local FBI.

In establishing the website, Paul had committed an offence: solicitation to murder. Had anyone acted on the invitation, Paul would have been guilty of being an accessory. The FBI naturally took the complaint seriously and began the process of tracking down a real address for Paul. Brandy knew that he lived in England, but had no more precise details than that.

Fortunately, Paul's emails to her contained not only his email address but also the Internet address assigned by his service provider to his computer each time he connected to the Internet. Using this 'IP address' and a public database of such addresses, the FBI was able to work out which Internet service provider Paul was using. Then it was only necessary for them to contact the relevant force and to trust that they were able to locate Paul through the details that they had provided. Here Brandy and her husband were lucky in that, at the time, the detective chief superintendent running the local CID was also the chairman of the Computer Crime subcommittee of the Association of Chief Police Officers and therefore extremely well placed to handle the request. Less than an hour after the FBI fax had arrived at the police headquarters, Paul had been identified and was being interviewed by uniformed officers.

Paul, the police discovered, was not a happy man. His argument was that the website had not been a public one. Although it *was* on the Internet, the name of the website had not been made publicly available. When pressed on this, he claimed that the website had not been listed in any of the search engines, and that therefore no-one would be able to find it. He explained that he had only wanted to 'frighten Brandy' so that she would want to come back to him.

The first request the police made to me was to address that question: would the website have been publicly accessible even if it had not been in the search engines? Even before proceeding with any analysis, I could note a quick reply to that: the website would have been accessible since it had a name registered in the domain-name servers and a publicly visible Internet address. If a website is accessible, then even though it is not explicitly submitted to the search engines, there are programs called 'crawlers' or 'bots' that explore the Internet constantly looking for new sites. The solicitation website would have been listed shortly after it had first been made accessible.

Beyond this, the stalking case seemed to have got increasingly complicated. After his interview, Paul had been arrested for solicitation to murder, at the request of the FBI, who believed that he posed a real threat to Brandy and her husband. The defence team had decided that Brandy had brought the situation upon herself, and they produced copies of Paul's emails showing that Brandy had represented herself as available and interested. In response, Brandy claimed that Paul had falsified those emails. She admitted exchanging email, but only about catering and more general things. She denied outright that she had ever told him that she loved him, that she wanted to be with him or that she was single and available. The police wanted me to establish whether the emails *had* been falsified by Paul, or whether they had been written by Brandy herself.

With the original PC on which the messages had been written, this would have been simplicity itself; even with the 'extended headers' on the email it would have been harder but still possible. With only the text of the messages, this was a challenging thing to try and do. However, I had been studying the work of Don Foster, an English professor in the US who specialized in 'attribution analysis': using clues in written text to ascribe authorship and responsibility. He had had a lot of success using textual analysis in criminal cases and I was confident that I would be able to use similar methods and have a good chance at building up a profile of both writers.

I also knew that computer writing had been successfully applied in a serious case. A friend of mine, Jim Bates, another computer expert witness, had been asked to examine a case in which a woman had been found dead. The police believed that she might have been murdered by her husband, but he produced a suicide note that he claimed she had written on the computer. Was the note written by the husband or by the wife?

To establish this, Jim had examined all other computer correspondence that unquestionably belonged to the woman and all writing that belonged to the man. He found that the man, unfamiliar with computers, typed in a very distinctive way: at the end of the line, instead of allowing the computer auto-matically to move to the next line, he would hit the carriage-return button, as though on a typewriter. He always put double spaces after punctuation and had other equally distinctive elements. All of his writing fitted this profile. Conversely, the woman was apparently more familiar with the computer and never ended lines with a carriage return; she also never used double spaces.

The alleged suicide note matched *his* writing style perfectly and was nothing like her style. The jury was invited to draw the conclusion that she had not written the suicide note. Of course, as Jim emphasized, this was not enough to form a proof of murder by any means: under stress of depression, she might have altered her typing habits, for example. Yet, though it might not be foolproof, the idea of textual analysis had appealed to me.

We had a good collection of non-contentious email messages from both Paul and Brandy, and a small set of messages that Brandy claimed had been falsified by Paul. I started by separat-ing the contentious messages into one pile and the others into piles of his and her writing. So as to have some control groups, I also collected a similar-sized collection of my own and several other people's email messages.

I began to analyse each pile in turn, building up a picture of common typing errors, grammatical and punctuation character-istics, typical word patterns, sentence and paragraph lengths, vocabulary and so forth. I constructed a detailed profile of each collection, giving them scores along a series of axes for each measured value. In each pile of writings, the individual mail messages all clustered around a common but distinct pattern of values – enough for me to be able to take mail messages at random and, by analysing them in the same way, reliably assign them to the correct pile even without knowledge of the author.

When I was sure that I could do this in a controlled and repeatable manner, I began to consider the email messages that Brandy claimed were not written by her but by Paul.

I was immensely pleased with the results as they emerged. The email messages were all consistent in their patterns and formed closely related groupings on the axes. Better, they all fell well within the range of values already associated with one of the 'innocent' email collections. Not surprisingly, the contentious emails fitted Brandy's writing patterns much more closely than Paul's – or anyone else's that I had analysed. Though it certainly did not excuse Paul from having threatened her life, it was apparent that Brandy had indeed 'led him on' as the defence insisted.

The analysis was not foolproof, however. All it really showed was that the text was more like hers than his. This could be because she did indeed write it, or it could be that he deliber-ately copied her writing style; or perhaps he started with a message from her and subtly altered it. It wasn't safe to assume *in a court* that she had necessarily written it. This is what is called a 'jury point' and is one of the hardest things for an expert witness to appreciate.

An expert is allowed to express an opinion, but only on the things for which he is an 'expert'. I could express an opinion about the operation of the computer, and that the analytical method that I had used to derive the results was valid and applicable. But I am not an expert on psychology, which is what would have been needed to provide an opinion in this case. In court, I could only present the results of my work – that the disputed writing was more similar to Brandy's than it was to any other person's analysed – but I could not express a view on what that *meant*. It had to be left to the jury to form an opinion.

I don't think we will ever truly know whether Brandy did write the disputed messages, though my feeling is that she probably did and then regretted it when her husband found out. But I had learned a great deal about the techniques of textual analysis that I could use in studying computer writing.

When the case came to court, the jury was instructed to ignore the issue of whether Brandy had or had not lied to Paul. They were asked simply to consider whether or not Paul had written the website, made it available to the public and used it to threaten her life. In expert testimony, I was able to show that the website was indeed available and as a result Paul was found guilty of soliciting the murder of Brandy and her husband, received a suspended sentence and was bound over to keep the peace. It was undoubtedly a fair sentence.

As with the Gary Glitter case, I was particularly pleased that the forensic work was moving from simple laboratory exercises – as with the study of bank computers that had allowed us to find Sir Paul McCartney's details – to more intelligent analyses of evidence. Now we were undertaking more than simple technical donkey-work. But the next case that was brought to our attention was more demanding still, forcing me to concentrate almost exclusively on the legal and moral issues involved, and not at all on the technical aspects of evidence seizure.

9. **Stopping a Crusader**

Although computer crime is increasingly common, and although viruses, denial of service and even defacement of websites are now widely understood, prosecutions of computer hackers are still rare. In the UK, the Computer Misuse Act is nearly a decade and a half old, yet there have been only a tiny number of prosecutions brought under the act.

For that reason, when a hacker *is* brought to justice, it is particularly important that the prosecution is well founded and well managed. Unfortunately, even with the best-organized case and the most obvious breach of the law, sometimes things still go wrong. And sometimes, the difficulties that are faced in a particular prosecution can throw confusion over an entire aspect of the law itself, let alone the specific case being brought. Such was the situation in 2001 with the prosecution of a young hacker whose legal team managed to locate – though fortunately not exploit – a substantial and deeply disturbing failure in the law controlling computer crime.

It was a confusing and worrying case to have to address, and one that has widespread implications for computer crime in the UK.

Raphael Gray is a young Welshman who made himself famous for having uncovered Microsoft chief Bill Gates's credit-card details during a high-profile hack in 2000, using them to order a supply of Viagra to be delivered to Gates's Seattle mansion. (However, the Viagra was not delivered, since the card number Gray had found for Gates had been a dummy card number used as a test value in a new website.) Gray, who called himself 'the Crusader', had made a particular nuisance of himself since the start of the year, hacking into a series of online shopping services, starting with a web server in Thailand. At first his activity went unnoticed apart from by his victims. He targeted websites throughout the world that were running the popular but all too insecure Microsoft Internet Information Server web-server software. He used a vulnerability that had been made public a few months earlier: a weakness in most implementations of the web server that allowed an Internet user access to parts of the web server that should have remained private. In particular, Gray delighted in obtaining credit-card details from the back-end databases supporting the online retailers.

What Gray seemed to want to do was to publicize the vulnerability and poor security of Microsoft web-server installations, though whether his target was Microsoft itself (for having produced such a poor application) or the sites using it (for being so foolish as not to protect it) was unclear.

Over a period of a few weeks he had gradually garnered more attention for his protest, though at first he was ignored by all but a few journalists. Eventually, to create more publicity, he had taken to posting some of the credit-card details on the Web and banner advertisements on his site. (According to some reports these were paid for with the stolen card details.) As the press began to take notice, he had given increasingly outrageous interviews, lambasting system managers and the police for their failure to implement adequate security and to track and catch him.

He eventually had managed to collect details of some 26,000 credit cards and the attention of a security expert in Ontario, Chris Davis, whose company was retained by the Canadian victims to try and locate the hacker. Davis found it surprisingly easy to do, using an audit log from one of the hacked servers to track Gray back to his Internet service provider. When it was established that this was a company in Wales, the FBI contacted the Welsh police and Raphael Gray, an eighteen-year-old from outside Swansea – whom I thought in the newspapers looked a lot like a young Jimi Hendrix – was arrested.

That was at the end of March 2000, and at the time I had laughed along with everyone else at the audacity of the young man ordering Viagra for Bill Gates.

Gray was charged with several counts under the Computer Misuse Act and also two counts under the Fraud Act relating to his use of the credit cards to purchase the web services that he had used to publicize the credit-card details. Later, he was charged with having committed offences under the Data Protection Act, of having processed personal data – the credit-card numbers – without authority.

At the time I had a certain amount of sympathy for the cause that Gray was promoting. Having spent a huge amount of time testing the security of Internet systems and electronic commerce sites, I was all too aware of just how inadequate protection levels were. The exploit that Gray had used was one that we had used time after time throughout 2000, with almost universal success. Even now, three years later, we still find that there are sites vulnerable to the scripting exploit on poorly maintained Microsoft web servers. In a way, Gray and I were in the same business, though the notion of stealing and publicizing individuals' credit-card details would be anathema to any reasonable security professional. When *we* test a site's security, we do so in confidentiality, with advance permission and legal restrictions imposing a degree of liability should any part of the service fail. Gray had not done any of these things. He was like a joy-rider who claims only to be trying to demonstrate that cars he takes and crashes should not have been parked where they were.

Hacking is not a victimless crime: real people suffer as a result of the attacks, as their credit-card details are exposed to fraudulent transactions. Even if the companies exposed by Gray were negligent, they still do not deserve to be pilloried just so that he could prove a point. I found Gray's whole crusade annoying and so was more than happy to assist when the police asked me to.

It was shortly before Christmas 2000 that I was contacted by Dyfed Powys Police. In a lilting accent that was hard to follow over the crackling telephone line, the officer explained some of the background to the case and that there were serious objections being raised by the defence expert, Mr Peter Sommer, objections that they had been told by counsel would need a computer expert to address.

I was immediately on my guard. Peter Sommer is well known among expert witnesses for computer-crime cases. Back in the early 1980s, he had written one of the first published works on computer-hacking, *The Hacker's Handbook*, under the pseudonym Hugo Cornwall. Twenty years on, he was a senior research fellow in computer crime at the London School of Economics and an eagerly sought-out expert for the defence, having scored some notable successes in high-profile hacking cases. In 1994, two hackers had managed to break into and download sensitive data from the USAF research laboratories at New York's Griffiss Air Force Base. Science-fiction enthusiasts, they had been searching for information about the notorious 'Area 51' in Nevada, trying to see whether details about a supposed UFO crash really did exist. They were spotted and traced by Air Force investigators and intelligence operatives, who believed they were observing a major international espionage incident. Embarrassingly for the investigators, their 'international Communist spies' turned out to be a sixteen-year-old music student and the twenty-one-year-old son of a Welsh policeman.

Peter Sommer was able to help in deconstructing the arguments and the technical evidence that were supposed to help put the pair in jail for hacking, if not for espionage. He had shown that, far from being highly skilled 'keyboard spies', the pair had simply guessed a password, which had been the name of one of the system managers' pets. From there they had merely accessed the systems with anonymous, guest-access accounts that were open to anyone.

One of the hackers was found guilty of minor computer-misuse charges and had to pay a small fine. The charges against the second hacker were simply dropped by the CPS when it became apparent that they had little chance of success.

Now Peter Sommer was on yet another Welsh hacking case, and he had managed to find some clever angle to that one as well. I was curious to see what he might have uncovered. A few days later, two detectives made the long journey to London, carrying a box full of the documentation that I would need to study before, they insisted, they would pass me Mr Sommer's defence-expert witness statement.

Reading through the evidence that had been collected into two densely packed ring binders, it was extremely difficult to see what Sommer could possibly have found to object to. The evidence had been collected in what seemed to be a well-managed process, including submissions regarding telephone billing, Internet access and well-secured audit logs obtained by Chris Davis in Ontario from the computers in various organizations.

I ran through the audit logs, following the sequence of Internet commands that had been issued from Gray's computer. He seemed to have run two popular hacking exploits on the computers he had conquered. The first was a 'buffer overflow', aimed at disabling the audit routines operating on the target computer by flooding the auditing program and hence crashing it.

The buffer-overflow exploit usually works by sending many more input characters to a particular program than it is expecting. I had first come across this in the 1980s when I was asked to analyse the infamous 'Internet Worm' that had been written by Robert Morris Jr in the US. This program had crashed almost all of the Internet throughout one November night. The Morris worm had been the precursor to the current spate of

Internet worms and hacking attacks, exploiting a security weakness that had first been discovered by Morris's father, a senior official at the American National Security Agency. Morris Senior had realized that many programs that interact with users put the input characters into a fixed-size portion of memory, called a 'buffer'. If the amount of input is more than the size of the buffer then strange things might happen. If the program has been properly written then an error message will be displayed; but if it has not been properly written then the program will continue adding characters into memory beyond the end of the buffer. In the most optimistic conditions the program will then fail. However, Morris Sr realized that if the characters placed in the input buffer were in fact program instructions then the software could be persuaded to execute them. His son was the first to make this possibility a reality, and his Internet Worm exploited that weakness to spread unchecked throughout the Internet.

Gray had not been trying to do anything quite so sophisticated. His exploit filled the input character buffers of victim computers with garbage characters so as to crash an auditing program, so that the audit logs would not record what he was doing on the computer. Unfortunately for Gray – but fortunately for Chris Davis in tracking him – he seemed uncertain as to how the overflow was supposed to work, and hadn't generated enough overflowing character sequences to stop it recording. As a result, the audit and logging program had continued to operate, capturing all of the subsequent activity.

The second hacking exploit that Gray had used was a way of running specific operating-system commands on a vulnerable web server over the Internet. A default installation of Microsoft's web-server system includes a preponderance of additional functions that aren't used by all websites. Often, instead of disabling those functions by uninstalling them, web administrators simply leave them in place, in the default configuration, i.e. out of the box. That was the case with the exploit that Gray seemed to have used: a function that allowed commands to be run and files viewed on the web server, even though those commands and files should not have been visible over the Internet.

To run the specific Microsoft web-server commands, all he had to do was to write the name of the command in a particular sequence of code characters in the 'Address' box at the top of the web browser. Following through Gray's actions, I could see him specifying to the web-server function that it was to display the credit-card database and other details exactly as though they had been valid web pages on the site.

The audit log that Gray had failed to stop had recorded the Internet address from which these commands had been issued and to which the results had been returned. That IP address had been assigned to a home-based computer on a dial-up connection. The account for that dial-up connection had been in Gray's name, and the actual telephone number used to connect had been registered to Gray's parents' house. Finally, though I wasn't shown the actual contents of Gray's seized computer, I was told that the files recovered from there matched those shown in the audit log records precisely. It seemed clear-cut.

I called Dyfed Powys Police headquarters. Thirty minutes later I was holding a copy of Sommer's witness statement. And ten minutes after that, I saw that he was trying not to undermine the evidence in the case of Regina versus Raphael Gray, but the whole applicability of the 1990 Computer Misuse Act to the field of modern, web-based hacking.

The 1990 Computer Misuse Act was developed following a string of failed computer-crime prosecutions in the UK – most famously, the case of Gold and Shiffreen (see p. 45). It was created at the same time that other countries, notably the US, were also developing statutes to outlaw what was becoming an increasingly challenging problem throughout the 1980s: intrusive hackers and destructive computer viruses.

There are two simple models for computer-crime statutes to outlaw hacking. In the first model, the crime of fraud is considered to have been committed. The hacker has defrauded the owner of the hacked computer in some way, so as to cause the computer to do something that the owner would not have wanted it to do. The US Computer Fraud and Abuse statute follows this model, and has proved to be successful up until the present time, when new statutes have been devised and introduced following the terrorist attacks of 11 September. In the US, computer-hacking is an offence that is investigated by the Treasury through their own investigation service, the Secret Service. Bizarrely, China followed the US lead in defining hacking as fraud, even though fraud is a capital offence in China: computer hackers in China – and particularly in Hong Kong – face the death penalty.

Executing computer hackers for their misdemeanours is perhaps a little excessive, but viewing this crime as fraud is understandable. In the UK, though, we took an alternative view. The second model is that of trespass: the hacker is considered to be an intruder, who has gained access to some part of a computer without the permission of its owner.

The UK law under which Gray was charged provides for three offences. Section One is often called 'simple unauthorized access', where an intruder has gained access to a computer or part of a computer knowing that they have done so without the necessary permission from the system owner. This is a relatively minor offence, included – I've always thought – to reflect the relatively trivial damage that was considered to arise out of the curiosity of a non-malicious, non-criminal, non-damaging hacker. This is punishable by a small fine. In physical trespass terms, it would be the offence of ignoring a warning sign to keep off someone's land but not doing any damage once on it.

Section Two is more serious and carries a larger fine and the threat of imprisonment: it is often referred to as 'unauthorized access with intent'. In this, the intruder has gained access to a computer without permission and has then done some further things that would be criminal offences. In real-world terms, they have trespassed in order to break into a house or to steal something. This was included in the act to reflect the growing damage that became possible as determined hackers were able to gain access to sensitive systems controlling banking funds, for example, with the intention of stealing money.

These first two sections therefore sought to outlaw intrusion into computer systems either for simple curiosity or in order to commit a further crime. One key element of the two sections – and, indeed, of the activity they were intended to criminalize – was that the hacker actually *gained access* to the system: they were *on* the computer to which the indictment referred. In the situation of computer viruses – a growing threat throughout the late 1980s, and now of epidemic proportions – the 'criminal' did not gain access to any of the victim computers. Instead, it was simply a program written by them that intruded and caused damage. To address this, Section Three of the act made it an offence to modify the contents – programs or stored data – of a computer without the owner's permission.

To the lawmakers back in the late 1980s this had seemed a more than adequate set of legal controls. Given the difficulties of obtaining evidence and of encouraging victims to press charges, the law has never been used heavily and there have only been around two dozen prosecutions under the act in the first fourteen years of its existence. However, it did seem as though the act had adequately specified the offences, even if they were hard to prove in reality. As time wore on, additional criminal opportunities came to light, testing the scope of the act quite severely.

I already knew that there were problems with the application of Section Three – not to computer viruses, but to the increasingly popular denial-of-service attacks.

Back in the early days of computer-hacking, we had considered a denial-of-service attack to be the last refuge of the incompetent. Unable to gain access to a target system, they instead lashed out in angry impatience to prevent any others from being able to use it legitimately.

Over the years, as the Internet grew to become a commercial domain relied upon by organizations wanting to transact business online, denial of service became increasingly important as a threat. Before the Gray case I had been involved with an extortion attempt mounted against an online gambling site, using a determined denial-of-service attack to prevent it from doing business unless it paid 'protection money' to the hackers based in Russia.

Unfortunately, other than when there *was* an extortion, it seemed likely that the denial-of-service attack did not form an offence. By definition, no access was being gained to the computer – and so Sections One and Two of the Computer Misuse Act did not apply – and there was no 'unauthorized modification' to the contents of the computer, so that a Section Three offence wasn't relevant either. Provided that the denial-of-service attack simply stops the computer from working – without changing any stored data or programs – then it does not appear to be illegal under the current definition of the law. This might be the situation, for example, if the access connection to the computer is simply being swamped with excess network traffic which is not in fact entering the computer at all.

This is an enormous grey area that has yet to be challenged or addressed in court. The precise wording of the Computer Misuse Act talks of 'intent to impair' the operation of a computer through modification. Clearly, in a denial-of-service attack there *has* been that intent. Also, it says that the intent need not be directed at any particular element of data or software. So the police and prosecution have become increasingly wary of applying Section Three to these attacks. As with so many elements of the law, only decisions in court will be able to clarify the situation.

I therefore already knew that the Computer Misuse Act was failing in some regards, but Sommer was proposing that it was not relevant in the case of Raphael Gray and hence not relevant in other, similar hacking situations. He was attacking Sections One and Two of the act, and doing a very fine job of it as far as I could see.

Gray had been charged with offences under Sections Two

and Three of the Computer Misuse Act. The Section Three offence arose from his use of the buffer overflow, which changed the contents of the victim computer by causing the logging procedures to fail. Was that an 'unauthorized modification of the contents' of the computer, as required under the act? It *was*, Sommer allowed; or rather it *would* have been, had the prosecution been able to bring any evidence to show that it had in fact happened. The only audit logs that the prosecution offered as exhibits were those that had not been disabled by the exploit: those in fact where the exploit had failed. That is, those where no modification had occurred.

Where the 'unauthorized modification of the contents' had taken place, there was no evidence; and there was evidence only from those places where the attempt to perform the 'unauthorized modification' had been unsuccessful. Sommer was right: the Section Three offences relating to the disabling of the audit process had to be discounted for lack of evidence. It was a damnably clever defence and altogether typical of the imaginative way that Sommer has learned to weave technical and legal aspects into a successful argument. There was no way of countering him on this.

The Section Two offences with which Gray was charged related to his unauthorized intrusion into the web servers with the intention of committing a further criminal offence: a Data Protection Act offence of publishing the credit-card details, and an offence under the Fraud Act of using the stolen card details.

That seemed unquestionable: Gray had hacked his way into the innards of the database storing the credit-card details by subverting the web server, and had done so with the intention of publicizing the credit-card numbers and, apparently, of using at least some of them. Sommer's response was that Gray had had no way of knowing that he was not authorized to access the credit-card database.

In the wording of the 1990 act, a Section Two offence is a 'Section One offence committed with intent . . .' and a Section One offence is committed if three conditions are satisfied. The user has to have made the computer give them access, that access has to be unauthorized, and the user has to *know* at the time that the access is unauthorized.

Sommer's argument was that Gray had not been challenged to present access credentials; he had not had to ignore a warning message telling him that the access was not permitted; and that the very nature of the websites we all visit is that anyone is allowed to visit them and to see whatever the website presents to us.

On that basis, Sommer argued that Gray had not known that he was exceeding his intended, authorized access and that he could not therefore be guilty of the Section Two offence. Another very clever defence.

I cursed his cleverness and settled down to try and find a way of countering what seemed like a killing blow – not simply because it would destroy the case against Raphael Gray but because it would damage every other attempt that might be brought to prosecute web hackers. I had to counter his argument in this specific case, and I had to find a way of countering this objection more generally.

When the 1990 Computer Misuse Act was framed, computers were accessed by presenting acceptable authentication credentials. Usually these would be a username and a password. A person who could provide the password corresponding to a valid username was assumed to be the authorized individual, and was given the access that had previously been negotiated for that specific person. Some users might be relatively un-privileged in the programs they could run and the data they could see or change, where others might have almost complete access; some users might be billed for their access, others given access without charges. The entry credentials – the pass-word in particular – mediated this access, and the law was framed on that basis. Intruders were assumed to have pretended to be authorized individuals when in fact they were not – and indeed, the most common kinds of hacking in those days revolved around the use of pilfered passwords, exactly as Gold and Shiffreen had demonstrated in the landmark case of their hacking of BT Prestel that had led to the framing of the act.

Systems on the Web are not accessed in quite this way. As far as the web server's operating system is concerned, all those browsing pages on the server are the same, anonymous user-name associated with the web application itself. Provided that the remote user's browser – Microsoft's Internet Explorer, most commonly – presents a well-formed request for a valid page, then that page will be transmitted by the server back to the IP address associated with the response.

The pages themselves are simply text files in a particular 'hypertext' format stored in a particular place in the file system, as are the pictures, programs and other elements associated with the web pages. The portion of the web server's file system dedicated to the web pages is often called the 'web root', and it is usual for all the pages to refer only to other pages within this web root. The anonymous user associated with the server application is not presented with any files from outside that web root.

However, as Gray had found, there are a number of ways of fooling the web application into giving access to files outside the web-root portion of the file system. In the case of the exploit used by Gray, a particular application running within the web root *is* permitted to access external files – so as to read or write entries within an associated database. Gray persuaded this application to access non-database files, so as to read the files he wanted to see and to send them to him as though they were in the web-root portion. Other exploits involve persuading the web application that the anonymous web user is allowed access to external files.

In all cases, the commands are typed in the browser's location box, exactly as though valid web pages – files within the web root – are being requested. Those commands are executed without any username or password being requested. Sommer's assertion that Gray was not doing something he knew to be unauthorized looked as though it might be quite difficult to refute.

There were two ways that I could see of possibly countering his argument. The first was to address his assertion that Gray had not known that the access was unauthorized.

Exceeding authorized access on a given computer is a 'security breach'. On the web pages that Gray had used to publicize the pilfered credit cards, and in the many interviews he had given to journalists, he had made it clear that he was trying to illustrate the poor security of the websites. He was trying to illustrate that he could exceed his authorized access. That is, he was doing and boasting about those things he knew involved exceeding his authority, and he must therefore have known that he *was* exceeding that authority.

It seemed a little nit-picking, but no more than Sommer's point about the denial-of-service attempt. In my own expert witness statement I therefore used the evidence of Gray's various activities and published material to illustrate that he knew his access was not authorized. I felt that I had managed to deflect at least one of Sommer's bullets.

Next, I had to counter the assertion that there was no authority involved in the web access, and that all access to a website – where no username and password were being requested in order to control access – was therefore 'authorized' in the meaning of the law. This was perhaps the more important point, since it had a bearing not simply on this case but potentially on all future prosecutions of web hackers brought under the 1990 Computer Misuse Act. I *had* to win this argument.

There are two 'normal' ways to access web pages. The first is simply to type the name of the web server in the location bar of the browser: for example, 'www.bantam.com'. This makes the browser read the file called 'Index' in the web-root folder of the Bantam server. From there, the index file provides a series of in-page links specifying subsidiary pages, which themselves might then contain further links. This 'web of links' is what gives the World Wide Web its name.

The second way, though, is to know the name and location of a specific web page within the structure of pages organized beneath the index page at the web root and to type the address in directly. (This might be because the page is specified in a search engine, or it might be that user has visited the page before and has kept a record of the page location.) An example might be something like 'www.bantam.com/books/list.htm', which instructs the Bantam web server to look in a folder called 'Books' within the web root and to transmit the web page called 'List'. The user in this case is 'teleporting' directly to that page without going via the index and any intermediate pages.

In this example, the web page specified within the 'Books' folder is a valid and reasonable one. Although the access command that Gray had specified was loosely similar to that, it was in fact an instruction to access a web page outside the web root by tricking the web server. The question seemed to me to become: is that type of access 'authorized'? I argued that it was not, because it was performed with the intention of exceeding authorized access. If it produces a valid page from within the overall structure beneath the web root, I argued, we would have to assume that it was valid. Using the scripting trick on vulnerable web servers to 'teleport' the user completely out of the web-root structure could only have been done with that intent.

In his witness statement Sommer had established an analogy for the type of access that Gray had been able to achieve on the vulnerable web servers. Sommer asserted that it was like going into a shop in which customers are able to wander freely, both within the 'true' shopping area and also within the 'back office' area where they are free to see customer details displayed. A customer like Gray wandering through the shop and passing no 'Private: Staff Only' sign would have had no way of knowing that he was not supposed to have been permitted to see those details.

It seemed impossible to tackle Sommer on the argument of interpretation of 'unauthorized' in the meaning of the law; that would require a decision on the part of the court. It was a 'jury point', meaning that it was not something either he or I were qualified to decide, but only to present. But it *was* possible to tackle him on the basis of the analogy he had chosen.

By arguing that the website was like a shop through which one could walk, Sommer was asking one to consider a shop in which the public and the private areas were not apparently distinctive. He was assuming that all parts of the shop were connected and traversable. I responded by arguing that the *public* areas were traversable, by means of the web-page links connecting areas together, but that the private area had in effect been reached by 'teleporting' through a wall that was specifically intended to keep customers away from the back-office areas. I argued that there was no doorway, open or otherwise, between the shop and the office.

For the prosecution, I would try to counter a defence assertion by using similar words and terms, so as not to confuse a jury. I said that implied authority to access a web server extended only as far as the published web-page locations; and I said that Gray must have known his access was unauthorized since he had claimed it as an indication of poor security.

The scene was set for an interesting and important courtroom battle that would directly determine whether or not the 1990 Computer Misuse Act needed urgent rewriting, and whether or not current hacking practices are in fact illegal. And, of course, an interesting face-off between Peter Sommer and myself, which was a prospect that I was frankly relishing, having such a huge respect for him but believing that in this case his interpretation was not correct.

Disappointingly, at the very last minute before court was due to sit, Raphael Gray took the advice of his counsel and changed his plea to guilty. He walked away from court in South Wales with only a community-service sentence. Obviously I was pleased that the prosecution had carried the argument. In the battle for the right computer expert opinion between Peter Sommer and me, it looked as though I had won, but only by default. But I was immensely disappointed that a series of crucial points were not going to be considered by the judiciary.

Afterwards, Peter Sommer phoned me, the first direct contact that we had been able to have since beginning the exchange of carefully worded arguments. It was a friendly though decidedly cagey conversation, as though between two people who had narrowly avoided a fight. The gist of the conversation was that our argument was a fundamental and important one that would have to be revisited sometime soon. We were both convinced – I still am; I'm sure Peter is too – that the law needs the most urgent reconsideration if events that we would wish to define as illegal are indeed going to be successfully considered as against the law.

At the end of the call, we wished each other well and promised that we would, in due course, see one another in court, where this most pressing of arguments will be decided. In the mean time, the most important law framed to prevent illicit activities involving computers remains unrepaired and in dire need of attention.

10. **Head-hacking**

All computer crime involves manipulating computer systems for criminal purposes. Usually, that manipulation is technical in nature: hacking, viruses, or hands-on alterations to the computer contents. But an ever-popular way of manipulating computers is not, in fact, to manipulate the computers at all, but to manipulate the people who use the computers.

This is called 'social engineering'. It can be thought of as 'hacking heads', since it is about finding and exploiting weaknesses in thought processes or management disciplines. I began my career in computer security fascinated by the system aspects of programming and manipulation; now, increasingly, it is the psychological manipulation of head-hacking that fascinates and excites me. People are far more interesting and satisfying than computers, and social engineering is the most enthralling hacking activity. Especially when it can be applied to head-hacking the computer criminals themselves, as I found in two similar though unrelated cases in 2001.

The two companies were within yards of one another in London. The first company was a huge retail organization, the second an insurance company. Both had near-identical problems: anonymous, damaging disclosures of company-confidential information on public websites. Both wanted my help to track down the people concerned.

For the retailer, my initial meeting was with the head of Internal Audit and Investigations, an ex-police officer who met me in a large corner office on the top floor of their building. The floor itself was nearly empty, with removal crates and empty desks along one wall, and a peculiar island of activity in one corner, surrounding the auditor's office. He made a joke about being the pariah of the organization, having watched departments come and go in the shared floor. A spare, pale-faced figure with thinning ginger hair, he was cheerful and energetic, leading me at a trot over to his office, obviously eager to work out the answer to their problems.

Their problem was an interesting one. Like all companies whose shares are listed on the stock market, their fortunes were closely related to the performance of those shares – and that performance in turn was closely related to any rumours and reports regarding the company that might appear in the media. Like similar companies they had a well-managed press and public relations department, and knew the influential journalists and editors for both the specialist and the general media. Senior executives would brief journalists and shareholders; publicity about takeovers, mergers, new product lines and both failing and succeeding aspects of the business was carefully controlled. Apart from the most energetic of the rumour mills: the Internet.

There is nothing to prevent *anyone* publishing *anything* on the Internet, and there are a wealth of places where they can do so. There are newsgroups covering every imaginable subject, whose popularity ranges from one or two dedicated people to hundreds of thousands spread throughout the world. There are chatrooms, online communities, web-published diaries, visitors' books and dedicated websites that can be set up in moments to be visible around the world, twenty-four hours a day.

There are two important websites that are noticed by investors in large companies. One is called *Interactive Internet Investor*, and the other is *Motley Fool*. Both publish stock-market information, titbits of gossip and influential opinions that are acted upon by a growing group of so-called 'day traders'. These are individual investors who use online banking and stock-market facilities to manage and dispose of their shares themselves rather than by means of the traditional stockbroker. These day traders often buy and sell shares within the day, showing either huge profits or huge losses depending on their day's luck. They often rely on the rumour mill of relevant websites; they can move many shares and have a significant impact on the companies concerned.

The websites themselves have two distinct areas. First, a general news area, with articles culled from other, more established publications and giving web links that can be followed to those articles. There are also comments from the operators of the site, acting like any classic investors' digest that might be distributed within a stockbrokers' community. The second area is what makes them different and, for the companies discussed, potentially dangerous. Here online discussion groups are supported, one for each of the stocks – individual companies – that might be tracked by users of the site.

Within these discussion groups, opinion, fact or just rumour can be posted and read by site users. And no matter how well or ill formed, no matter how useful or useless, no matter how intelligent or idiotic the comment, it all gets published. It is all published under nicknames, hiding the true identity of the authors, yet this information might be believed and acted upon.

The retail company monitored those and other websites on a constant basis, with repeated keyword searches to look for anything that might be damaging to them. Beyond that, there was little that they could do. They didn't want to respond to particular threads within the discussion groups, since that might be seen as legitimizing the discussions so that the participants would then pay more attention to the anonymous rumours.

All the company could do was monitor the websites. It was during just such a monitoring session, the former detective explained, that a series of postings concerning their company had been uncovered. And these, he went on, placing a series of printouts on the table in front of us, were particularly worrying.

It was easy to see why the company had become concerned. The printouts showed a sequence of several different discussion 'threads' from the two websites. In each of the submissions one particular author seemed very well informed, sometimes giving definitive information about the company's profit and performance. My host assured me that it was all accurate information, previously not in the public domain, and known only to the most senior managers of the company.

Was it a lucky guess on the part of the writer? Apparently not. Over a period of a few weeks the postings covered a wide variety of topics and were equally well informed, giving detailed information that was not then in the public domain. Unquestionably it was the work of an insider.

There were three possibilities that I could think of. The first was the easiest: the individual posting the material was a current, trusted employee of the company who was using his position to collect and publish confidential information. That was the easiest for several reasons, most obviously because it gave us a reasonable chance of tracking them down cleanly and knowing they could then be disciplined.

The second possibility was that the individual could be outside the company but close friends with a trusted employee. It could be that they were being passed confidential information, wittingly or unwittingly – pillow talk, perhaps; or by going through the employee's papers, for example – and then posting the details on the website.

The third possibility was the most worrying of all. The individual could have gained illicit access to the information – perhaps by having hacked into the computer network. This could be in order to gain unfair profit, or even to damage the company's reputation and performance.

Establishing which of these was the culprit would depend on the nature of the information being revealed: how accurate it was, when it had been made available within the company and to whom. That could only be worked out by studying the postings and collecting any others that the individual might have made, perhaps about other stocks, then doing careful analysis with the data available within the company. If the data was collected from many disparate sources at the time it was revealed on the website, then we might very well be looking at a hacker. Otherwise, an insider – leaking the information by one or another mechanism – would be the more likely.

I was fairly certain that we would be unable to rely on information from the websites themselves. If this had been a police investigation, it would be possible to have access to the records, logs and audit data within the sites themselves, under the authority of a full warrant. As it was, the company could either request assistance from the websites, or try to use a form of civil search warrant called a 'production order'. Both of these were possibilities, but the manager explained that they wanted to reserve that until they had exhausted any other avenues that our investigation might present to them.

I collected together the relevant papers and promised him that I would have some detailed investigation plans within a few days.

Although they had a broadly similar problem, the meeting with the insurance company couldn't have been more different.

Instead of a near-empty floor high up in the building, this was a claustrophobic, crowded basement. Instead of a former police officer already well aware of what might need to be done, I met a relatively junior technical manager. Instead of a well-indexed file of relevant material, all she had was a single, well-thumbed piece of paper.

Although this company was also worried about information posted on the Web, that material was not company-confidential, was not necessarily from an insider and was not available on the Web any more. All that now remained was the printout of the relevant section of a page from a site whose name was an insulting but otherwise obscure version of the company's name.

She explained that they had had the website contents drawn to their attention by a customer and had visited it, collecting just the single screenshot page that she offered to me. Since it was a self-evidently malicious misrepresentation of her company they had instructed lawyers to contact the author using an email address that had been provided for 'feedback' on the original pages. Within a few days of the email having been sent, the page was replaced with a much shorter one, saying simply that the original had been 'censored' and was therefore no longer available.

I confessed to her that I was confused. If the material was no longer available, what was the issue they wanted me to address? She insisted that the lawyers had advised them they could still prosecute the person responsible, but only if they could track them down. She had been instructed by the company's management to find a way of doing just that.

Curious, I read the screenshot, wondering what the author could possibly have said that was so bad. To me, it simply read like a list of complaints – a poorly structured, rambling series of paragraphs, with a lot of repetition and more irrelevant material. I couldn't honestly see that it could pose a serious threat to the company, but I agreed to try and locate the person for them.

I explained that this was possible but unlikely. Websites have to be registered, and the owners have to give at least some information about themselves. In this case the owner would probably give false details. Because the web pages had been removed, any identity clues in the source code of the web page would also be missing, though there was a possibility that the code might have been preserved, or 'cached', on the computer that she had used to capture the screenshot. I thought that was worth a closer look, if she could bring me the specific computer. Other than that there was little that could be immediately achieved without investigating to see who the company hosting the site was and whether they were prepared to assist. And, of course, discovering whether the hosting company itself had accurate information about its customer.

The preserved web page had been obtained by the technical manager herself and she was happy to let me have a look at the cache contents before I took the single sheet away, so as to plan

some form of investigation. However, I drew a blank: her system had not preserved the web page. Perhaps it would have
been available had we forensically imaged the system, but there
was no guarantee that it would not have been simply a waste of
time to try.

Unsure how I was going to proceed, I slipped the page into
my briefcase and promised that I'd be in touch in a few days'
time.

The retail company's problem was the easiest to come to grips
with when I got back to the office. We had a mass of information and an obvious focal point for the investigation.

I began by asking what other stocks the anonymous author
had shown an interest in. If they had similarly detailed knowledge about other companies, unrelated to our client, then it
would make it more likely that they were an outsider with some
ability – whether by hacking or through some other means – of
obtaining sensitive information. If they didn't, then we might be
able to rule that as being less likely.

I signed myself up for membership of both sites and then ran
an author search based on the nickname that the culprit was
known to have used in writing about our client. On the *Internet
Investor* site I found three distinct stocks they had posted discussion articles about; on *Motley Fool*, only the articles relating
to our client. Interestingly, the *Motley Fool* postings – all of
which we had already been given by our client – were old, the
last one being several months earlier than the *Internet Investor*
set. Even more interestingly, those earlier postings had con-
veyed no substantive information, simply quoting articles from
the day's paper. I felt I could safely ignore that site for the rest
of the investigation.

The *Internet Investor* postings were much more interesting,
and fell into two categories. The postings relating to our client
were all enthusiastic about the company's performance, and
more often than not backed up that enthusiasm with detailed
insider information. The category of postings relating to other
companies, which were in wholly unrelated industries, were

much more varied – some enthusiastic, others critical – and gave absolutely no detailed information.

The first observation that we could make from the postings was that the detailed information almost certainly came from someone within our client's company. The second was that the author did not have similar access to detailed information from any other companies.

The other fascinating aspect of the postings was their support for the company. Almost all of them argued that the company was worth the investment. The author defended the company's performance when it was criticized by others submitting to the discussion thread. When a posting *was* critical it was always backed up with recommendations, almost all of which sounded well considered and rational.

It struck me as being most likely that the postings were being made by someone working for the company and, moreover, someone who was enthusiastic in their support for it. It *could* have been an outsider who was particularly close to an employee – a husband or wife, for example – but it seemed unlikely that even they would be quite as supportive as a company manager could be expected to be.

The next thing I wanted to do was to see what the nature of the postings themselves could tell me. First of all, I looked at the *time* that the postings appeared. Every posting had a date and time associated with it, but was that time stamp associated with the computer from which the message came – and therefore perhaps capable of being altered – or was it applied by the computer hosting the discussion group?

To see which it was, I sent a message from my own computer and then altered the local date and time. Then I sent a second message. It was a crude way of working it out but it was effective, showing that the time stamp was applied by the remote computer. That meant that I could rely on the time stamps – at least, up to a point – to illustrate the times of day at which the postings were being made.

I made a chart of the times for the postings. On the whole, they were in the early evening throughout the week, but spread fairly evenly through the day at the weekend. There were none in the early hours of the morning, and none late into the night. The timing data didn't add greatly to my understanding, but it did support the tentative conclusion that I was forming: the author worked through the day, going on the Internet in the early evening and at weekends, most probably when he or she was at home. Also that author was in a similar time zone to me.

Although the majority of the postings fell into the evening and weekend range, there were two or three that were in the working week; there were none on bank holidays, and only a few during one particular week, when perhaps the author was on holiday. Interestingly, the postings that appeared during a working day were all in what seemed to be angry response to some particularly wrong-headed postings that immediately preceded them. Had he or she perhaps sent these postings from their desk? Were they monitoring the site quite closely, and couldn't resist replying immediately to something? It seemed possible, which might then present us with a good potential for locating them.

Before I could proceed with a deeper analysis of the *Internet Investor* postings, I had to make at least some progress on the insurance-company case if I was to keep both clients happy.

Though I had no particular plan in mind, there were some immediate steps that I could take. First of all, I could get the registration information for the website's domain name. Internet computers all have a numerical IP address, and these addresses allow communication traffic to be sent to or from them. However, to make it easier to remember and specify the computers, they all have more intelligible names, called 'domain names'. A set of computers called domain-name servers, DNS, contain the mappings from names to numbers.

When a new domain is registered – say, for a business – the IP address and name have to be passed to the DNS systems if that domain is to be available to the rest of the Internet. In that registration – handled by a small set of specialized registration companies – the owner has to provide their own contact details. Unfortunately there is no way of ensuring that those details aren't falsified.

Fully expecting that I would not find anything useful, I had to start with the registration service. I was not surprised: the owner's name was evidently made up, and the contact telephone number simply returned the 'unavailable' tone.

The next stage of the investigation was to see if the company hosting the website might be forthcoming. Again, that inform-ation is available through the registration process, where it lists its address and the owners of the systems that will act as the primary contact computers for the domain being specified. I expected the anonymous author would have chosen a sufficiently anonymous hosting company. Again, I was not surprised to find that the company was based outside the UK. I didn't believe any useful purpose would be served in trying – as a civilian 'private investigator' – to get in touch with it.

Browsing the website itself, it was clear that it had served its function for the author and had been closed down. Just one, short page remained, with the title 'Censored', and a brief para-graph explaining that the site had been shut down, and a button to click to send email to the author. That was all that remained, with no clues in the source of the web page and no pages hiding behind that one.

I had two obvious options, one positively illegal and the other slightly dubious. The illegal option was to hack the web-site itself and see if there were any useful records remaining on the server. It didn't look as though it would be too hard, since the site was plainly running an old version of Microsoft's IIS Web Server – a superseded version that I knew a handful of ways of circumventing – but I couldn't guarantee that I would find anything and I couldn't guarantee that I wouldn't be detected. I was confident that I could do it without being traced – years spent tracking hackers meant that I was pretty sure I knew how not to be tracked myself – but it would still have been a bit awkward to explain later.

The second option was to contact the author directly and to

see whether I could persuade him or her to start communicating with me. I decided that was the more prudent course. Instead of hacking their website, I would try to hack them through social engineering.

At the simplest level, social engineering can be just a question of phoning a company and pretending to be an employee having difficulty accessing the network. At the most sophisticated level, it can be a complex 'sting' operation. In this case I didn't have to be particularly creative, but I still needed to have some form of cover story for the sting to work. I needed some way of enticing the author to talk to me, so that I could perhaps track them by means of their email headers. To be on the safe side, I needed to provide sufficient enticement for them to come back more than once to the discussion.

Reading and re-reading the original screenshot of their web-site, the thing that leaped out was just how *angry* the author was. The typing was full of mistakes – the sort of mistakes that come from typing quickly rather than badly. The tone of the language and the choice of words were all those of an angry person – perhaps not a particularly articulate or well-educated person, but definitely one who had a point they wanted to stress and that they wanted to make to as many people as they could. They were hiding behind the anonymity of the Web, instead of facing the company directly, and they had, in effect, run away as soon as they were challenged. The site was closed down, and there were no other instances of the material on the website. This was an angry coward.

That was my opportunity. This person wanted to express their anger to as many people as possible, while hiding safely away. If I could promise them a way of expressing that anger effectively, to a lot more people, safe from the target of their anger, then they would leap at the opportunity. The obvious thing was to pretend to be a journalist wanting to interview them and write about their problems.

I couldn't aim that story at the target of the person's anger – that would be a little too obvious. Instead, I decided to have an anger of my own, which they could feel they were using for their own ends. I needed to let them feel that they were being the clever manipulator, not me.

The main word on the remaining website was my trigger. I decided that I would be angered by censorship, that would be my crusade. I would be angry at the growing tide of restrictions imposed on Web citizens by big business crudely throwing its weight about, stamping on the individual. Deliberately, I worked myself into an annoyed state about it all. I scrawled down all the petty elements of commercial arrogance on the Internet that had ever irritated me. I provoked myself to think and feel exactly like the person I was trying to be would feel, and then I wrote my email message.

I told the author that I was a journalist researching a story on Internet censorship and that I had come across their site and wanted to interview them so that they could tell their side of the tale. I didn't flavour the email with a false attempt at anger. Instead, I tried to write genuinely, with that sense of burning anger at injustice and corporate bullying fresh in my mind. Calming down, I was pleased with the result: it could almost have been written by any one of my friends in the civil-liberties community, and I found that I had unconsciously copied a lot of the ways of writing that my friends in the campaigning press would tend to use in their own email.

Next, I needed a nicely anonymous email service from which to send the message. I was hoping to be able to track this person through their email; the last thing I wanted was for *them* to be able to track *me* through mine. I had said that I was a freelance writer, so at least I didn't have to worry about trying to spoof an originating address within a national newspaper or magazine – but I couldn't simply send the message from within my company. Instead I used a FreeServe dial-up account that I set up specifically, confident that it would not be traceable – unless the author was able to get access to systems I knew were well protected by friends of mine working for FreeServe.

All FreeServe connections to the Internet go through one centralized point called a 'proxy' server. It takes all the Internet requests from FreeServe customers and funnels them down into one, very high-speed connection to the Internet. It has the effect of making Internet access much cheaper than it would otherwise be but unfortunately means that all FreeServe account holders appear to have the same address as far as the rest of the Internet is concerned. A nuisance when we are tracking hackers, but a boon when we want to hide.

Knowing that I was well hidden from my target, and that this was probably my only chance of tracking him or her, I fired off the email message and crossed my fingers. For the time being, it was all I could do.

While I waited for any kind of result with the insurance company, I had the chance to go back to the other project. I had a mass of written material from each of the discussion postings, and the first thing I wanted to do was to try and profile the author based on their language. This 'textual analysis' can be very useful when there is no evidence other than written material.

I looked through the material for some simple clues. The first question was whether the submissions were all written by a single person writing alone. 'Committee' writing has a number of distinctive elements. If there are several people throwing in ideas for a piece of writing, the tone, the tense and the form of the writing often changes abruptly from fragment to fragment. These samples were all consistent so it seemed most likely that they had all been written by just the one person – and because the writing style didn't change from day to day, it was likely that this was the same person throughout.

The second question was the author's sex. As a crude differentiation, women often say 'we' whereas men say 'I'; women say 'feel' whereas men say 'think'; women sympathize and attempt to expand on problems, whereas men try immediately to find solutions for them; women ask, whereas men tell. Obviously no such analysis can ever be 100 per cent accurate, but it can be a good indicator. In this case, I was fairly certain that we were reading a man's writing – and a fairly assertive, bullying one at that.

The third question was the author's education level and background. Grammar and vocabulary are the best indications of education. There are a number of objective measurements of these, with some standard formulae we use. The formulae can be used to calculate, for example, what grade of education might be required to read and understand a particular fragment of text. They can never be considered as wholly accurate, and indeed the science behind them is not as reliable as one might hope for. Nonetheless they provide a useful indicator, especially since the formulae are built into the standard grammar-checking utility in Microsoft Word and are therefore easy to obtain and use.

According to the results, the author had a reasonably high degree of education and familiarity with English. It was consistent with him being a manager in the company, though obviously it *proved* nothing.

Background and accent can often also be determined from written text, particularly by looking at mistakes. Many foreign-language speakers might omit the definite or indefinite article, and often misspellings are a good indication of the writer's 'internal accent' – the way they say the words in their heads. For example, many of those I grew up with would write 'should of' instead of 'should have'. Even the author's handedness can sometimes be determined from mistakes, by determining which side of the keyboard is the one at which most 'finger-fumble' typing mistakes occur.

What I was trying to establish here was not the writer's identity. Rather, I wanted to establish some unique indicators so that when – or rather, if – we did find the writer, we might be able to confirm his identity through textual comparison with his other, non-suspect writing. I was doing this analysis in anticipation of having to do the scene-of-habitation analysis at some later point, establishing the writer's identity by investigating his usual behaviour patterns.

The work was intensive and time-consuming, and demanded huge amounts of concentration in the reading and annotating of the textual material as I worked through into the evening on it.

I have to confess that I was more than a little irritated when my system beeped to tell me that I had new mail. But that irritation vanished when I saw who the email was from.

The author of the website attacking the insurance company was not using a Hotmail account, which was something of a surprise. Hotmail is more or less anonymous, in that it has no checks on the accuracy of any signup information, and is widely used. Instead, the author used the email service from the foreign hosting company that had supported their website. The email name they were using was a generic one that told me nothing about them, but the 'extended headers' *did* give me the address of the computer that had passed the original email message to the email servers for transmission, along with some details about the computer itself. It told me the type of computer and the type of email application that the writer was using.

Unfortunately, I knew the originating address that the headers showed all too well: it was the address of the 'proxy' for the FreeServe Internet-access service, the very same system that I had hidden behind in communicating with the author. Just as I knew it would effectively protect me from them, I knew it would hide them from me.

I had no way of tracking them – at least, not yet – so I had to continue the exercise of negotiating with them. In classic negotiating, the mantra is 'Keep them talking.' The more some-one can be made to talk, the more chance there is that they will make a mistake: that they will give something away, or that they can be persuaded to do something. In telephone-based negotiating this involves keeping them on the line for as long as possible, using verbal tricks to get them to fill any silences in the conversation.

In email negotiation, the basic principle is the same, but the mechanism is different. Short, sharp messages, with quick replies; tags to encourage the correspondent to reply; and always more and ever more questions – open and closed – alongside the offer of encouragement and the promise of concessions and additional information.

With that in mind – and conscious that the author must be on a dial-up line, given the time of evening, from home – I needed to reply as quickly as I could. First, I had to make sure that I didn't make the mistake that I intended to force the author into making. I wanted to finesse them into a position where they gave away their location through carelessness, but I had to make sure I didn't do the same. Before I could reply, I had to dial in to FreeServe myself and then bounce the next, encouraging email along to them.

The person's email had reiterated the points that I knew they had already expressed on the original website – though I had to pretend I hadn't seen that. I didn't write a lot in my reply, just a simple request for information about when they had been censored and by whom.

The writer was obviously still online: the next message came through almost immediately, with details of the lawyers' original email to them and some justification about why they had had to take the site offline. Again, I typed a rapid follow-up, asking how they felt about it. I wanted to try and establish whether this was a man or a woman and whether there was just the one of them. But I was having to do this rapidly and off the top of my head, almost as though they were sitting in front of me.

The cleaners were bustling through the office as I sat tensely typing up the next email. All in all, we bounced half a dozen messages backwards and forwards, and over the period of the exchange they became more and more revealing. Eventually the author signed himself 'Rob'. That was an interesting titbit, but the main thing I wanted to do was to draw him deeper and deeper into the communication, as rapidly and as completely as I could, because I wanted to move the conversation from the evening at home to wherever he worked. I was sure that if he did work, and I could persuade him to send me email *from* work, then I would be able to track him. It was a little like playing a fish: I had to let him have enough line to persuade him that everything was safe, before the strike. And the bait I dangled was that I had, I was sure, in my files some stuff about the company he had targeted. I promised that I would send it and then simply stopped sending him further emails that night.

It was late by this time, but I knew that I had lured him into the idea that he would get some interesting material from me . . . and I was sure he wouldn't be able to resist the temptation of at least checking, and I hoped sending, email from his desk the next day.

The next day, before I could return to 'Rob' and his email, I had a meeting with the retail company. I could tell them that, even without knowing the full documentary history of the information disclosed, I was reasonably sure that it was someone in the organization who was responsible for it. And I could give them a number of possible ways of locating the person.

One option, just as with the other case, was to entice the person into email. That would be relatively long-winded, but not particularly difficult: it would be an exercise in social engineering again, and I had already worked out some of the psychological characteristics of the individual that would allow me to do it.

The second option was much easier, provided that the company had a well-run computing infrastructure. Just as all FreeServe users access the wider Internet by going through the service provider's proxy, users in any large organization would go through their own proxy. Most companies buy only a small number of Internet addresses, and then share them between the hundreds or thousands of employees that might need access. The system that makes this work is called a proxy, and it has one IP address that it uses on behalf of all users. When a user makes a request for a page from a particular website, the request in fact goes to the proxy instead of the website itself. The proxy then makes the request directly, and returns the web page to the user's computer.

This has two advantages. First, it makes it easier to manage the internal network. Second, and more crucially, it makes it possible to *log* every user request to the Internet.

If the retail company's network was correctly set up, the

proxy would log all access to the Internet – including the insider's access to the *Internet Investor* site. Since I knew exactly what a message-submission request looked like – having made them myself the day before – I could be confident that we would find the submission requests.

As before, the meeting was in the internal audit and investigation manager's office, but this time I had asked him also to invite someone who would know about the proxy configuration. I explained what we had found, the nature and timings of the postings, that it was almost certainly an insider, and that the proxy log would show precisely who it was. I had a printout of a fragment of the log from my company's proxy, with the message-submission text highlighted, but as I showed them the date and time of the anonymous insider's submission the system manager shook his head sadly. Whilst they did indeed log, they didn't keep the logs for more than a few days.

That left the second observation, though: that the insider had apparently replied almost immediately after several provocative postings, showing that he was watching the site almost constantly. Perhaps he still was?

The audit manager now shook his head and commented that there were probably a lot of people in the organization who would be watching the site – including himself – especially amongst the senior management. But he was prepared to have a look. From the audit manager's office workstation, the system manager connected to the proxy server and started a simple program to monitor the audit log. Sure enough, there were two dozen internal computer addresses highlighted that had connected to the *Internet Investor* website within the last three hours. As expected, one was the audit manager himself, who had reviewed the discussion-group postings shortly before our meeting had started. Others were scattered throughout the building.

We needed a way of filtering out all those who were simply curious about the company's performance, to leave the one that was our anonymous poster. Then I realized how to do it: if the insider was lurking on the discussion groups relating to this company, he might also be lurking on the discussion groups relating to the three other stocks we knew he had an interest in.

It was the job of a moment to filter the log readings to show just the three specific web addresses that we were interested in within the *Internet Investor* site. Sure enough we found one internal-network address that had connected to all of them that very morning. We had our man – or rather, we had the network address for our man. All that remained to do was to check the network address database to locate the specific workstation. Five minutes later, the system manager read out the office number of our suspect, a middle manager in the Accounts Department.

Flushed with that success, I made my way back to my office – and there, waiting in my inbox since 9.30 a.m., was the email that I had been hoping for.

It was from the second anonymous author, wondering when I was going to give him details about the insurance company. The extended headers showed, as clear as day, that it had been written on a different computer, with a different network address. These headers showed an internal network address for the workstation used, and even the name of that workstation; they also gave a network-gateway address through which the message had passed, and *this* gave the domain name of the company at which the anonymous author was working.

I knew now where he worked: a large consulting firm in London. I knew that his first name was possibly Rob, and I knew the name and location of the workstation he was sitting at within the company. I might not have been able to give his home address but I was confident that I had enough information for the client to be able to track him down through the consulting firm's own records. I confess, though, that I was still feeling excited and confident from having found the suspect for the retail organization, so I decided to press my luck slightly further.

The trail of extended headers showed not just the workstation but also the names of two further servers through which the message had passed. As with most large organizations, those names, although slightly cryptic, were comprehensible. The mail-server name, for example, hinted that it was a Microsoft Exchange server based in London. The other server had a similarly cryptic name, but networks in large organizations usually map onto departments, buildings, sometimes even floors; and servers are usually dedicated to those same subdivisions. The most obvious reading of the server name was that it acted as the mail gateway for the IT help desk at 'Rob's' workplace.

For any social engineer, the IT help desk – trained to be helpful to those who need assistance with their IT infrastructure – is a familiar target. Directory Enquiries gave me the switchboard number for the company's main office in London, and the switchboard happily put me through to the help desk. Worried that the answer might be 'Rob who?', I asked the first person who answered the phone what Rob's surname was, saying that 'My manager wants to know.'

There was only one Rob in the department; I had found the second of my targets.

The retail company gave their manager a written warning, but no further action was taken. He had been acting out of misplaced enthusiasm, initially wanting to correct some misunderstanding on the discussion group, and using material that he knew was available in the office. Not being privy to the company's public-relations plans and imperative, he didn't appreciate that the publication of the data might be damaging – but since he had no criminal intent, a warning was more than enough.

'Rob' turned out to be a past client of the second company. When his basic complaints were investigated they were found to be wholly justified – though, of course, the company was still not happy to have had its failings so publicly discussed. I was told that an accommodation had been reached with him, but not what it was.

For me, the few days of intense activity had been an

interesting combination of standard investigation and standard hacking tricks used to solve two interesting and knotty problems.

My final thought was how far from the truth the popular view of anonymity on the Internet really is. With enough capability and enough imagination it really is possible to work out who you are dealing with – a vitally important lesson when investigating computer crime, and an equally important lesson to teach corporate victims of those crimes: report the crimes, because we may very well be able to pull rabbits out of hats that will surprise you.

11. The Rolex Robbers

The overwhelming bulk of my work in computer crime has been in obvious areas that one would expect. From Internet paedophilia through hacking to email stalking and information abuse, these are all common types of crime with computers. It is understandable that the vast majority of computers or case files that make their way to my Buckingham Gate offices will fall into that category.

Increasingly, however, an interesting collection of new and different kinds of offence has started to appear: criminal cases in which the computer evidence has been secondary to the main crime. Cases where the computer has been used by the criminals exactly as it might be used by ordinary people for legitimate purposes.

Email, web-browsing and general communication facilities over the Internet are a part of everyday life now for us all – and that includes criminals. Because of this, we are presented with new sources of evidence in traditional crimes. The computer can be as useful as a set of fingerprints or a CCTV picture in capturing criminals.

The first such example of this that I personally encountered was in the context of armed robbery, where computer contents helped to put a gang of hardened criminals behind bars. And made me realize for the first time that I faced threats to more than my peace of mind from my work in computer crime.

The detective who arrived at my offices in early 2000 was from the Metropolitan Police Flying Squad. I was somewhat in awe of such a high-profile, energetic group of detectives. I imagined them handling armed robbers and murderous drug dealers, speeding in fast cars through the narrow streets of south London. The officer who turned up hadn't disappointed us. He introduced himself just as 'Dave', and arrived in an unmarked, turbo-charged Saab with bulletproof vests and the trademark baseball caps in the boot alongside the evidence bags containing the computers he wanted us to examine. Dave was a good four inches taller than my 6' 1" and, dressed in jeans and a casual bomber jacket, he did not look like a man to cross. He looked and sounded the part of the hard copper, until his mobile phone went off and the entire office collapsed laughing as the *Sweeney* signature tune sounded through the office.

The case he had brought to me was an everyday one for the Flying Squad, even if it was unusual for us: armed robbery of jewellery shops in the London area by a gang intent on stealing Rolex watches. The crimes had been foiled by observation and intelligence work, culminating in a 'take-down' as the gang had made their way to a target in Kingston-on-Thames on 5 November 1999. For the Flying Squad, it was a near-textbook operation, but they wanted an additional topping on the case, from information they were sure would be stored in the computers but which they were unable to examine until we had 'made it safe' for them by imaging the computers.

This was the first real indication that I had had within my work of the way that computer evidence could be of importance in traditional crimes. The police believed that no actual criminal use of the computer had taken place: there was no suggestion that the robbers had hacked into the jewellery shops' websites or business-management computers. Instead, the computer was believed to have formed a supporting tool for the robbery, which made sense: computers and the Internet are key parts of legitimate business, so why not of illicit business?

Pleasingly, when the computers had been seized by the investigators, they had also been preserved. For several years I have been involved with Police National Training, now going by the name of Centrex and based in purpose-built accommodation to the north of London. I have worked hard and long hours, for free, to educate detectives in the handling of computer crime. In the early days of that training effort one of our greatest worries had been that important computer equipment would either be overlooked – so that diskettes or back-up tapes would not be seized – or that enthusiastic officers would examine un-imaged computers and thereby destroy their integrity. If the computers are not handled in the correct, forensically sound manner, any evidence obtained from them becomes immediately suspect and is easily challenged in court. That happened so often – usually by police officers who believed they knew a little about computers – that we worked hard to introduce general guidance literature provided to every police officer, telling them the most fundamental element of computer forensics: *Do not touch!* That a group of officers widely perceived to be 'gung-ho', on a case in which care of the computers was not an obvious priority, could have been so careful and so correct in their handling of the computer material was the best indication that the education programme within the police force was having an effect.

Even had we not been able to help with any aspect of the Rolex case, I would have felt a sense of victory just because of that.

Dave had brought us three computers from two sources. From the house of the gang's leader they had seized a tower computer and a laptop; a second tower computer had been seized from the house of an accomplice. This second man was the 'fence' who was believed to have agreed to resell the stolen watches for the gang.

Dave briefed me on what the Flying Squad detectives wanted us to do. First of all, Dave wanted my help to emphasize the careful planning that had gone into the robberies. He wanted to show that it wasn't an opportunistic, one-off attempt on the part of the suspects, but a well-managed, well-researched criminal 'business venture'. He was sure the leader of the gang had researched the ideal shops to target through using the Web, first to locate shops that dealt in Rolex watches and then to obtain location maps so that they could plan approach and getaway routes. Second, Dave had a good idea that the gang leader had communicated and planned the disposal of the stolen watches by using email to the fence, and that some indication of this might be found on the fence's or the gang leader's computers. Finally, Dave wanted to discover whether or not the fence had planned to try and use the Web as a means of selling the stolen watches.

Dave listened patiently as I outlined what I would need to know to direct the computer investigation: the date and time range over which the planning was believed to have occurred; the names of the relevant shops and gang members; the items of interest to the gang; and the names of associates who might not be involved.

If I'd been pleased to hear that the Flying Squad hadn't accidentally mishandled the computers, I was ecstatic when Dave calmly handed me a collection of A4 sheets when I had finished describing what I would need. The sheets contained all the necessary detail; they had anticipated everything that would be necessary to make the computer investigation straight-forward. More than any other factor in my experience in computer crime, that made me believe that we were finally beginning to get things right.

Stepping first through the configuration and registration details of the laptop files, I could see that the laptop was registered as belonging to the IT support company that employed the gang leader's girlfriend. Email packages store the messages sent or received in specific places on the computer and there were several hundred messages, all of them to or from her, none of them to or from the fence. Files created by office-automation applications are usually stored either on the user's desktop or in a specific set of folders. These contained documents and spreadsheets, the overwhelming majority of which had been created by her or by others working for her company, none of which had anything to do with jewellery shops or Rolex watches. When a user accesses the Internet, a record of sites visited and of pages downloaded is retained by the computer and is of crucial importance in a computer investigation; this collection of files showed only access to websites related to her job, and none that had any bearing on the case.

So the laptop appeared to have been used exclusively by the gang leader's girlfriend to support her job. It did not even contain any games, nor any messages between her and her boyfriend. It was as clean a system as I have ever examined, and seemed to have been seized by the police in error. We carefully stored it away in a spare laptop-shipping box and called Dave to have it returned to the girlfriend's employer.

The other computer seized from their house, however, was much more interesting. The tower unit was a medium computer case, small enough to fit under a desk and the typical size for a home or office computer. Roughly eighteen inches deep, eighteen inches high and six to eight inches wide, this type of case is designed to be easy to access and typically has enough working space within the enclosure to make it reasonably straightforward to get at the disk drives within it.

A set of six cross-head screws had to be removed before the outer casing cover could be lifted clear to expose the internal modules. As with almost all modern computers, the case contained a floppy and a CD-ROM drive, accessible from the front panel, and a larger-sized hard-disk-drive unit mounted below that, connected by grey ribbon cable and a black and red power cable to the backplane itself.

One of the first things to check with the larger computer cases is the number of disk drives contained within the case. Although I've never come across this personally, other investigators have told me of suspects – particularly in paedophile cases – who have had multiple disconnected disk drives hidden within the tower chassis. A hurried investigation would not uncover those suspect drives. But there was nothing like that in this case: the chassis contained only one disk drive, about two-thirds the dimensions of a paperback book.

There are two connections and four grub screws used to secure a disk drive inside most tower cases. The power cable – ordinary, coloured wires twisted together – is usually simple enough to pull clear, though most investigators use sharp-nosed pliers so as to avoid skinned knuckles. The grub screws – or rather, the rearmost pair of grub screws – usually present the greater problem, simply because of how awkward they are to reach and how firmly embedded they can become through the surprising amount of dust that collects inside the cases. Once those are clear, though, the disk drive can be lifted clear, and the final ribbon cable – which carries the data to and from the disk drive – can be carefully wriggled off.

The disk drive itself is surprisingly heavy. Usually silver-coloured, moulded metal, it is stamped with the manufacturer's details, including the disk capacity. In this case, it was a 6Gbyte disk: not huge by modern standards, but still large enough to hold between five and ten thousand books' worth of information, a good-sized library.

To copy this kind of disk we put it inside a caddy: a removable box version of the mounting from within a tower chassis. A power cable and a data-ribbon cable are attached to the drive, and again grub screws are used to hold the drive securely – important, since the spinning disk can often make the unit vibrate annoyingly. This caddy is then slid into a corresponding slot on the front of the laboratory computer system, and a second disk – called the 'forensic target' – is also slid into place. We store this in a sealed container in the Chubb safe once it has been copied.

As with the laptop, there was no encryption in place. This was hardly surprising, since the gang leader was not particularly computer-literate, unlike the hackers and paedophiles I was more used to dealing with. The first thing to establish was whether or not the computer did contain information relevant to the investigation. Dave had provided me with a list of the shops and the items that had been stolen. These formed the first basis for my investigation, and I used the search facility of the forensic software to collect every occurrence of those names.

The police case, Dave had told me, had been built on information from an informer. This person had told the police that the gang had begun hunting out information about the jewellery shops and watches in early October. The computer evidence supported that totally. On the timeline, before October there was only casual use of the Internet – about which, more later – but from October there were records of specific web searches with the Google search engine to find details about shops. There were copies of maps from the *Multimap* website, centred on the postcodes of the targeted shops, and we could even see records of some of these maps having been printed – including the map for the shop outside which they were finally arrested.

We had also been given the Flying Squad's observation records, showing the times and dates at which their suspect was known to be in the house: these matched perfectly with the timeline information showing the usage pattern for the computer. And for the dates and times at which their informant claimed the planning process was going on, there were usually records of web searches.

The only thing I could *not* find was any reference to the alleged fence, nor indeed any installation of an email package, though I could find indications of use of several web-based email services similar to the Hotmail application.

It seemed likely that the police case regarding the use of the computer in planning the robberies – and their assertion that therefore the robberies were carefully planned – would stand up in court.

But there was one problem with the computer evidence. Just as with the laptop, I examined the registration data for the computer and found that it was registered to the gang leader's girlfriend. Worse, the Internet account that had been used to access the Web – and hence the jewellery shops – was in her name as well. A possible objection that the defence could raise at trial was that the contents of the computer had nothing to do with the gang leader – that it was only in fact used by his girl-friend. I could imagine a defence barrister creating a tale of searches for jewellery shops, and even Rolex watches, by the girlfriend hunting out birthday presents or some such.

It became important to establish whether or not the computer was being used by the gang leader exclusively, by his girlfriend exclusively, or by both. And this was precisely the problem for which I had devised the scene-of-habitation analysis, used successfully in cases ranging from the Gary Glitter prosecution to the later online stalking exercise. It seemed odd to think that it would be useful in a case such as this, but I saw no reason why it should not work.

Scene-of-habitation analysis depends on deriving infor-mation on computer usage patterns *distinct* from the allegedly criminal use of the computer. In this case, that meant discounting everything to do with jewellers' shops, maps and so forth.

It proved surprisingly easy to establish the identity of the computer user. The accessed and altered files over the last few months of the computer's use seemed to divide into two categories. First there were the operating-system files, indicat-ing the periods that the computer was booted and rebooted, checked for viruses or similar. Second, there were files related to the operation of the Internet access: cookies, stored web pages, downloaded pictures. There were no other files: no documents, spreadsheets, game applications; absolutely nothing. It seemed that the computer was used for no other purpose than to access the Internet.

The next step was to determine what *type* of Internet access was recorded, and this could be achieved by looking at the Internet history and at the files, pictures, pages and cookies downloaded and stored automatically by the system. Other than the jewellery shops, the browser seemed to have been used to visit search engines, four different web-based email services – all of them in the gang leader's name and not the girlfriend's – chat services, and a truly *immense* number of 'adult' sites. Indeed, by far the overwhelming majority of Web- and Internet-related material on the computer was pornographic in nature.

Examining the search-engine records, I could locate several hundred records of distinct searches. Other than the few related to the case, all of them were attempts to find sites featuring heterosexual sex – with anal and 'doggy'-style sex requests being the most common. Of the pictures that had been down- loaded and preserved automatically by the system, the bulk were of evidently heterosexual pornography – with anal or doggy-style sex featuring quite heavily.

Finally, there were preserved fragments of many Internet chat sessions. The computer user in this case had apparently used chat frequently, exclusively in adult, sex-oriented chat- rooms. To use the service it is necessary to provide an email address; the address given was one of the web-based email services set up in the gang leader's name. It is necessary to give a 'sign-in' name or 'handle' by which others will know you in the chat session. The name given in all cases was 'Doggy-style'.

The preserved fragments of the chat sessions all had a common feature: the user signed in as 'Doggy-style' and propositioned anal sex with each person identified as female in the session. That seemed to be the sum total of the user's involvement with the chat sessions that they joined. It seemed fair to conclude that this would be more likely to be male than female behaviour.

Despite the fact that the computer and the Internet account were associated with the gang leader's girlfriend, it seemed to us beyond reasonable doubt that the principal user of the computer was our suspect.

We now felt confident that the illicit activity recorded on the computer could safely be associated with the gang leader, so we turned to examining the rest of the data for additional clues. The most obvious thing that we wanted to discover was any association with the alleged fence, though we weren't hopeful. While I had been examining the gang leader's computer, we had taken a copy of the fence's computer – another tower system – and had found no mention of Rolex watches, jewellery shops or association with the gang. In fact, it seemed from the contents that the computer had been used only by the fence's teenage son to do his homework. But we still had to examine the email that might have been preserved on the leader's computer. Perhaps there would be evidence of him contacting the fence? Unfortunately all the email addresses referred to *web*-mail services.

There are two ways of using email on the Internet. The first is for the mail messages to be collected by the user from a mail server, using a specific mail-reading program – typically something like the Microsoft Outlook application. This connects over the Internet to the mail server and then copies all the messages to the local computer, where they are saved and read. When a user has one of these services, we would expect to find most of their email on the computer when we analyse it, as we had done with the laptop examined earlier. The other type of service is accessed over the Internet using the web browser, just like visiting any web page: Hotmail, for example. Individual email messages are then displayed just like other web pages, but are not stored on the local computer. Sometimes, as with any other type of web page, there might be fragments left on the disk of messages viewed or written, but not always.

In this case, we were unlucky. We found only tiny fragments of mail messages remaining, certainly not enough to say anything more than that email *had* been used by the suspect, but not enough even to be able to say to whom it had been written. This was disappointing, and meant that there was no way of using the computers to determine whether or not there had been a conspiracy between the fence and the gang leader.

Despite this, the Flying Squad were happy: we had managed to establish that their suspect had planned the raids with great precision, had undertaken research over a period of several weeks before his arrest, and that it was indeed him that had carried out the research. All we had to do now was to write our report and wait for the trial.

*

The report was written for the police at the start of April 2000. Based on previous experience with the slow-grinding wheels of justice, I hadn't expected to hear about the case again for several months. Astonishingly, it was as quickly as the end of June that I was called to give my evidence at the Old Bailey.

To anyone involved in crime in the UK, the Old Bailey is a name to be conjured with. For many, the face of English justice is represented by the fine, high-arched entrance to the impressive courts on the Strand, near Fleet Street. There are always banks of cameramen and journalists, and the bustling flotilla of black-gowned counsels and their assistants wheeling trolleys of case papers over the two zebra crossings from the Temple alleyways to the courts. But this picture is of the excessively grand Royal Courts of Justice, not the Old Bailey. That is an altogether more dour, relatively modern building, a stone's throw from St Paul's, just off the Holborn Viaduct.

As a name, the Old Bailey evokes the picture of famous trials. As a reality, it's a depressing building, with narrow windows set into thick, concrete walls. I'd driven past it in taxis any number of times before, on my way to or from clients in the City. I'd always been amused to watch the hordes of photographers, and the peculiarly British tradition of the artists' chalk sketches propped against nearby windowsills to be filmed, like the work of court-fixated pavement artists. I'd always wondered what stories and events had brought the sombre-suited, stone-faced witnesses and policemen to that ugly building. Now it was my turn to experience what the place was like.

The taxi driver who dropped me off at the top of the street leading down to the courts explained that he couldn't get any nearer because of a police cordon set up to keep the press at a distance. I could see what he meant: there was a scrum of journalists on the opposite pavement, with a shaky-looking camera platform built of scaffolding poles and planks. It seemed a bit extreme, all that attention simply for a small gang of failed jewellery robbers?

As I paid him, the taxi driver wished me luck – and I wondered if he thought I was a defendant in something important. I wanted to explain that I was a witness – an *expert* witness, one of the good guys – but he was gone before I could think of a way to frame it.

I stood then for a moment, slightly uncertain about what to do and where to go. It isn't that obvious exactly where the entrance to the courts actually is, and the thought of exploring my way around the narrow, hot street under the glare of photographers and TV cameras wasn't exactly enticing. The thought of standing in the witness box and presenting to judge, jury and the gallery didn't faze me one bit; but the thought of making an idiot of myself in failing even to find the front door had me sweating.

I was saved by the appearance at my shoulder of big Dave and a crowd of his colleagues and of uniformed police officers. Dave swept me up with them and, ignored by the press, we made our way in through the police officers' smaller entrance, through the security checks and on up to the rooms reserved for the CPS and police.

Dave explained that the press weren't there for the 'Rolex robbers' but for the culmination of a much larger, gruesome case of abduction and rape. Eager to sort out his own exhibits, Dave introduced me to one of the officers in that case and left me to have coffee and listen to the queasy details while I waited for counsel to find time to chat with me about my evidence.

I felt even more queasy as the prosecuting counsel began to explain what would meet me in the court itself.

By the time of the Old Bailey appearance, I had appeared in a number of courts of varying kinds: modern ones, in places like Newcastle and Birmingham; and older, traditional ones, such as a court in South Wales – for a paedophile case – that didn't seem to have changed since the days of 'Hanging Judge' Jeffries. From the ancient to the modern, though, they all had a uniform arrangement: the judge faces the defendant, with counsel sitting between them; to one side of the judge, the jury sits in two rows of seats, facing across the court towards the witness box and, behind that, the public and press gallery.

Every witness is told that, though the questions will be asked by counsel, and occasionally by the judge, all their answers must be addressed to the jury. Naturally, this is hard for most people to manage, but the more traditional judges are emphatic that 'professional' witnesses, including the police officers, *must* do this. I have heard nerve-racking stories of poor police officers being upbraided by the courts for giving evidence badly – and defence counsels in particular take great delight in baiting expert witnesses.

In this court, though, I was warned that it was going to be even more difficult, because the jury had been moved to sit out of sight of the public gallery – actually underneath the gallery – and therefore behind the witness box. I would have to take questions from counsel and then physically turn in the box so as to address the answers to the jury members in an artificial and clumsy way.

That was a concern, but even more of a worry was when the prosecuting counsel casually mentioned why the jury had been moved. There had been a fear that associates of the gang would threaten jury members or their families, so that the jury had to be protected by anonymity. A major exercise had been going on throughout the course of the trial – which was in its third day by then – to ensure that the jury was brought to and from the court in secrecy.

It had never occurred to me that a trial could lead to threats of violence and that, as a professional witness about to give evidence that might help convict violent criminals, I might be in some danger. The prospect of being threatened – or, worse, of my family being threatened – didn't exactly fill me with relish. But even had I wanted to back out, it was too late to do so now. I had no option but to take a deep breath and go through with it – and hope that, since the computer material was useful but not central to the case, I would not be in any danger.

Usually, there's a pattern to the presentation of information in computer-crime cases. First there is the description of the fundamentals of the computers themselves. Unlike any other aspect of crime, we cannot assume that the jury will have even the first idea about what a computer is and how it works. If the case involves a car, say, then we can assume at least some level of familiarity: we don't have to explain that the car has a number of wheels, and that those wheels have tyres, and that those tyres have a pattern that can be examined. But in computer cases, we have to start with the most basic of explanations.

Common practice is now for the prosecution and defence expert witnesses to agree a description of these fundamental concepts that both sides will work with. This describes the computer and its basic operation in simple terms, including the existence of files and of collections of files into folders; of disk drives, diskettes, printers and the like. Indeed, there is now a move that I'm involved with, planned by the Crown Prosecution Service, to introduce a simple, single booklet of agreed descriptions – including pictures – of the computer elements that are most commonly encountered in court.

The first task of the expert witnesses is usually therefore each to define and then mutually to agree on the descriptions that will be used, so as not to tax the jury with multiple types of description – a valuable lesson I learned from the 'Christopher Robin' paedophile trial. The second type of information that must be given is the basic concepts from which any argument has been constructed. So, if the argument is going to involve the computer's time stamps or file storage elements, then these must be described for the jury. The final element of the information is what we think of as the 'argument'. These are the elements of the computer evidence over which the two sides might disagree – usually the expert interpretation or opinion built upon the factual presentation. Again, this is a lesson I learned from that earlier case: to ensure that the jury understands what it is that the prosecution and defence disagree over in the evidence.

In the case of the Rolex robbers, the description fundamentals were of the computer operation; the concept fundamentals were over the time-stamped material showing the user visit a number of websites; and the potential disagreement was over whether that showed the computer to have been used by the defendant alone, to plan the robberies.

The defendants had not appointed their own computer expert witness. This might be thought of as a good thing for the prosecution, since it meant that what I was about to present, and my opinions about it, were unlikely to be challenged. However, it also meant that *I* had to explain all of the concepts involved, in an accurate and even-handed manner.

To the outsider, it appears that the prosecution and the defence are set against one another. That is true, but only partially. It is not the role of the prosecution to show only the things that make the defendant appear guilty, whilst the defence show only the things that make them appear innocent. The prosecution must present the *truth*, while the defence tries to make the defendant appear in the best possible light given that presentation.

An expert witness is there to help in achieving this, but their role is to assist the *whole* court to understand the complicated concepts that might be involved. The expert witness is a servant of the court and is paid by the court to appear, not by the Crown Prosecution Service or the defendant. Indeed, in civil cases it is now common practice for only one expert witness to be appointed, as a 'friend of the court', and for both sides to use them in the collection and presentation of evidence. This makes sense, but it places a huge responsibility on the single expert witness to ensure that the evidence is fairly and correctly presented.

This was the position I was in for this major criminal case. I sat outside the courtroom, nervously rehearsing what I would say and how I would explain it all. In most situations where I have had a nervous wait, there has been some fixed point in time that the wait will come to an end: the exam will start at a particular time; surgery must finish within a few hours. But waiting to appear as a witness isn't like that. What is anticipated as only being a short part of the evidence can end up taking hours and even days to present, whilst complex subjects might be accepted in a moment.

As I waited on the hard seats outside the court, the morning drifted inexorably towards the lunch break. By midday, I had exhausted any interest I might have had in re-reading my witness statement and the original reports, and was reading a book I had thought to bring – another lesson learned from previous cases. Lunchtime came and went – sausage, egg and chips with the Flying Squad detectives – and the afternoon wore on until at four o'clock I was finally released, with a request to return the next morning.

I had wasted an entire day, sitting bored and nervous outside the courtroom – but then, as I'd already found countless times before, the courts aren't there to serve the interests of the expert witness. All I could do was content myself with the comfort that the day was a chargeable one, and return as instructed.

I finally took the stand a little before eleven o'clock the next day. The court was every bit as impressive as I had imagined, with dark-wood panelling and the gallery hanging over my head. This was the first time I had seen the defendant, whose interests I had studied minutely in the reflection of the computer evidence, and he struck me as a hard case, sitting bolt-upright and glowering from the dock. The usual formalities of swearing in and giving my name and occupation were done on automatic as I felt the gang leader's gaze boring into me across the length of the courtroom. It must have been difficult for him. Everyone has private, personal fantasies, sexual interests that they assume will stay a secret. The contents of the computer had shown me his fantasies even more clearly than reading a personal diary would do. Now, not only did he know that I had read my way through them, and him, but that they were now about to be shared further and used, at least in part, to convict him.

Giving the evidence was very difficult. I found that I had to answer each question at least twice, because of the positioning of the jury behind me. I had to turn so as to give my answers to them, and then to repeat the answer to the judge who, almost always, needed further explanation of the answer. That explanation then had to be repeated to the jury, and was then clarified by a further question from counsel. Throughout this awkward procedure, the defendant did his best to disturb me, glowering, sighing, snorting and shaking his head in disagreement or disbelief at what was said. It was gamesmanship, I knew, but it still made it hard to keep focused on the questions and answers, with that ever-present physical intimidation as a backdrop to the presentation.

It seemed to take an age, but eventually we had gone through all the material that I had to present. It might have taken longer, had it not quickly become obvious that defence and prosecution had come to an agreement over the sexual material. It was relevant to establishing identity, but not to the case itself. As I had started to explain how we had shown that only the defendant had used the computer, the prosecution had interrupted and told me that the attribution of responsibility was not disputed by the defence.

Perhaps it would have damaged the defendant's position to have had his sexual fantasies discussed, and I must admit that I was relieved not to have to try and describe them to the court. At first, though, I was disappointed that my attribution of usage through scene-of-habitation analysis wasn't going to get an airing in court. But then, it had obviously served its purpose by establishing that a challenge to the attribution wouldn't have served the defendant's overall best interests.

A week later I heard from the Flying Squad that the robbers had been found guilty and were all to serve at least three years in prison. My evidence had been important because it had allowed the prosecution to establish that it hadn't been a spur-of-the-moment robbery but a meticulously well-planned exercise. It had helped to establish that this was no casual group of robbers, but a professional and well-managed group. They were convicted as such, all of the gang going to prison rather than receiving the suspended sentences that the defence had argued for.

The case underlined a number of important lessons for me, not least of which was the threat of violence or intimidation. Though the threat hadn't been made against witnesses, it made me think more deeply about the nature of the crimes that I would have to consider as the use of computer evidence moved from being related only to computer crimes and became more general. Computers can be used by murderers, by terrorists, by blackmailers – and I have been involved with both the investigation and the prosecution of all of these. Unlike the usually physically harmless computer hacker or white-collar fraudster, these can be particularly scary individuals.

I had – and have – no desire to be threatened in the course of my work for the police. But the work that I do is important and useful, in two senses. It helps on specific cases, where my computer-crime knowledge can be used to convict or to acquit a suspect; and it helps more generally, through the education and training of those involved in computer crime. Neither of these is something from which I would happily walk away.

This is particularly true because the use of computers in 'ordinary' crime is assuredly going to increase. Ever more blackmail and threatening letters are being sent by email; ever more planning of bank robberies involves the Internet. Stolen goods are increasingly being sold online.

That was an important thing to recognize, and it could be used to inform a variety of different aspects of our work, particularly given the gruesome nature of a second important case that I was involved with during this period. Unfortunately, this second exercise was nowhere near as successful as the first.

12. Getting It Wrong

Where the Flying Squad surprised us with their awareness of the issues, in this second case a company which should have known better surprised us with its ineptness.

It could almost have been a scene from a gangster movie, had it not been so horrifyingly real. The group of thick-set young men followed their prey through the inner-city housing estate, past burnt-out cars, broken bottles and discarded needles. They moved quickly and confidently, a pack hunting, as frightened bystanders scuttled out of their way. The gang cornered their victim in his flat. They forced their way into the room and pushed, kicked and punched the man until he lay crying on the floor. They stood angrily over him.

Himself a crook and a hard man, their victim was not surprised by the punishment. He owed money, and in the cruel world in which he operated a beating for non-payment was the norm. He might not like it, but he could expect to endure it. Until, that is, one of the young gangsters produced a shotgun, pushing it into the terrified and bloodied face that lay at their feet. Maybe the gunman was worried that his nerve would fail, or maybe he simply wanted to end the cruelty quickly. Whatever the reason, he hardly gave his victim time to react to the sight of the huge barrels in front of his eyes before pulling the trigger. Both barrels blew a hole through the victim's face, killing him instantly and splashing blood, brain and fragments of skull deep into the carpet.

Standing back from the corpse, one of the gang lifted out a mobile phone and used a speed-dial setting to call their boss, to tell him that the job was done and that the defaulter was now well and truly dead.

But computers throughout the telephone network took a note of that transmission: the local phone mast recorded the location of the call; the central switching computer recorded the number dialled and the cell's duration. Ultimately, those logs would be collated and stored, to be accessed and analysed by the police. And eventually they would find their way into court in a deeply disturbing, deeply frustrating murder prosecution that would, unfortunately, end in a dismal failure.

After St James's, Green Park is my second-favourite park in London, lying just to the north of Buckingham Palace, a pleasant stroll from my office at Buckingham Gate. It was summer 2001. I had just finished giving a talk at a conference at the Park Lane Hotel and was looking forward to a relatively relaxing day. It was not to be: I was barely through the park gates when my mobile rang and a gruff voice introduced itself as a detective superintendent in need of some assistance.

I moved to the side of the path to sit on a warm bench and began to scribble on the back of my presentation notes as the detective explained that he was the senior investigating officer in a serious murder case. He described how a group of well-known criminals had been paid to murder another well-known criminal in what the press had called a 'gangland shooting', and that computer data from the mobile-phone calls was going to be vital. It was precisely this, the man emphasized, that the defence had chosen to challenge, arguing that the call records were not reliable and had, in fact, been falsified by the police.

In most cases, those sorts of wild accusations of police falsification can be easily countered through demonstrating the reliability of the forensic procedures and through allowing the defence the opportunity to repeat the prosecution analyses independently for themselves. To do this forensic procedure for the computer material from the telephone companies, the defence had hired not one but two computer expert witnesses. They had produced separate reports, both challenging the evidence and the police handling of the data. According to the detective superintendent, both reports asserted that the records of the calls had not been preserved in such a way as to prevent alteration. Without saying that the telephone records *had* been falsified, he explained, the expert witnesses had shown that there was no way of proving that they had *not*.

The detective wanted me to examine the evidence for myself, and then to try to counter the defence assertions. He was at pains to point out just how important the mobile-phone evidence was. With it, they were sure that the gang would be convicted; without it, they were almost certain to walk free. There were no additional witnesses, no fingerprint or physical evidence; there wasn't even the shotgun itself, presumed to have been destroyed. Everything hinged on the mobile-phone calls, which the police believed first set up and then confirmed the shooting.

I agreed, though I realized that it was a tall order, because the case was due to be heard the following week. I had only days in which to examine databases of mobile-phone calls, study over a hundred pages' worth of experts' reports and write my own in reply. I swallowed hard, mentally rearranging my diary, and agreed that I would help.

The huge pile of documentation relevant to the case was delivered to my office the following day by a police courier. I had just five days – seven, if I counted the weekend – in which to address computer evidence and two experts' statements. Thankfully, the first expert's report was an intelligently concise one, basically reiterating some of the objections stated in his colleague's document. But that second expert's statement was huge.

Over recent years, I have been involved in training Crown

Prosecution Service lawyers in how to handle computer evidence and, more importantly, how to handle computer experts. I emphasize the importance of asking closed, well-defined questions of the experts; of having them agree a common vocabulary between prosecution and defence; and most importantly of having them write *short* reports. A short report is a clear report and one in which complex arguments have been distilled, meaning that they have been expressed as compactly and as cogently as possible. Short reports are much easier for judge and jury to read and understand. The purpose of the computer expert witness is to help the court to understand the arcane aspects of computer operation that are important to the case at hand, not to explain every fine detail of that operation.

A bad report is almost always a long one, with complicated bridges of argument and explication, masses of details and several intertwined threads of argument. A long report can seem to have been written to confuse rather than to explain.

I was not sure if the second expert's report had been written to confuse, but it certainly ranged over a huge variety of topics. It covered data-protection issues in the delivery of call data to the police, the history of telephone-metering, and the question of preservation of computer evidence. It called for the defence to be granted access to the telephone companies' complete databases – clearly an impossibility, since it would breach confidentiality – and for the programs used for analysis to be released to the defence – again, an impossibility since those programs were commercial applications.

The statement also referred to a document that I had had a hand in preparing. Written for the Association of Chief Police Officers, it was a best-practice guide for the handling of computer evidence. It drew at least partially on work that I had done several years before while working as a consultant in computer-crime investigations at the Inland Revenue. The expert's report had cited the best-practice document to show that the way in which the mobile-phone evidence had been collected, preserved, analysed and presented was not in line with the 'correct' way of working.

I was confident that the expert witness had made a mistake in mentioning the best-practice guide in this way. The guide was never meant to be used as a reference for evidence collections such as those obtained by the police from telephone companies. Rather, it was written to show police officers how to handle personal computers that had been seized, most usually during a raid on a suspect's house. It was expressly *not* intended to be used in the situation where evidence is provided to the police from a third-party computer system; indeed, the very first sentence in the document states precisely that. The defence expert witness's references to the guide could therefore be safely dismissed. However, I could recognize that there was the germ of a significant objection to the computer evidence embedded in the detail of the statement, one that was going to need a lot of attention.

The basic objection was that the original source of the call-data evidence had been lost, because the mobile-phone company had destroyed the magnetic tape on which it had been stored. Tapes cannot be stored in perpetuity – the cost would be horrendous – and so some storage criteria have to be applied. Here, the tapes had not been seized by the police – a mistake, of course – and had been overwritten as the cycle of tape reuse had proceeded. Worse, though, the controls on the production of the exhibits from that lost original evidence had not been sufficient to ensure that they could not have been tampered with.

Worst of all, the defendants claimed that calls that they *had* made were not present in the call records, and that call records were present to illustrate calls that they had *not* made. Without the original records, and without being able to show that adequate controls were in place to protect the only copy, the police could not do anything other than put their word against that of the defendants as to whether the call-data evidence had been falsified.

It was a wholly unacceptable state of affairs, and unusually I found myself in complete sympathy with the defence expert witnesses. I was being put in a very difficult position: I might well find myself having to defend the indefensible in this prosecution, which was something I was not prepared to do.

Because of the high risk of violence associated with the defendants, the court was well guarded. All visitors to a crown court have to pass through a security screen, just like at an airport, to have bags and coats searched. But all this bustle was now being watched over by two armed police officers, wearing bulletproof vests and futuristic radio headsets. They had holstered handguns and were carrying large machine-guns, obviously taking the threat posed by the prisoners more seriously than even the senior investigating officer's initial telephone call in Green Park had led me to expect.

There were more armed officers throughout the building. They were a watchful presence at the top of the stairs and in the lobby area outside the courtrooms themselves. To get into the court, we all had to run a gauntlet of further security checks, watched over by half a dozen more armed officers. Even in the courtroom there were two officers in bulletproof vests, though their guns were either well hidden or left outside the room.

Though the armed officers were all friendly, even chatty, the presence of their weapons drove home far more solidly than in any other case that there was a very real risk associated with the delivery of prosecution evidence. I was getting more uncomfortable by the moment: I was being asked to defend the indefensible, in trying to prove a case built on sand against dangerous criminals who deserved an extensively armed guard. For the first time ever, I wished that I had not become involved in a particular case.

The more I had studied, read and questioned the mobile-phone operators themselves about the evidence chain leading to the call-record analysis the more concerned I had become. Call-data records are created automatically by the telephone switches and are collated by analysis computers used by the telephone companies to create bills. The records are stored on magnetic tapes, which are kept at an off-site facility once the bill has been prepared. It is these tapes that the police request in the course of an investigation, passing them to a specialized forensic company to produce court exhibits showing calls made or received, along with details of the mobile-phone cells that processed the calls. When the police request call information for a particular phone over a particular period of time, the relevant tapes are signed out of the storage repository and couriered across to the specialist forensic company. Here, the tapes are placed in a second secure storage cabinet until an engineer is able to examine them.

Up until this point in the chain of evidence the process looked forensically ideal. The initial data were produced and collated by automatic programs, and the accuracy and dependability of those programs were something the telephone companies measured and had provided statements for. The storage, transportation and receipt of the tapes were equally well controlled, with a clear record showing that nobody could have accessed and altered the sealed tapes' contents.

Unfortunately, after this stage the process became dramatically less secure, since the engineers working for the forensic company appeared to have kept no record of what they did next. The tapes could easily have remained out of the evidence store for hours or even days before they were analysed, with nobody responsible for their security. They could have been modified, with records of calls perhaps altered, to show them occurring at different times, from different places or to different people. Entire telephone calls could have been invented or destroyed, with no way of establishing what was true and what was fiction.

Even worse, the process for analysing the tapes seemed almost totally unsound, with the engineers theoretically able to alter the exhibits produced from the tape. The tapes were restored to a computer on which they could be analysed so as to generate a printout, and it was this printout that formed the exhibits relied on by the prosecution. Unfortunately, the computer on which this was done handled the data as simple text files that could easily be deleted or altered, again with no way of proving what had happened.

There was no record of what an engineer might do to the contents, nor was there any way of guaranteeing that the correct data were being processed. Those data were then not presented to the court on an unalterable CD, but rather as a paper printout from a simple floppy disk; worse, the floppy disk wasn't even set up with the write-protect tab set so as to prevent alteration.

It seemed a horrendous muddle of an exercise and not one that I would expect to see presented in court. Worse still, the defence expert witnesses had pointed out that the printed records contained a series of errors: some phone-cell sites had completely the wrong postcode for the address quoted, showing that the cell-site reference data was not trustworthy. The print-out was neatly arranged, showing that it had been edited in some fashion after the data had been input. And in a final stroke of ineptness, the 'last modified' date and time stamp on the file on the diskette was for the day before the court case began, showing not only that the file could have been altered but that it definitely *was* edited in some way immediately before the court case. Even if that editing was simply to format the data, it was still a massive *faux pas*.

As the defence experts emphasized, there were periods of time in which the data could have been modified, deleted or added to, without any controls to prevent it. There was no auditing of the procedure and no way of proving that the data was not wholly fictitious. I had to agree with them. The exhibit should not be admitted in court, let alone relied on to try and convict someone of murder.

Because the hearing was a so-called '*voir dire*', about what evidence was going to be allowed to be seen and heard, the judge was sitting without the jury, and the form of the hearing was a little more relaxed than a full trial. Despite that, the defendants were present, with friends and well-wishers in the public seating area.

The courtroom itself reminded me strongly of the first such place I had worked in years earlier for the 'Christopher Robin' case, though now I was at the other side of the procedural and technical objections. It was a modern, light room, with fixed chairs and polished lime tables. Unlike the first paedophile case, the defendants were behind tough-looking screens and surrounded by tough-looking guards. The prisoners were brought in daily in an armed convoy of vehicles, and they looked bored and sullen at the abstruse arguments raging over their telephone calls.

I made my way forward to the stand and took the oath. It was the first time I had been before a lord justice. I had to fight hard to remember to call him 'Your Lordship' instead of 'Your Honour', as the counsel for the prosecution took me carefully through the gist of the arguments concerning the telephone records. They did not all hinge on the records so badly mishandled by the forensics company; there were parallel records from other telephone companies, which had been much better prepared and presented. Counsel had me describe the nature and form of this data, and the way in which such records are produced, maintained and used. I was asked to detail the way in which computer date and time stamps operate, and the way in which distinct database records can be correlated. Counsel didn't raise the problem with the evidence, and I didn't volunteer it. There seemed no reason to, when we were certain that the defence would do so as soon as they had a chance.

The defence counsel was a small, sharp-faced man with a patrician bearing and a very composed voice. He seemed in no hurry, taking the questions carefully and slowly, almost excessively polite in his demeanour. Even so, it took only three very general questions before he focused on the main issue. He asked me about the way computer forensic evidence should be handled. I described the good-practice measures almost exactly as they had appeared in the second defence expert's statement. He asked me about the production of the prosecution exhibits derived from the telephone company's database. I explained how I believed them to have been produced, and, at his prompting, the failings associated with this. He even asked me whether I would allow someone working for me to produce an exhibit of that quality, and I had to admit that I wouldn't: they would have been warned and then sacked for such shoddy work. He asked me whether I agreed with the defence experts in their opinion of the work, and I said that I did.

This was perhaps the hardest time I have ever had in giving evidence as an expert witness. Although experts are usually employed by one side of a particular case, we are not 'on their side' once we are in court. We are there to help the court, as explained in the preceding chapter. We are there to see that justice is served, not simply to say only those things that are of relevance to 'our side'. Though my expert evidence was undermining the prosecution case, I could have no choice in what opinions I gave. For my opinion to have any value in court it has to be both expert and impartial. What I said was the truth, the whole truth and nothing but the truth. But even so, I could see from the dagger-glares of the prosecution counsel and lawyers that they were not best pleased.

The integrity of the basic telephone data as evidence was severely undermined. It was, however, not completely ruined; the basic data could not be relied on solely, but had to be supported by the testimony of those people working for the forensics company and handling the data. Instead of being able to rely on the processes that went into creating the evidence, the prosecution had to rely on the trustworthiness of the individuals concerned. Fortunately for the prosecution case, the forensic engineer in question was a stolid, reliable-looking individual.

Naturally he admitted that the work had not been performed to the forensic standards expected. But, he emphasized, he had *not* altered, added to or subtracted from the data. He was adamant – and believable – in his assertion that the data could be relied upon.

It was a very close-run thing, but by the time I was released from the court on the third day of the *voir dire* hearing the call-data-record evidence had been allowed as a part of the main hearing. Unsurprisingly, the prosecution decided they would not call an expert witness for the telephone records, but instead rely on the forensic engineer alone. I can't say I blamed them, and I can't say that I was eager to have anything more to do with the prosecution. I breathed a huge sigh of relief.

Driving home at the end of that final session, I had mixed feelings about the case, especially in the context of the earlier exercise with the Flying Squad. Then, detectives who really couldn't have been expected to appreciate the finer points of computer evidence had shown themselves to be highly effective. They had done *exactly* the right thing with the computers. In this case, those who should have been operating to forensic standards had mishandled the computer material to a quite startling extent. In fairness to them, they were not *computer* forensic specialists and had never been told that they had to operate to those standards. But the principles of forensics are essentially independent of the field in question. I felt that they should have been able to get it right, especially since computer forensics is not a particularly difficult thing to do properly. It's a process that requires care, auditing and the consciousness that actions will be questioned closely by experts.

After the work with the Flying Squad I had begun to feel that the basic lessons of computer forensics were starting to be learned and applied. Now, I was faced with the reality that they might not be, and that there was still a lot of ground to be covered in the work of education and awareness.

A few weeks later, as I feared I might, I took a second call from the senior investigating officer in the case. It was the eve of his retirement party, but he was calling to give me the result of what was now his last major case. One of the accused had already pleaded guilty and had in fact given evidence against some of the others. They in turn were found guilty of manslaughter. But the two who had been accused of organizing the killing – and for whom the telephone records had been an important element in the evidence – had been acquitted. The defence had indeed been able to throw doubt on the trustworthiness of that evidence, and the defendants had benefited from that doubt.

Good application of forensic disciplines to arcane and

complicated computer data can help to convict those who are truly guilty. Inadequate or careless application can render the data unusable, and under those circumstances defendants cannot be safely convicted. Obviously I have no idea whether, with the correct handling of the computer data, those defendants would have been found guilty, but in my teaching of police officers and prosecutors I have now taken to using this case as an important lesson.

Though we have come a long way in improving the handling of computer evidence, we still have a long journey ahead. With increasing numbers of serious cases now involving computer evidence, we *must* handle it properly. The need for that education is more urgent now than at any other time.

13. **Real Men**

Susan Kent had been a single mother of one, who had lived in Medway in Kent. At midday on 24 November 1999 she was raped and murdered in her own home, just before she was due to leave for work. The attack was apparently by someone she knew, since the door had not been forced. But this person had somehow managed to tie her hands behind her back, rape her, score her body ritualistically with a knife, and cut her throat before leaving her face-down on the bed to bleed to death.

Her bound and semi-clothed body was discovered by her mother and young daughter on the afternoon of her murder – a terrible and immensely disturbing way of learning of the traumatic death of a loved mother and daughter. Susan's daughter had returned from school and her mother – worried at not having heard from Susan during the afternoon – arrived at the same time in a taxi. Together they went into the house, followed by the taxi driver when he heard their screams.

Susan's body had been deliberately posed on the bed, with her thighs slightly parted and bottom lifted towards the doorway. The effect seemed intentional – a lewdly shaming exposure for a woman past being able to defend and cover herself. A final insult to her from the murderer? Or an insult to those unfortunate enough to discover her? Or perhaps the completion of some scenario staged and acted out thousands of times in the murderer's imagination, now being played for real?

Outraged and disturbed, the taxi driver covered her with a blanket and contacted the police.

Along with the first responding police officers, an ambulance and a doctor were despatched to the Medway house, and Susan was officially pronounced dead at the murder scene. Throughout the rest of the day, and in the weeks that followed, the lumbering beast that is a major incident investigation rolled over Susan's house and her life, following the preset programme of events so familiar to us from a hundred different TV shows.

A senior investigating officer – Detective Superintendent Dennis McGookin – was assigned from the Maidstone headquarters of Kent Police. An investigating officer was assigned from Medway CID, Detective Chief Inspector Martin Henneker, a stolid, grey-haired officer of immense calm and charm. An incident room was established at Medway, and the white-suited scene-of-crime officers were despatched to collect and preserve the available physical evidence at the house, and make a videotape and endless rolls of photographs of the body and the room. Hearing that she had been covered by the taxi driver, the forensics team removed the modesty blanket, and Susan was taped and recorded for posterity exactly as her callous murderer had left her.

Contrary to the impression given by popular fiction and TV, murder is not a common way for someone's life to end, and even when someone is murdered the culprit is generally easily found. Most murders are committed by close family members – spouses in particular – and in the heat of the moment. There are usually witnesses, an easily discovered motive and an equally easily discovered murder weapon. Most killings are solved within twenty-four hours. In real life, murder mysteries are very rare.

Susan Kent's death, though, *was* a mystery. First of all, the murder bore all the hallmarks of a sadist's activity. She had been tied and quite deliberately hurt – tortured, in fact, using a knife on her breasts – at the same time that she was raped. Sadistic murderers are rare and generally there is a build-up, a progressive series of increasingly sophisticated and controlled attacks, culminating in a killing – and sadly, sometimes several related killings.

There had been no such progressive series of attacks reported in the area, making this single killing highly unusual. Of course this might well be the first of several if the man was not quickly discovered. Even more worrying, it was apparent that Susan had been 'well managed'. The murderer had controlled her with the minimum of 'accidental' injuries to her, and had not attacked her in a frenzied and unsophisticated manner. He seemed to be a *practised* sadist and not obviously one beginning his 'career' as a sadistic killer. Had he in fact already murdered before, the body or bodies not yet discovered?

Susan had been murdered in broad daylight – rare enough – yet as police officers went from door to door to question neighbours, it seemed that no-one had heard or seen anything or anyone. Most murderers – even 'clever' ones – leave some physical evidence at the scene: fibres, fingerprints, or fluids. There was, at least on first inspection, no physical evidence such as semen found that could obviously be tied to the murderer.

Despite these problematic areas, the juggernaut of investigation proceeded. Susan's body was cleaned and examined by a pathologist, and photographs of the waxen figure and its now bloodless puncture wounds found their way into the growing investigation files. The police began the painstaking process of tracing and interviewing all those who had known Susan in life: friends, lovers, workmates and relations. They even went so far as to have an appeal for acquaintances broadcast on the local news.

David Ferguson had been drinking in a Medway pub with friends when news of the appeal was broadcast. He had not been a boyfriend of Susan's but had known her as a friend;

and his mates knew that he had known her. They were adamant that, if for no other reason than to rule himself out of the inquiry, Ferguson should make himself known to the police.

Ferguson hesitated and prevaricated, explaining that he had been chatting with friends at a local tattoo parlour almost all day on 24 November. There had been a lot of people he had met and had chatted with, he claimed, who would surely all remember him and show that he could not have been anywhere near Susan's. Was there, he demanded, any reason why he should let the police poke into his business? His friends insisted, and finally Ferguson capitulated, calling the incident-room number and arranging to see a uniformed officer.

Ferguson was a muscular man of medium height, with a shaved head, neat moustache and bearded chin. Extensively tattooed, he looked a somewhat dangerous individual – a pub brawler or a biker – but the answers he gave to the officer from the incident room were calm and measured. When had he last had contact with Susan Kent? Not for several months, he replied. Had he gone to her home? Again, not in several months. Could he account for his movements on the 24th?

He could. Ferguson had two alibis, one of them apparently rock-solid. He told them of his time at the tattoo parlour – which could be easily checked – but more importantly he showed them a new medicine bottle, with the chemist's label clearly showing the date and time at which the prescription had been collected. It was almost exactly the time at which the pathologist had confidently stated that Susan's life had ended.

David Ferguson was ruled out of the inquiry and the investigation continued. It was a slow, laborious period of time for the investigation team, checking alibis of acquaintances and friends, following up leads at knife shops, trying to trace Susan's movements in the period before her death. Trying to find someone who could be put into the frame for her killing.

A valuable source of information, about suspects or about the lifestyle of a victim, is the telephone records: numbers called, but also crucially those who have called that particular number. As a matter of course, the telephone records for Susan's number were requested from BT, and in due course they were delivered to the incident room. The long process of investigating the numbers began.

In the 1970s, at the time of the infamous Yorkshire Ripper serial murders, the amount of paperwork generated threatened to break the floor in the incident room at the police headquarters in Leeds. Vital links and correlations were missed, simply because of the unimaginably huge amount of data that had been collected. As a result, although Peter Sutcliffe had appeared in the investigation team's records and should have been identified, he was released and allowed to continue killing. Because of this, a project to produce a computerized solution began – culminating in the introduction of a major-incident investigation system called 'HOLMES'.

Computers may be the bugbear of police officers when they have been used to encrypt or to hide vital evidence, but in major inquiries they can be used *by* the police to discover and flag correlations that might otherwise be missed. David Ferguson – whose interview report was flagged to show that he had had no contact with the victim for several months – was found to have phoned her number and talked for a long period of time the night before her murder. Reinterviewing Ferguson became an urgent priority for the investigation team.

Within seconds of the officers stepping into Ferguson's house, the decision to arrest him had been made.

With that assertiveness peculiar to police officers the world over, the detectives had eased their way into Ferguson's home when he had answered the door to their unannounced visit. Then they had stood in open-mouthed amazement at the sight of wall after wall decorated with the most bizarre and outrageous pornography, both photographs and drawings. Picture after picture showing women bound, cut and raped – including a large number of line drawings of a muscular, bald-headed, tattooed man having anal sex with a bound woman as he sliced her throat.

Here was the story of a murderer's mental progression,

tracing a developing fantasy of coercive, sadistic sex with a bound and helpless woman, tortured and eventually killed with an oversized knife. They had a man who knew the victim, who had lied to them, and whose fantasy life would seem to encompass the very things that their victim had suffered.

As they questioned him, it became increasingly obvious that Ferguson was uncomfortable, evasive and providing far from satisfactory answers. Finally he was arrested and brought in for more detailed questioning, and a search warrant was sworn to allow the officers to search his house more thoroughly. The police then had twenty-four hours in which to interview him and establish a good reason, if one existed, to charge him with the murder.

Once given a 'good' suspect, the investigation team could move into a higher gear. Officers with the search warrant took over Ferguson's house, collecting the pictures from his walls and various other items of pornography in his property. One set in particular caused great concern: a photograph collection showing Ferguson and an unidentified friend apparently acting out an abduction, bondage and rape scenario with another, unidentified young woman. Was she too a victim? Had Ferguson practised his 'technique' on this woman, before proceeding to attack Susan?

Fearing for her life, a priority for the officers was to identify, trace and – they prayed it was possible – interview the woman. In due course, she *was* located, alive and well, but terrified at the discovery that what had been for her a frivolous sexual game had been something much more for Ferguson – and indeed, something much more for another female partner. It had been *practice*.

The interviews of David Ferguson make fascinating reading, as the officers grow increasingly frustrated at his obstinacy and at the near-perfect quality of his alibi from the pharmacy label on his tablets. Eventually, as the twenty-four-hour period is coming to an end, they realize that there is a source of potentially new and interesting evidence available to them: a computer that has been seized from his house.

*

The Kent Computer Crime Unit is not as old as the original, Metropolitan Police unit, but none the less it is well established and well staffed. Two people in particular were already well known to me: a civilian computer technician called Chris Crute, and the detective sergeant of the unit, Nigel Jones.

Despite their competence, the pair of them were severely tested in the rapid turnaround that was required to handle Ferguson's computer. With the clock ticking down to the time at which Ferguson had to be charged or released, Chris used the computer forensic application to 'preview' the disk drive in the computer. As well as making a perfect copy of disk contents, forensic applications also allow the investigator to examine the disks in a way that is guaranteed not to alter them. This is 'previewing', in which access to the disk is controlled wholly by the forensic application rather than by an operating system.

Using this, Chris began to work his way through the disk, and encountered a bizarre collection of files. There were stories – some at least written by Ferguson – in which he wrote of using his '12″ of rape meat' on helplessly screaming victims. The phrase was repeated often throughout the files, and in fragments of email apparently sent to a collection of websites. There were also details, again written by Ferguson, of his plans to establish a 'Rape Club': women who consented to 'rape encounters' with members of the club would all wear a lapel pin symbolizing their acquiescence.

It was all rather juvenile, but deeply disturbing. The nugget of gold, though, came in a collection of preserved web pages from a site called *Real Men*, including a snippet of text – apparently written by Ferguson the night before the murder – in which he stated that he would 'become a real man in less than twenty-four hours'.

Chris and Nigel rushed to access the *Real Men* website. Apparently run out of America by someone calling himself Louis Cipher – presumably in reference to Lucifer – the site contained spurious and laughably implausible advice on what it takes to be a 'real man'. Real men, it claimed, keep themselves fit and well muscled, but not to the point of a body-building fixation. Real men have few friends; those they do have are loyal to the death and speak seldom, but always to great effect. Real men are tattooed, with shaved heads and physically demanding jobs. Real men take what is owed to them, be it property or women. Real men feel no compunction, no hesitation at killing if that is the only way they can get what they want.

It was hard to take seriously, but Ferguson apparently had. Not only was the description of a 'real man' close to his own physical appearance, he had also submitted a number of postings to the site. He had expressed pleasure at finding a site that matched his interests; he had laid out his 'Rape Club' plans, to the appreciation of other users of the site; and he had made a posting to the site's discussion group, the one in which he had said that within twenty-four hours he would be a real man. The posting was still visible on the website and was comfortably within the window of time in which Susan Kent had been killed.

On Sunday 12 December 1999 David Ferguson was formally charged with the murder of Susan Kent.

Because Kent Police were going to be relying, at least in part, on the evidence derived from the computer, they needed a computer expert witness. In these circumstances, the expert's role is to testify that the procedures adopted in preserving and handling the computer evidence are valid, and to see if there is anything more that can be deduced from the material.

DS Nigel Jones phoned me shortly before Christmas. Although he gave me no more than the barest details about the case, I agreed that after the holidays I would drive down to the Maidstone headquarters to review some computer evidence with him and Chris Crute. We made an appointment for 10 a.m. on Friday 7 January 2000.

I had expected to meet Nigel in the crowded Computer Crime Unit office at the headquarters, and to have a chance for a gossip. I had known and liked Nigel for several years by this time, and I knew that he was then only a few short months away from retirement. Tall, thick-set and with a headmaster's bearing, Nigel had been the secretary to the joint industry–police Internet Crime Forum, of which I had been a founder member. This was the group originally chaired by the senior detective in the police force involved in the online-stalking case of an American woman. Now the forum is chaired by the head of the National High-Tech Crime Unit. Involving representatives of the intelligence services, the police forces, government and the Internet industry, it has become one of the greatest forces for the correct handling of computer crime in the UK. But barely had we greeted one another and got a mug of coffee each when two of the murder-squad detectives arrived to join us in the canteen. After handshakes and introductions, the senior detective explained that they wanted us all – including me and Chris Crute – to be briefed on the case.

It seemed fair enough. Not knowing what to expect I followed them through to a stuffy briefing room at the far side of the canteen. We all sat around a battered and coffee-ring-stained table, at one end of which an oversized TV and video had been set up. My heart sank as the junior detective, intro-duced to us as the 'exhibits officer', took a video tape from a tatty wallet folder and slipped it into the unit. The senior of the pair explained that he wanted all of us involved in the case to know what had been done to poor Susan Kent. I was going to have to watch a video of a real-life dead body, and the idea sickened and frightened me far more than anything else has ever done in my career.

I am hopeless at horror movies and hate to read scary books. I have a rich imagination, and once didn't sleep for days after having read a Clive Barker novel. Even knowing that it was all fiction, I still found it the stuff of nightmares. The idea of having to sit through something that I knew to be all too real was an order of magnitude worse.

Nigel Jones and Chris Crute sat impassively, and I envied them their calmness. Had they had to do this before? Could it be possible to become immune to the horror of a murder scene? Obviously yes, because the two murder-squad detectives looked to be relishing the prospect of watching the video – or of inflicting it on some poor innocent computer geeks.

Trying desperately not to show how scared and upset I was, I folded my arms across my chest – to hide the fact that my hands were shaking – and stared at the screen. As the video ran, I imagined a white-boiler-suited scene-of-crime officer slowly and methodically making his way up the front drive of the house. The view swung easily and smoothly, showing that the front door hadn't been forced, showing the scuffing of the carpet, the first flecks of blood at the top of the stairs. The view shifted to a child's bedroom, lingering for a moment on stuffed toys and scattered books before moving on. A bathroom, old-fashioned but pristine; the landing and spare bedroom, both untouched. Then, an unseen hand must have pushed open the master-bedroom door, and the cameraman inched slowly into the room, pausing to sweep the camera in a scene-setting arc.

Her blood had soaked the bed brown-black. Not a pool, but a complete colour dip for the crumpled sheets and bedding on which the woman had been left, face-down. She was wearing a blouse, though it wasn't possible to tell the original colour, and her hands had been fastened behind her with what looked like stockings or a scarf. Her heavy buttocks and legs were bare, pale, almost blue-looking against the darker stain beneath. It was a pornographic scene, as though she were posing, her thighs spread, bottom provocatively exposed to the camera. Perhaps that had been exactly the effect the murderer had intended, aiming to shock whoever discovered her.

Dispassionately, the senior detective described what had happened, as the camera lingered on close-ups of her slack face, on the gaping wound at her throat and the knife cuts which marked her bottom and thighs. I swallowed, trying to force my breathing to be regular, trying to retain a façade of ease, as though this was something that I did every week. But I knew that the explicit, specific images – of her hands cruelly twisted, the staining and bruising where she had been raped, the half-open eyes – would remain with me for a long, long time.

That video played out in my dreams for several weeks afterwards, and gradually the sense of shock turned to one of anger. There was no reason that Chris Crute and I needed to sit through that video: it added nothing to our understanding of the computer, nor indeed of the crime. Making us watch it seemed to me to have been an initiation ceremony into the world of murder investigation.

We passed the initiation, but to me it seemed childish to make us endure it. For cases related to murder or extreme pornography taken from computers, I now no longer allow the images to be used for shock value. I avoid exposing myself to them, and I ensure that those working for me don't have to view the images. In most cases, we are interested in the *properties* of the computer-held pictures rather than the *contents*. Only the jury need to be exposed to the images themselves, so as to make their judgement, and I certainly don't envy them that experience.

The work that the murder squad wanted me to do was fairly straightforward, once we had escaped from the picture show. I needed to establish that Chris had handled the material properly and that the computer could be argued as having been Ferguson's responsibility. The murder team also wanted me to examine material that had been delivered from the American company hosting the *Real Men* site. And, if 'Louis Cipher' was ever located (which he wasn't), to examine any material provided from that source.

Establishing that Chris had done the correct things with the seized computer was a straightforward task. He showed me that he had referred to the 'Good Practice Guide' developed for police investigations into computers. He described the way he had used the forensic application – first to preview and then to copy the computer – and even that he had used an alternative imaging application as well, so as to ensure that a true copy had been taken. He described the way the material had been analysed, and the way in which copies had been retained for use by the defence. Finally he gave me a copy of the computer contents on a pile of CD-ROMs so that I could do my own analysis back at the office. It seemed completely in order, and I promised Nigel Jones that I would write a statement to that effect, and do my own analysis as well.

Although the investigation team were confident that, in Ferguson, they had found the killer, there still remained the problem of his alibi. The tattoo-parlour aspect wasn't particularly difficult to address. Ferguson had certainly been in there during the day, talking pointedly and extravagantly with a number of people – almost, the officers guessed, as though he had particularly wanted to be remembered. But the times that people could definitely recall him being present didn't coincide with the time at which Susan was killed. The officers were confident that he could have easily travelled between the shop and the house in the time available.

But this still left the issue of the chemist's label on his medicine, placing him categorically some distance from Susan's house at midday. A number of explanations were possible. First of all, that Ferguson wasn't the killer. This, though, was ruled out of the police consideration at this point. Ferguson matched the psychological profile that had been constructed, appeared to have told someone that he was going to take a major step in the 'next twenty-four hours', had lied about contacting Susan, and was self-evidently fascinated by sadism, bondage, torture and rape. If it was not Ferguson, then it was someone very like him who had killed the poor woman. The second possibility was that the medicine had been collected by someone else for Ferguson; and the third was that he had somehow faked the label.

But neither of these two had in fact happened. The medicine had been signed for by Ferguson, and the staff in the chemist's remembered such an unusual and distinctively tattooed person collecting the medicine. The chemist's copy of the medicine label confirmed the date and time printed on the bottle. There was no doubt about it: Ferguson had not faked, in any way, the label on the medicine; it was 100 per cent genuine. Nor could he have made his way from the chemist to Susan's house and killed her at the time that the pathologist had said she died.

Could the pathologist have been wrong? Checking the medical facts took the team some time, but the pathologist was absolutely definite. The bedroom was a well-controlled environment, not like an outdoor murder scene where unusual temperatures and fluctuations can fool the scientific measures. Indoors, the rates of mortification for different parts of a corpse are remarkably well understood. Susan had been found within hours of having died. Her body core temperature was almost perfectly aligned with the expected values for her body mass, age, sex and posture at death. Rigor mortis had barely begun, the blood remaining in her body had not begun to pool. The pathologist went steadily and methodically over each of the steps that led to a confident assertion that Susan had been alive in the morning, had met her death at midday, and had been dead for more than three hours when she was discovered.

So, perhaps Ferguson *wasn't* the killer?

Frustrated, annoyed and confused, the officers made their way back to the incident room and discussed the nature of the computer evidence that was being handled by Chris. They had a series of questions to ask of Nigel Jones and the Computer Crime Unit, as part of trying to establish that – with or without an alibi – Ferguson was a highly probable killer. The officers wanted to know, first of all, how many people in Kent were on the Internet. Nigel made an educated guess. Around half of British households then had some form of Internet access, and based on that he provided a 'finger in the air' estimate that seemed to satisfy them.

How many of them, asked the officers, had visited a sex-content website? Biting back the obvious retort – 'Probably nearly all of them' – Nigel explained that this was impossible to determine, given the nature of the Internet. Well, OK, they went on, so how many people in *Medway* would have visited a bondage or sadomasochism website? Again, Nigel explained that this was impossible to say.

To the investigating officers, more used to the real world of shops and clubs, it was an obvious thing to want to know: the Internet version of asking how many people would frequent a particular sex shop or blue cinema. But the anonymity and sheer scale of the Internet – and the immense quantities of hard-core sex sites of various sorts available on the Web – made this an impossible question to even begin to work out how to answer. The investigators must have felt like they had run down every single blind alley that was on offer. They had no-one better than Ferguson, but there was still the problem of the chemist's label.

Until, that is, Nigel pointed out that it had been printed on a computer. He asked whether anyone had checked that the pharmacy computer that had created the label was working correctly. Was it possible that the computer was showing the wrong time?

Not only was it possible, it turned out that it was *true*.

The officers discovered that the clock on the computer at the pharmacy was an hour fast, probably having not been reset to Greenwich Mean Time at the end of British Summer Time. This was the breakthrough that they needed, and Nigel and the Computer Crime Unit team raced to seize and analyse the computer, establishing that the record of prescriptions was a consistent hour out across the whole period of time the murder squad were interested in. They did this by comparing stated prescription times with the shop's opening and closing times, showing that prescriptions had apparently been issued when the shop was in reality closed and locked.

It was a complete fluke, but one that had provided Ferguson with a near-perfect alibi. There was no suggestion that Ferguson had somehow managed to create the alibi – though he might have previously realized that the clock was wrong and taken advantage of it – but with the correction in place, his alibi collapsed. There was now no doubt in the officers' minds: David Ferguson had murdered Susan Kent.

*

Back at the office, I began my own analysis of the material seized from Ferguson's computer, starting by ordering all of the files in sequence according to their date and time stamps. This allowed me to pick through Ferguson's activity on the computer, to see if I could separate out the activity that was unrelated to the actual murder.

It was all but impossible. Since it had been bought and installed only a few weeks before the murder, the computer had been used almost exclusively to search out websites specializing in bondage, sadomasochism, rape and killing. In fact, looking at the search terms that had been used in the America On-Line search engines, I was struck by how Ferguson had immediately begun to use the 'correct' search terms for the material he was interested in. Generally when we see people searching for specialist sexual subject matter, we see a progression in the way that they search for it. They might start using everyday terms and words, and gradually refine them as they gain an understanding of what is meant.

The material that Ferguson was interested in is generally indexed amongst the 'bondage, domination and sadomasochism' collections, the usual term for this being 'BDSM'. Ferguson had clearly gone directly for this, indicating that he was already well familiar with the terms, concepts and nature of the material he was searching out – almost certainly through prior exposure in practice or in non-Internet literature.

This was an important point. One question asked by the police was whether 'Louis Cipher' – operator of the *Real Men* website – carried some responsibility for having encouraged Ferguson in his activities. Since we could show that Ferguson had this level of familiarity already, it seemed unlikely that Louis Cipher had encouraged him to be interested in something he wouldn't otherwise have been interested in.

Beyond that, though, I wanted to see whether the scene-of-habitation analysis could be used to ensure that Ferguson alone had been using the computer. It didn't seem that I could do that from the evidence available: the scene-of-habitation analysis was no use when there was plainly no 'habitation' on the system. Fortunately, Ferguson readily admitted that the computer was his and that no-one else had had access to it; he accepted that he carried out the searches and wrote the emails – though of course, he denied that the 'twenty-four-hour' message was a reference to his plans to kill Susan.

It was disappointing that the analysis method I had worked so hard to develop could not be used for this most important of cases, but the timeline analysis of Ferguson's activity and the recovered material proved useful and interesting during his trial at Maidstone Crown Court in October and November 2000.

I was booked to attend on 10 October, and travelled down by train early that morning. The court itself is a squat block, a fifteen-minute taxi ride from the station, and for once I arrived in good time, met there by the young exhibits officer whom I remembered from the video briefing at the start of the year.

Chris Crute was scheduled to go into the witness box immediately before me, to explain the analysis that had been performed on the evidence. The senior investigating officer, Mr McGookin, explained that Chris would simply present the computer material as a factual exhibit, which should be fairly rapid. Then I would be asked to comment on the accuracy of his procedures, and then in much more detail on the interpretation – most particularly concerning the clock error associated with the pharmacy computer. This, McGookin emphasized, was vital if we were to convince the jury that Ferguson's alibi was worthless.

Fortunately, McGookin explained, the computer evidence was no longer the central element of the case. In the months since we had begun to consider that evidence, physical evidence had also emerged: fluids recovered from the murder scene were found to match Ferguson's DNA. No detective is relaxed before the final verdict, but McGookin and his team appeared upbeat and hopeful for a victory.

It seemed a fairly straightforward situation, and I composed myself to follow Chris Crute into court reasonably quickly. But as the day wore on and on it became apparent that Chris's evidence was causing the court some problems. At lunchtime he emerged. He and I weren't allowed to chat, since I hadn't given my evidence, but his raised eyebrows and wry smile were eloquent enough.

At the end of the day, the exhibits officer – who had been slipping in and out of the courtroom throughout Chris's evidence – explained that there was no problem as such with the computer material. There were no objections being raised, nor any serious challenges from the defence to the exhibits and the procedure. It was simply that the jury had no experience of computers whatsoever and that they were struggling to understand the most basic elements. In a world of juries unfamiliar with computers, we seemed to have got the extreme.

Poor Chris spent a day and a half struggling to describe how computers work, what the clock and file time stamps were about, how web searches work and the rest of the detail important to the court. In all fairness, that explanation role should have been mine, as the prosecution computer expert witness, but the court was reluctant to release Chris and the Crown Prosecution Service did not want to suggest any break in evidence presentation that might jeopardize the trial. As a result, it was the following day before I was able to get into the witness box to give my testimony, increasingly concerned as to whether I too would face such a daunting task.

It was just before lunch that I was sworn in, and I ran through the usual litany of standard questions to give my name, occupation and qualifications. Then I stood ready to field a similar battery of questions to those that had been fired at Chris Crute. I got only a half-dozen questions, all of them simple, all of them straightforward clarifications of elements already presented by Chris. I was dismissed before lunch, bemused at how fickle the courts can be.

On Monday 20 November 2000, Nigel Jones phoned me from Maidstone to tell me that David Ferguson had been found guilty of murdering Susan Kent and that Lord Justice Hidden had sentenced him to life imprisonment. Since that moment I have never dreamed about the murder-scene video again.

14. **The Future**

In planning and researching this book, I was struck by two observations in particular. First of all, the startling breadth of criminal activities that I have observed and been asked to handle, from obvious crimes such as hacking, through paedophilia, threats against life, extortion and copyright breaches, on up to rape and murder. And that's not all, of course. Like everyone else, on 11 September 2001 I watched open-mouthed as two planes destroyed the World Trade Center in New York, and plunged the world into crisis. Unsurprisingly, the planning of that event had involved computers and the Internet. Inevitably I can now expect my work to extend beyond murder to active terrorism.

The second observation was how little time the events and developments described cover: from February 1995 to February 2003. Eight short years, but what important years. They have seen the explosive growth of the Internet as an engine of the modern economy, and with it the growth of overtly criminal use of hacking techniques; the development and introduction of evidence-handling protocols; the recognition of international co-operation for handling computer crimes; the expansion of education of computer-crime investigators; and the formation of the UK's National High-Tech Crime Unit.

What of the next few years? Criminals and terrorists will not stop using the Internet. Why should they? It's where the money is; it's where the victims are; and, despite the phenomenal steps we have taken to date, it is still not as well policed as the high street. But with a growing number of police officers trained to patrol that beat, with dedicated police units in developed countries, and with computer experts willing and able to assist, the next few years will see yet more exciting developments.

There are new laws and new powers being proposed and reviewed, in particular a rewriting of the Computer Misuse Act 1990. Prosecutors are being taught about handling computer crimes, and the judiciary will be trained in the necessary disciplines. There are also proposals for clearer and fairer inter-action between the Internet industry and the police, including specifications of how long crucial data should be stored for. I am intimately involved in all of those steps, and fascinated to see the impact that they will have.

The new laws to counter terrorism have also had clauses introduced to cover deliberate damage to computers, making computer-hacking a terrorist crime for the first time. It seems odd to think that an activity that, for me and for many others twenty years ago, was a harmless hobby should now count alongside bombs, kidnapping and torture in the eyes of the law. But again, this is a reflection of how far our dependence – legitimate and criminal – on computers has come.

Unfortunately, the technology will change and make the role of investigator and computer forensic scientist ever more difficult. Most obviously, the growth of mobile and wireless networking will make the job of tracing offenders all but impossible.

A few months before writing this, as a part of a legitimate test, I sat in a City wine bar with a friend who specializes in wireless networking. We were across from the Royal Exchange, the very heart of the City. From the top-floor window of the wine bar, we could see the Bank of England building and a host of major financial organizations. By now I must have visited each and every one of those buildings in the course of my career, and I knew that each was physically secure. There were guards on the doors, locks that needed card passes to be opened, cameras and infra-red detectors. Getting into any one of the buildings would be difficult; connecting a computer onto their network undetected once we were inside would be even harder.

Instead, we used a wireless-networking card connected to a laptop. It took a moment or two for the card to find all the available networks, but soon it presented us with a list of around a dozen private networks that could be connected to. Without walking into the buildings, the private-office networks were open and accessible to us, and from there we could have accessed the Internet. Anything we could have done – any frauds we committed, any hacking that we'd performed, any paedophilia we had uploaded – would have been tracked back to the company, and certainly not to the wine bar across the road.

As more and more companies employ these wireless networks – for the convenience of not having to install expensive wiring in their buildings – this threat will grow. Companies will be hacked, and the hackers will be all but untraceable.

This is a development that we can anticipate. Although we have little or no idea at present how this problem will be solved, we none the less know that it *is* a problem, and that it *must* be solved. Perhaps by legislation on the operation of the wireless transmissions of the network; perhaps by enforcing adequate standards of information security inside organizations; or perhaps by enforcing operating practices for the wireless systems.

A second, equally worrying development comes from operating systems themselves. For example, in their latest systems Microsoft provide disk-level encryption that will mean that *every* file on the disk is encrypted. We will no longer be able to gain access to encrypted files by looking for plain-text versions of the file, since there will be no plain text to see. Even deleted files may become inaccessible to us, since Microsoft is introducing automatic overwriting on deletion so as to render deleted files unrecoverable. Naturally, this will create more secure workstations and personal computers, for which as a security consultant I am grateful. But it will also make the systems more secure for the criminals who use them for illicit or illegal purposes.

So, the landscape of criminality and the response to it will continue to shift and to evolve. Rapidly, on the part of technology; quickly, on the part of the criminal; more slowly on the part of the judicial response. But though that response will be slower, it will now be measured, thoughtful and appropriate – at least, that is our hope.

In writing this book, I wanted to show that computer crimes now touch all elements of criminal behaviour. I cannot now read the paper without wondering which of the many interesting crimes will result in a computer being delivered to my laboratory for analysis. Have I seen every aspect of computer criminology now? No, not by a long way. The next week, or the next month, will bring a new kind of computer crime, and a new challenge to be solved.

It certainly won't be boring, and I wouldn't have it any other way.

Index

access: authentication credentials,
174–5; mechanisms, 120–3; simple
unauthorized, 170; unauthorized,
175–7; unauthorized access with
intent, 170–1
administrator accounts, 116–17
aliases, 12
America On-Line search engines, 245
Association of Chief Police Officers,
222
attribution analysis, 159–60
Austen, Detective Inspector John, 46, 76
Avon and Somerset Police, 139, 147, 151

back connection, 54, 67
back-ups, 36
banner-grabbing, 63–4
Bates, Jim, 160
best practice guide
blackmail, 218
blocks, 79, 88, 146–7
Blythe, Andy, 93
bots, 159
Boy Scouts, 9, 15, 28
Bramshill, police staff college, 75–6
Brandy (of death-threat case), 156–62
Britton, Paul, 141
browsers, 175
buffer-overflow exploit, 167, 173

bugging, 109
business cards, 50–2

CCTV systems, 2
CD-ROMs: copies of computers in
hacking case, 80, 94, 101–2; copy of
computer in paedophile case, 36–7;
copies of end-of-life computers, 131,
136; imaging process, 143–4, 145
Centrex, 203
Channel 4 News, 129, 134, 135–7
chatrooms, online, 7
child pornography: computer-bases,
11–12; images, 8, 9, 12, 18–20; legal
position, 9, 11, 38
China, computer hackers, 170
Chris (Christopher Robin): appearance,
21, 28; collection of images, 15,
18–20, 29; computer evidence, 35–7;
court cases, 20–1, 27–38, 214,
226–7; defence, 21–2, 30–2, 38–9;
emails, 13–15, 32–3; framed?,
10–11, 141; investigation of case
against, 16–18, 22–7, 33–4, 35, 140;
meeting, 13, 21; paedophile charge,
6, 8–9, 11; pass phrase, 86;
postgraduate work, 6–8, 15–16;
Scout activities, 9, 10, 13, 15, 28;
sentence, 38